A Killing Art

A Killing Art

THE UNTOLD HISTORY OF TAE KWON DO

UPDATED AND REVISED

ALEX GILLIS

ECW

Published by ECW Press
665 Gerrard Street East
Toronto, Ontario, Canada, M4M 1Y2
416-694-3348 / info@ecwpress.com

Cover design: David A. Gee
Cover photo: Martin Crawford
Author photo: Michael Phang

LIBRARY AND ARCHIVES CANADA CATALOGUING IN PUBLICATION

Gillis, Alex, author
A killing art : the untold history of Tae kwon do / Alex Gillis. — Updated and revised edition.

Issued in print and electronic formats.
ISBN 978-1-77041-300-9
also issued as: 978-1-77090-694-5 (PDF)
978-1-77090-695-2 (ePUB)

1. Tae kwon do—History. 2. Choi, Hong Hi. 3. Kim, Un-yong, 1931–. 4. Gillis, Alex. 5. Martial artists—Biography.

I. Title.

GV1114.9.G54 2016 796.815'7
C2016-902319-2

The publication of *A Killing Art* has been generously supported by the Canada Council for the Arts, which last year invested $153 million to bring the arts to Canadians throughout the country, and by the Government of Canada through the Canada Book Fund. *Nous remercions le Conseil des arts du Canada de son soutien. L'an dernier, le Conseil a investi 153 millions de dollars pour mettre de l'art dans la vie des Canadiennes et des Canadiens de tout le pays. Ce livre est financé en partie par le gouvernement du Canada.* We also acknowledge the Ontario Arts Council (OAC), an agency of the Government of Ontario, which last year funded 1,709 individual artists and 1,078 organizations in 204 communities across Ontario, for a total of $52.1 million, and the Ontario Media Development Corporation.

PRINTED AND BOUND IN CANADA

PRINTING: MARQUIS 5 4

PEOPLE

I love Tae Kwon Do and martial arts, mainly because of the empowerment and enlightenment that comes from facing violence and fear. I began writing *A Killing Art* in 2001 to figure out how Tae Kwon Do grew out of a history of violence and corruption to become an empowering and popular martial art. Since the first edition was published in 2008, nearly a thousand readers have contacted me with opinions about the book, most of them positive. For this second edition I have updated every chapter as well as added new chapters. The book is leaner and faster, with more names, scenes, and stories, especially about the brave martial arts leaders who stood up to dictators, bullies, thieves, and cheaters in Tae Kwon Do.

The book is heavily referenced so that readers can discover where Tae Kwon Do's incredible and astounding stories came from. I would like to thank many people for telling me the truth, especially Chang Keun (C. K.) Choi, Jung-Hwa Choi, and a handful of martial arts masters and grandmasters, such as Bob Hardin, Jhoon Rhee, Joe Cariati, and Joon-Pyo Choi. Rhee in particular set me straight on much of Kim Un-yong's and Tae Kwon Do's history in the 1960s and 1970s, in spite of Rhee's involvement with violent espionage missions and a cult that bankrolled Tae Kwon Do events. Jung-Hwa Choi was open about the art's history from the 1980s to the present. Former South Korean general Sun-Ha Lim, a friend of Choi Hong-Hi's from the 1940s, told me about Choi and his country during the Second World War and the Korean War. The work of historian Bruce Cumings provided a context for Tae Kwon Do's role in North and South Korea.

Some grandmasters bravely recounted what others were reluctant to share: Nam Tae-hi, Kong Young-il, and Jong-Soo Park (my former instructor). And thank you to the martial arts instructors in my nearly thirty-five years of training: Yoon Yeo-bong from the World Taekwondo Federation (the WTF, perhaps the most unfortunate acronym in sports history) and Park Jung-Taek, Phap Lu, Alfonso Gabbidon, Park Jong-Soo, and Lenny Di Vecchia, whose intense martial arts instruction inspired me to write the first edition of this book.

I would never have finished *A Killing Art* without my black belt friends — Floyd Belle, Martin Crawford, Marc Thériault, Tourage Mahdi, Duane Cato, Karen Chen, and others — who meet with me every Saturday to practise Tae Kwon Do without politics or talk, an increasingly rare situation in the world of black belts. A martial artist once telephoned a famous grandmaster, Duk-Sung Son, for an interview, but Son said, "No, no more talking. I'm going to train now," and hung up.[1] My training with Floyd, Martin, Marc, and others countered the darker parts of this book. Many times I'd finish a difficult interview or chapter and trudge to the gym, hoping to find them there — for more training and less talk.

For editing or research support, thank you to Hendrik Rubbeling, Thomas Kuklinski-Rhee, Manuel Adrogué, Loren Lind, Mark Dixie, Susan Folkins, Jane Ngan, Katie Gare, Diane Gillis, Renée Sapp, Laurie Gillis, and Hana Kim, who was the Korea Studies Librarian at the East Asian Library at the University of Toronto. John Koh was an excellent translator and interpreter who offered insights along the way. Thank you also to the Ontario Arts Council for grants and to Nancy Foran, Crissy Calhoun, Troy Cunningham, Michael Holmes, David Caron, and Jack David at ECW Press, and to my agent, Hilary McMahon.

Alex Gillis
Akillingart.com
@GillisTKD

ABOUT KOREAN NAMES

Tae Kwon Do is usually spelled "Taekwondo" for the Olympic sport (run by the World Taekwondo Federation) but "Taekwon-Do" for the traditional style (the International Taekwon-Do Federation). Instructors from both styles sometimes use Tae Kwon Do, and there has been so much overlap between the different Tae Kwon Do federations, and their offshoots, that I have stuck with the dictionary spelling of Tae Kwon Do throughout the book, except in titles and quotations from documents.

Most Koreans have three names and write their family names first, but some switch the order, and others change the spelling. Names can be confusing when you read different sources. Kim Un-yong, for example, can be written "Un-yong Kim." A hyphen connects the first names, with the second word of the first name often beginning with a lower case letter (Un-yong), but many Koreans begin both with an upper case letter, with or without a hyphen (Un Yong and Un-Yong). I settled on using either what the person in question uses or on the Korean standard, which is last name first (Kim Un-yong).

To make things more confusing, Korean names can be spelled in different ways. Un-yong, for example, can be spelled "Un-young" or "Woon-yong" — and those are all correct spellings! On top of this, many otherwise good sources spell names incorrectly. I have provided the various spellings in the index but have used only one consistently throughout the book.

Whenever possible, I used McCune-Reischauer spelling for Korean words.

INTRODUCTION

FUNNY OR PHONY?

Tae Kwon Do is about self-defence, but if you enter the backrooms of its history, you'll discover a killing art — and an empowering art. I learned this the hard way on April 20, 2001, the Year of the Snake. I walked into the Novotel Hotel in Toronto, Canada, to wait for the "Father of Tae Kwon Do," General Choi Hong-Hi, who was leading a three-day seminar for black belts. I was naive then and revered the eighty-two-year-old as well as the other founding members of Tae Kwon Do, including a man named Kim Un-yong. I felt intimidated walking into the seminar, partly because Choi was a taskmaster. He had become a major general in the South Korean army at the age of thirty-three, and even though he had retired from the military in 1962, he was still known as "the General." He and his men had sacrificed their bodies, careers, and families to perfect a martial art now practised by an estimated seventy million people in nearly every country in the world.

I can picture the first day of his 2001 seminar as if it were today: I wait in the Amsterdam Room of the hotel with 100 black belts from the U.S., Canada, Chile, Peru, Paraguay, Uruguay, Argentina, and Honduras. Standing among the bowing, whispering martial artists, I feel like I'm waiting within a palace of the *Chosŏn* dynasty in the 1300s. I imagine ancient warriors waiting for dynastic rulers, the floors heated in the old style (invisible and underground), and Korean geisha girls ready to sing the *p'ansori* verses that praise Confucian values and sagacious leaders.

The General and his men are extremely late, however. He is upstairs, talking and arguing with his son and the masters and grandmasters who will help during the seminar. These men once fought, parted, and threatened to kill one another over politics, but the masters and grandmasters know they owe their fortunes and reputations to the General, and everyone is trying to reconcile past threats with present ambitions. Few young people in Olympic Tae Kwon Do know about Choi, who more than anyone deserves the label "founder" in this martial art. Other founders — and there are many (some of them in this room) — erased him from the popular record long ago.

The General takes lineage and loyalty as seriously as others take love and death. He has charted his family tree back eighteen generations to the *Chosŏn* dynasty, when, in the mid-fifteenth century, a king ordered a military noble, Choi's ancestor, to move to a northern part of the Korean peninsula to protect several towns. The *Chosŏn* aristocrats, who reigned for 500 years, structured society around the Three Relationships and the Five Injunctions, summarizing the world with lists and blood.[2] The General and his men seem plucked from that ancient time. They are working on the Fifth Injunction — Let Faithfulness Unite Friends — temporarily abandoning the other four injunctions (Honour Your Ruler, Honour Your Father, Honour Your Elder Brother, and Assign Man and Wife Different Duties).

For an outsider, especially a non-Korean, it is difficult to understand the cultures and conflicts of these men — conflicts that have lasted decades, which might as well be centuries. Stories from the *Chosŏn* era are full of dynastic leaders with godlike powers, and for fifty years, the General has quoted poet Po-Eun's call to loyalty from that time: "I would not serve a second master though I might be crucified a hundred times."[3]

We are expecting a good seminar and no crucifixions, but the General is late, the floor is cold, and the women have mastered head kicks rather than geisha songs. The seminar will be the General's last in Canada; he is more than eighty years old and is rounding up his former enemies and old warriors for a new mission that I find difficult to believe: he wants to help reunify North and South Korea by merging his Tae Kwon Do (based in North Korea) with Olympic Tae Kwon Do (based in South Korea). I wonder if the General is a megalomaniac. He does want to take over all of Tae Kwon Do, and there are rumours that he will meet Kim Un-yong, the president of the World Taekwondo Federation (WTF), which runs Olympic Tae Kwon Do.[4] Kim is the General's enemy, but an enemy worth negotiating with, because one of Kim's coughs is worth a thousand of our yells.

Choi is "the General," but Kim is "the President." Kim is not here, but he is in spirit. In the 1960s, he began a patriotic career as a spy in the violent Korean Central Intelligence Agency, working within one of the world's most successful dictatorships. In the 1970s, he stole the General's "Tae Kwon Do" name. In the 1980s, he inserted the sport into the Olympics. By the 1990s, he had become a powerful, corrupt leader in international sports. The only goal Kim has not achieved is immortality, and he is working on that by helping to reunify North and South Korea, who have been at war for fifty years. Both men have similar goals, and both countries are in the middle of negotiations. Part of the plan is to hold joint Tae Kwon Do events in the autumn, assuming the men and countries do not destroy each other first.[5]

The rumours are unnerving many black belts, because Tae Kwon Do is supposed to be apolitical and nonviolent, and instructors are weary of the espionage, gangsterism, and cheating that has plagued their martial art, but the reunification goal is admirable — and attainable — if you consider the history and culture of these men and their art. These elders are modern *yangban* — men of the sacred bone, the upper castes of Korea.

Tae Kwon Do supposedly flourished 1,300 years ago under a general who held an extremely high rank in the *Silla* dynasty, perhaps even the rank of "sacred bone," which meant people treated him as if he was immortal. Choi acts as if he holds that rank. He is also known for being generous, funny, and approachable. Most of us in the room have read "the bible of Tae Kwon Do," as Choi dubbed his training manual,[6] and most of us have trained until we bled. But most of us are naive, believing that the General is like a god — in the same group as the other men who developed a martial art in the twentieth century: Gichin Funakoshi (Karate), Kano Jigoro (Judo), and Morihei Ueshiba (Aikido), all of whom were Japanese. Many Olympic Tae Kwon Do students place Kim Un-yong in the same pantheon.

"Attention!" someone calls. We stop chatting, General Choi enters, and we bow. Seeing him in person is my first shock: he is puny — only five feet tall and about a hundred pounds. Men always pushed him around, no matter how politically cunning he was and no matter how many barroom tables he pounded with his bare hands. He often faced bigger opponents — generals more powerful and presidents more ruthless.

I sit on the carpet with the other black belts as one of the grandmasters attaches a microphone to the General's shirt. Before starting the action, the General introduces the men at the head table, including Grandmaster Jong-Soo Park, who owns the gym that I attend but who has not worked with the General in more than two decades.

"Most of you do not know him," the General says. "He is one of my most beloved students. Give him a big hand."

We applaud, not seeing the trap. It has taken me years to learn the rule of opposites, a rule I discovered as I studied my martial art: when someone says something dramatic of an opponent, such as "He is a beloved student," listeners should automatically assume the opposite, or close to it. According to this rule, Park is not the General's "most beloved." They are attempting to reconcile though. Both men stopped speaking to each other in the late 1970s, after the General accused Park of co-operating with the Korean CIA in a kidnapping plot. Park denied the charge. He is a renowned martial artist who introduced Choi's version of the art to the Netherlands and Canada in the 1960s,[7] so it seems odd that the General once accused him of a plot.

It is difficult to understand the gap between feelings and words

Jong-Soo Park springs into a jumping kick. PHOTO COURTESY OF PARK.

in these men, between truths and half-truths. Ambivalence and shame creep through the seminar. When someone announces that Park's demonstration team can begin, no one stands. Team demonstrations are routine events at these seminars, but Park has suddenly disappeared. There are at least twenty of his black belts here, a couple of them former world champions, but none rise. Some of us, the young ones, are bewildered and embarrassed; Park organized this seminar in honour of the General, so why did he not prepare a team? We soon find out.

The answer lies in the manner with which the General offers advice — his no-holds-barred method of teaching that leaves students stunned. You could call it the "old way," an approach that involves sticks on the shins, training until you vomit, and sparring after you bleed. He beckons one of Park's sixth-degree black belts, an American, to the head table. The General asks him to explain how one would teach a new student. The black belt begins talking, but the General immediately says, "No, stop!" and points out that the first thing to teach students is how to bow. Evidently, the black belt himself did not bow properly. "That's why your school never grows," the General scolds. "The students never listen." The implication is that if students are lazy about bowing correctly, how can they obey during strenuous classes. "Beware phony instructors!" the General suddenly warns.

The seminar continues in this manner while Park prowls the restaurant and hallways of the hotel. Most of Tae Kwon Do's techniques have changed during the lost decades in which he and the General have not spoken. The General seems so frustrated by our techniques, which in his view need updating, that he sometimes can only yell "Whaaa!" He is punishing us for the lost years and for Park's — unproven — betrayals.

In any case, the General and his men are still deciding how Park and his schools will join the General's International Taekwon-Do Federation — and how much the whole thing will cost. Much of the conflict is about money, but most of the General's criticism centres on techniques that distinguish his Tae Kwon Do from Olympic Tae Kwon Do and Karate. Park is not in the room to hear the rants and the "Whaaas!"

Those of us not being verbally attacked laugh uncomfortably. The General is a wicked, witty genius, but we are here to learn. A young woman rises to demonstrate another technique and does it incorrectly.

"You're a lady?" the General asks.

"Yes, I am," she replies.

He motions for her to sit down. Some of us look at each other, as if to say, "Did he really do that?" Misogyny is everywhere in this martial art, and the General believes that men and women should have different duties, so to speak. Choi waves for a man to stand and asks him to do a low block. The man's fist is off by a quarter of an inch, apparently.

"Who taught you that?" the General asks.

The black belt names the master.

"Don't know him," the General says. "You should get your money back."

I feel sorry for the black belt. Tae Kwon Do has always had a dysfunctional relationship with profit; the two are fire and water. For this seminar alone, black belts paid C$250 to C$410 each. Park organized the event, and I volunteered to help, so I saw what happened on the first day: most black belts were well behaved, but a few barged through the door without paying, and sixteen members of a South American team were either tricked into thinking that the seminar would be free or they lied. Further, sometime during the three-day seminar at least C$1,000 disappeared. This is what sometimes occurs when money meets the martial arts — a mix of warrior and clown, tradition and farce — and why Tae Kwon Do is sometimes pronounced "Take My Dough," as my friend Martin Crawford once pointed out.

Money is the least of our worries, however. What many of us do not know is that Tae Kwon Do has been connected with espionage, terrorism, and gangsterism since its birth — and many of these masters and grandmasters lived through that time and became ensnared in some brutal campaigns. The General bragged about sacrificing students and even his own children to promote the art,[8] a brag that, in some ways, is rooted in his personality — "a tornado," as he once put it.

Park is not having a good day with the tornado. The General says the word phony so many times during the seminar that, years later, when I tell Park in a relaxed moment that he is funny, he stops and asks, "What did you say?"

"I said you're 'funny' — your comment is funny."

He stares at me like a tiger measuring its prey.

"Funny sounds like phony," he says calmly.

Funny. Phony. I had never realized how similar they sound. Park is not phony — in a martial art filled with overnight grandmasters, he is a genuine pioneer — but I will never again tell a grandmaster that he is funny.

x x x

At the front of the seminar room, the General teaches a black belt from South America how to block.

"Always look your opponent in the black ball," the General tells him.

"Eyeball!" whispers his son, who is standing a couple of feet behind.

"Always look in the eyeball," the General corrects. He smiles and taps his forehead with a thick, callused finger. "I am getting old. Lucky I have a good son."

His son, Master Jung-Hwa Choi, lowers his head. He is forty-six years old and taller and stockier than his father and is another "beloved" master, if you know the history between the two men. He will be the General's heir, if all goes well. The two men have not been getting along for years, but they are trying now.

The younger Choi addresses his father as "General" or "Sir" in public, and their lives are filled with Tae Kwon Do. They have very few good personal memories together. One that Jung-Hwa Choi later describes is from his childhood in South Korea. He spent many nights lying on the floor behind his father as the elder Choi played poker with the other generals. The boy would inhale the smell of appetizers brought out one by one, the aroma floating through the comforting smell of cigarettes, sake, and Johnnie Walker. All the generals drank Scotch then. Jung-Hwa would hear his father's voice, the men's voices, strong, as they laughed. "Father, don't lose," Jung-Hwa would whisper as he tried not to fall asleep on the floor. "I never lose," the General would reply.[9]

It is Jung-Hwa's misfortune that his father never loses, that his father knows the outcome of a gamble before it begins.

"Tae Kwon Do is easy to learn," the General says into the microphone during the seminar. "That is why it has spread like wildfire all over the world. Someday, it will be on the moon and the stars."

It is day one of the seminar, and he is already dreaming about immortality.

He falls to the ground and does push-ups on his knuckles. We cheer; he is eighty-two years old after all. He tells us to read the books, his books, especially the *Moral Guide Book*, in which he encourages his readers to live justly and honestly.

"Tae Kwon Do is not only about punching and kicking," he reminds us. It is about doing the right thing, which he has tried to do all his life, even when he seemed not to. That day, the General insults the co-organizer of the seminar, Son Myung-Soo, and Son's black belts from the Royal TKD Academy all drop out.

XXX

The second day's demonstrations are much better than the first day's. A fifth-degree black belt jumps into the air, spins 180 degrees, and breaks four boards with a side kick while in mid-air. Later, after someone explains that Tae Kwon Do is the only martial art with a "twisting kick," someone else demonstrates by running, jumping, and breaking a board held six or seven feet above the ground.

But the General seems to be in a bad mood. Besides "phony," his refrain throughout the seminar is, "He'd be killed in combat," as if combat were at the next café. And he uses "suicide" as a verb. "The WTF," he grandly announces, "they don't know what they're doing. They all suicide."

The General loathes the style of the World Taekwondo Federation — the only style allowed in the Olympics and the style run by the General's nemesis, Kim Un-yong. He also hates Karate, even though he developed Tae Kwon Do from it.[10] Throughout the

General Choi blocks kicks from his son Choi Jung-Hwa (on the right) and Park Jung-Taek, my first instructor. PHOTO COURTESY OF GENERAL CHOI.

seminar, he makes fun of both martial arts. He asks a black belt to begin a pattern called *Toi-Gye* (which the General created and named after a sixteenth-century scholar of neo-Confucianism), and he instructs the man to redo a strike to the pubis, a technique called an "upset fingertip strike."

"Why do you withdraw your hand after the strike?" the General asks him.

The black belt explains that he is ripping off the opponent's scrotum.

"No," General says. "That's Karate and WTF style."

The mistake reminds the General of a joke: "A woman told another, 'Don't marry a guy who studied WTF.' 'Why?' asked the second woman. 'Because he has no weapon,' said the first."

We laugh, because there is evidently too much scrotum ripping in the WTF, but more than that, we laugh because he is not castrating *us* for these few minutes.

"I want you to laugh, because you're so serious," he says.

But on the last day of the seminar, Bob Wall, the legendary martial artist who won many Karate championships and who starred in three Bruce Lee movies, materializes to provide the biggest laughs. He stands at the front of the room to sell phone cards, credit cards, internet services, and "collectible items" such as postcards and key chains that contain photos of General Choi.

"You can imagine what these will be worth," Wall says. "The value goes up when the person is deceased." He adds that the General gave a ninth-degree black belt to Hollywood martial arts star Chuck Norris, who has 182 schools. Norris considers himself a student of the General's, as do movie stars Jackie Chan and Wesley Snipes. They own some of the cards, Wall claims, and we can collect points for airplane mileage just as they do. "You could have flown here free," Wall says.

As if on cue, the General stands and says, "Everyone should participate in this plan. You should tell your students. We'll make it the best martial-arts-run company in the world."

One of the grandmasters from Quebec, Tran Trieu Quan, falls asleep at the head table as Wall and Choi shill services that will empower martial artists while draining their wallets. Maybe Quan does not need phone cards, or maybe he is as stunned as I am by a group of men who seem like comic-book characters from a bygone age.

CHAPTER 1

THOUGH TEN MILLION OPPONENTS MIGHT RISE AGAINST HIM

The essence of Tae Kwon Do began during a poker game in 1938, the Year of the Tiger, when longing and violence stalked the world. It was the most reckless day of Choi Hong-Hi's young life. He lived in a small house in the village of Yongwon, in northern Korea, at a time when Japan was crushing the nation like a trap around a fox. The sun had set on the *Chosŏn* dynasty, but Choi was twenty years old, full of rebellion, and, like most Koreans, refused to forget his past. He had inherited his father's small, sharp eyes and chin, which usually tilted upwards or cocked to the side, making him look taller than his five feet.

On that day in 1938, he faced his mother under the dim light of a lamp.[11] He was preparing to travel to Japan in two days to complete his education, leaving behind his daughter and a wife whom he had married in his early teens.[12] In Japan, people routinely abused Koreans, but Choi would receive an excellent education there, the first in his family to complete middle school. The trip would be an honour, even though he had to adopt a Japanese name, as the Japanese government had banned people from speaking Korean and was forcing Koreans to change their identities.[13]

Choi's mother took a thick wad of money from her pocket. "Be careful not to lose this," she warned. She had worked hard, from dawn to midnight on many days, selling tofu and sewing clothes to save the money. She folded the bills twice, tucked them inside his belt, and sewed the belt shut. But after she went to sleep, Choi went to someone's house to play *Hwatu*, a popular Korean poker game. He had been gambling, drinking, and smoking since the age of seven — a partier, like his father. For many years, his father had owned a successful brewery, eventually deserting his wife and taking Hong-Hi and the two other children to live with a *kisaeng*, a Korean geisha. Living with *kisaengs* had been an old practice from the *Chosŏn* dynasty, but it should not have included abandoning the first wife, according to Confucian thought.

The *kisaeng* had ruined several men's lives already, but she made an impression on Choi; he thought she was worldly and sophisticated compared to his mother. Choi had been six years old when the *kisaeng* became his stepmother.[14] Those were the years when he learned how to gamble, smoke, and drink. She was an opium addict and ran a tavern, cooking her excellent food and singing her *p'ansori* songs, the classical music favoured by *kisaengs*. Choi saw how his father could be naive, obstinate, and deeply indulgent — how he gave her everything he had. Finally, his father lost so much money gambling that he sold the brewery. In those early days, the young Choi rarely visited his real mother, who was living in poverty in another part of the village.

One day, he tried to deliver soup to her, but the *kisaeng* found out and sent a thug to knock the bowl out of his hands. Choi was devastated as he watched dogs lap the food from the dirt. He would never forget that day, not even after the *kisaeng* died at the age of thirty-eight, when Choi was ten, and his father, as Confucian custom dictated, returned to the first wife. His parents rarely spoke to each other afterwards, and his mother, not his father, raised him for most of his life.[15]

To support the family, the boy helped his mother on their small plot of land, tending the garden, feeding the animals, and making tofu — sometimes on the lookout for his father's blows, which struck like lightening. The process of soaking, grinding, cooking, straining, and pounding tofu was so intense that for the rest of Choi's life he loved eating tofu because it reminded him of his mother. As was the custom during meals, his father ate first.

Choi's mother would place rice and side dishes on a table while the family waited. Choi and his brother would peek through a little hole in the door to see if their father would leave some of the rice uneaten, the delicious smell floating into their noses.

But now, at age twenty, Choi would flee all that. In 1938, after his mother sewed the money into his belt and went to sleep, Choi snuck out of the house and met Haak-Soon Huh (a local wrestling champion) and a few friends.

Choi loved the parties that went with poker, and he was excellent at *Hwatu*. He played so well that he could spot cheaters, which meant that he could cheat with the best of them, but he did not on this day because the others at the table were professionals.

In rapid succession, he and the others laid down the colourful cards and staked their money, but as the game progressed, Choi fared badly. "Strange," he thought. "I am not winning." He continued gambling, hoping to win back his losses.[16]

Some of the *Hwatu* cards have poetic names, such as *Crane and Sun*, but the poetry may have been lost on Choi as he detached the education money from his belt and gambled more. Soon, he lost all the money that his mother had given him, but he convinced everyone to continue playing. Dawn was still far away, Choi said, and they should wait for him to win back some of his losses.

Finally, the wrestler stood up. "The purpose of gambling is to win money," he said. "I've waited long enough."

Choi wanted to attack him but knew that would be like a fox jumping a tiger. Choi could fight a bit — at age fifteen he had learned some *T'aekkyŏn*, an old martial arts game, from his calligraphy instructor — but the wrestler loomed as a bigger and better fighter.[17] As he sat there, Choi saw a thick bottle of ink on a desk nearby. I wonder if he pictured the next few seconds in advance: the way the room blackened before his eyes, the way the wrestler put the money in a pocket, the way Choi's hand found the bottle of ink, and the way it sailed at the wrestler. The bottle smashed on his forehead — a lucky hit. The wrestler fell on his back, blood and ink trickling down his face. While the other gamblers watched, Choi walked to the body, pulled the money from the

Choi Hong-Hi stands on the left.
PHOTO COURTESY OF CHOI.

man's pocket, counted what he had lost, and fled. No one stopped him, perhaps because they knew the wrestler would hunt him down.

Choi rushed home, cold and sweaty, and wondered if he had murdered the man. All that blood! What would his parents do? He and his brother and sister had always obeyed their father, who had studied the works of Confucius and become a doctor of Chinese medicine before opening his brewery. Their minds were laden with obligations and traditions, a Confucian legacy so warped that Choi's grandmother kept her nail clippings because respect for parents meant respecting every part of one's body.

But non-Confucian values — those of the heart — thrived in Choi and his era, values related to superstition and intuition, freedom and insight, passion and drunkenness.[18] In Choi's household, obedience lived beside rice wine and geisha girls, and attacking a man after losing a poker game would create intolerable trouble for his parents.

As he walked home after the poker game, did he remember the first time he had created trouble for them, his birth in 1918? That was the Year of the Horse and a year in which the Japanese government arrested, tortured, or killed 140,000 Koreans who were suspected of resisting the Japanese empire.[19] It was a year when cunning and independence were at the centre of the world. Choi was born a runt and looked destined to die young. His mother came from a wealthy family but hated her husband. Each time she gave birth, she left him to bring up the newborns in her father's comfortable, Confucian home. But her father treated her like a servant because daughters, after marriage, were not supposed to return to their parents. She bore the humiliation for the sake of all eight of her babies, only three of whom lived past the age of two. She would grumble later, "After the greater ones are all gone, the worst weakling survived to give me a headache."[20] Choi, the weakling and the youngest, was sickly and short for the first four years of his life. In desperation, his mother tugged his legs night after night as he slept, trying to make him taller.

As Choi left the poker game, he wondered if the wrestler was dead. Afraid of his own parents, he avoided home, the police, and the entire town. He walked sixteen kilometres past cow-driven carts to a train station, travelled twenty hours on a train to a Pusan port, and caught a ship to Kyoto, Japan. That day marked him; for the rest of his life, he would embroil himself in conflict then flee.

Months after arriving in Kyoto, Choi met a man from his village who told him that the wrestler had recovered and was counting the days to Choi's return. Choi felt doomed and began training in Shotokan Karate to defend himself. Karate was a Japanese martial art that Gichin Funakoshi had transferred from Okinawa to Japan in 1922.[21] Choi had watched a class and concluded that it was devastatingly powerful; it aimed punches right to the heart, solar plexus, or whatever vital spot could lead to death.

Beginning in 1938, Karate strengthened a trait in Choi that Westerners associate with Japanese *kamikaze* pilots from the Second World War or with samurai warriors from a thousand years ago.[22] Choi called it Indomitable Spirit: "A serious student of Tae Kwon Do will at all times be modest and honest. If confronted with injustice, he will deal with the belligerent without any fear or hesitation at all, with indomitable spirit, regardless of whosoever and however many the number may be."[23]

But Choi did not practise Karate for long. He did train diligently for a few years in Kyoto, keeping the wrestler in mind, but he later claimed to have attained a second-degree black belt. Experts dispute this claim, saying that no one in those days could reach that level in such a short time, considering Funakoshi's standards.[24] In fact, only one Korean, Wok-kuk Lee, attained a second-degree black belt in Karate during that era. Choi likely exaggerated his rank, but he kicked wooden street poles, punched sand to toughen his fists, and trained so much that he failed his first year in middle school, which he thought was yet another reason to avoid going home.

The Karate also proved useful in Japan, where people insulted him and his Korean friends, told them they smelled like garlic, physically attacked them, and treated them like servants. Choi was constantly getting into fights. He was not special in this regard; Japanese bullies had been abusing Koreans for decades, and the nation of Japan had been trampling Korea since 1894. One of Choi's fights began after he warned two boys to stop bullying a friend. The boys took the warning as a challenge and followed Choi after school. As they approached him, he hit one in the face. The boy fell, and Choi immediately pinned him to the ground with a foot on his neck as the boy's wooden sandals flailed in the air. The second boy ran away, and Choi released the first, marvelling at his new-found power.

Scared of the wrestler and his parents, Choi stayed in Japan for four years, never visiting his village, telling his parents that he was too sick to travel. He saved money and sent it to his mother. At the age of twenty-four, however, after finishing middle school, he finally felt confident enough to face the wrestler and his parents. He returned to his village, proudly carrying a new sewing machine for his mother. It was 1942, the middle of the Second World War, and Japan was brutalizing Asia-Pacific, but Choi was concerned about the many villagers who were ganging up against him and, of course, the wrestler.

Shortly after Choi's arrival, the wrestler saw him in a pine grove near the village, kicking small trees and smashing clay roof tiles. He thought Choi was mad and having seizures, because from a distance Choi's fast movements did not look like any martial art that the wrestler had seen.

Choi was not insane, a friend explained to him. Choi practised Karate, a Japanese martial art that could kill with one blow. The wrestler chose not to challenge the wild claim and avoided Choi. In the end, the runt defeated his opponent without a fight — and that is when Choi's real problems began.

CHAPTER 2

A SUPERPOWER ON EVERY BORDER

Choi tried to escape the draft into the Second World War by starving himself and, when that failed, hitting a Japanese police officer, but in 1943 Japan forced him and 4,300 other Korean students to join the Japanese Imperial Army.[25] He was stationed with the 30th Division in P'yŏngyang, in what is now North Korea.[26] Unconquerable Japan, along with Nazi Germany and Fascist Italy, was taking over the world. Japan had massacred 300,000 civilians during six weeks in Nanking, China, and had conducted medical experiments on prisoners in Manchuria. It had worked prisoners to death in Burma and Thailand, and in Korea, it was forcing 100,000 girls and women to become sex slaves, so-called "comfort women" for Japanese soldiers.[27]

Many Koreans willingly fought alongside the Japanese, a fact not widely known even today, but Choi was a rebel, and in P'yŏngyang he joined a mutinous plot to escape his Japanese unit, a plot that would become known as the P'yŏngyang Incident.[28]

In those desperate days, Choi stole food from the horses and began losing his mind from the torture and death that he witnessed. A few soldiers rebelled within their Japanese units and ended up in military prison. A Korean soldier named Yum, for example, ended up in jail and pretended to go crazy as a way to escape. During a roll call, Yum climbed a wooden board above the prisoners and guards, balanced there, naked, and began urinating and yelling,

"You, Japanese, go drink my pee!"[29] The guards grabbed him and, three days later, returned him to his cell beaten and tortured. Yum's friends warned him not to goad the Japanese guards again, but Yum did anyway. He disappeared. After the war, a friend met Yum and realized that he had gone crazy for real, having lost his mind from torture and imprisonment.

Choi and a group of his Korean companions began plotting an escape from their Japanese unit — a mutiny. Another man in his division had succeeded in fleeing; the soldier had hidden in an air duct under loose floorboards for five days then run to a military ground, where he had lain in a straw-covered storage bin for forty days. Japanese soldiers practised their drills around him and had no idea that he was hiding inside the bin. The Korean civilian who owned the bin and worked for the soldiers fed him during the day, but the panic-soaked soldier lost his mind, died from typhoid, saw hell and heaven, and rose from the dead.[30]

Choi and twenty-nine other soldier rebels would perhaps accomplish a similar miracle. They hoped to win a gunfight against the Japanese and escape to join rebel leader Kim Il Sung, the man who would soon rule North Korea. But a spy, a fellow Korean soldier, betrayed Choi and the leaders of the plot, and in November 1944, the military arrested them. On the day of Choi's arrest, he had planned to meet people at a spot on the Boo-Jun Plateau. His mother did not know about the arrest and went looking for him in the bushes of the plateau. She trudged to a town where someone claimed to have seen him in a nearby village. She walked in the freezing cold only to find the village deserted, the doors squeaking in the wind. Meanwhile, the Japanese banished Choi's father to a remote mining village in the mountains, and the rest of the family fled.[31]

Japanese soldiers took Choi to a detention house after several days of interrogation. There, he turned to look at one of his friends. "Bastard!" yelled a guard in Japanese and slapped Choi's face. That was how Choi learned to look straight ahead at all times — until his probable execution for desertion.

Indoors, he and the other rebels sat like stones in their cells.

Outside, they stood motionless in the sub-zero cold with only one layer of clothing.

Over time, Choi pretended to completely repent, and his Japanese jailers allowed him to practise Karate in the detention house, which kept him sane. The martial art's punches and kicks — spear hand, sword foot, front kick, side kick — impressed some of the Japanese guards, but Choi expected to be sentenced to death during his upcoming trial. Still, the guards asked him to teach them Karate, Japan's martial art, and they transformed part of the detention centre into a gym. Choi relished the sound of martial arts cries echoing through the room. As before, he gained more than physical power from the techniques.

Seven months later, the Japanese military charged Choi with breaking a military-service law.[32] He was sentenced to seven years in jail and transferred to P'yŏngyang Prison, but he was happy because he had avoided execution. He assumed that life would improve now; after all, the new prison was bigger and contained Korean, not Japanese, guards.

On Choi's first day in the new jail, one of the guards led him to a prison cell. Choi stopped in the doorway. Inside, he saw three prisoners. One was leaning on a blanket that was black with dirt, pus oozing from wounds on his side, and the other two men looked deformed, their hip bones and shoulders protruding like pots and their skin covered in scabs. They are lepers, thought Choi. The cell walls were covered with bloody marks from smeared bed bugs. The toilet crate smelled worse than the sour sake it had once held, and the beds were slick with pus from the prisoners' skin. Choi was so revolted and horrified that he could only stand there.

"They should have killed this kind of bum," the Korean guard said of Choi. "What is the use of feeding him bloody beans and rice for seven more years?" He cursed Choi and the other Korean prisoners then kicked him into the cell.

Choi cried, and he had good reason to. What was his cellmates' skin disease? Someone told him that the leprosy-looking scabs were contagious. The prisoners believed it was caused by "bean poison" — because they ate mainly beans — but the truth is that it was caused by the filthy conditions.

If he did not die from disease, he would die from shame for the Korean guards who were Japanese collaborators. He asked himself how a Korean jailer could become as sadistic as a Japanese one; this was not Korea's war after all. When Japan took over in 1910, most Koreans — certainly anyone who was not part of the aristocracy — did not want to co-operate with the invaders. By the 1930s, however, Japanese oppression had a Korean face: Korean men had rounded up many of the Korean comfort women, and Koreans comprised nearly half of the Japanese-run National Police, with Koreans oppressing Koreans.[33]

In 1945, Choi was seeing the horror of this oppression in his prison, and even as he vowed to fight it and to make his woebegone nation stronger, his body became infected with his cellmates' disease.

One summer day a Korean guard, Mr. Kim, walked by with a bucket of cold water, splashing it and taunting the thirsty prisoners. (Kim, a popular Korean name, means "gold," the name of a long line of men who would tempt and torture Choi until the day he died.)

The prison guards rarely gave anyone enough to drink, and the splashes from Kim's bucket were excruciating. Choi was also suffering from the oozing skin infection that plagued every other prisoner. Each day, corpses on stretchers floated past his cell.

"Here, I have water!" Kim announced as he stood outside Choi's cell. "I am going to give a dipper of it as a prize for the cell that has a good singer. How about that?"

None of Choi's cellmates wanted to sing. They had no energy, no talent, and the game was yet another humiliation. In spite of his desperate state, Choi stood up and sang a popular Korean folk tune.

Kim gave him and the others a cup of the precious water.

Choi Hong-Hi (fifth from the left, in the third row from the front) studied in Japan just before the Second World War. As with many other Koreans, he had to use a Japanese name, Yuseki Nishiyama. PHOTO COURTESY OF CHOI.

"Sing another song," Kim ordered. "I'll give you another dipper."

Choi began a folk song.

Suddenly, a Korean guard in the backyard screamed in Japanese, "Who was it?" He rushed to Choi's cell like a tiger and flung open the door. "Who was singing just now?" he yelled.

"It was me," Choi said and raised his hand.

The guard slapped him and every man in the cell, and he handcuffed Choi's arms behind his back. Choi seethed; why would one guard ask him to sing and a second tell him to stop?

Later, alone in his cell, the pain in Choi's arms devoured his anger. He eventually lost all feeling in his arms. He tried to lie on his side, but this made his upper arm feel dislocated. If he lay on his front, his chin mashed into the ground. He was too weak to stand, so he sat all night.

When breakfast arrived in the morning, he was dizzy with hunger, but he pretended otherwise. His cellmates ate his food. Lunch arrived, but he ignored it. The men in his cell begged him to eat, but Choi had chosen suicide. Many men had suffered torture, malnutrition, and insanity in Japanese prisons during the Second World War. Some simply lay down and gave up the will to live.[34] Choi fainted.

He woke up around five in the afternoon, and the second Korean guard, the one who had slapped and handcuffed him, led him to the office of the chief of guards. "This guy is a good singer," the guard joked to the chief.

Choi could not believe it.

"Sing," the guard demanded as he removed Choi's handcuffs.

Choi looked at the two men, his arms dangling at his sides. "I cannot sing," he said. He did not mention Kim, the guard who had wanted songs for water. The chief did not force Choi to entertain them, and the guard returned him to his cell.

Kim soon visited Choi and apologized for the singing game, but the apology and jail politics did little to help Choi, who was so malnourished and sick that he thought he would die. However, since Choi had not mentioned the water torment to Kim's superiors, Kim spared him further turmoil, visited him often, and snuck in medicine for the skin disease. The two men eventually became friends, which perhaps demonstrates the jailer's foresight: Japan was losing the war by this time, and jailers would soon become prisoners.

Two months later, Choi heard speakers crackle in his cell. They had been off for the entire nine months he had been in prison, but they now bristled with what sounded like the impossible: the Japanese Emperor was crying and reading his nation's surrender. Japan had lost the war.

Long live Korea! Choi screamed to himself. He wanted to dance for joy, but Kim warned him to remain quiet because retreating Japanese and Korean jailers might kill prisoners. The next day, however, the guards fled, and Choi stepped outside the iron gates. Wearing a loose shirt, baggy black pants, and straw slippers, he followed Kim through jubilant crowds, past the Korean flag at P'yŏngyang's city hall, and into Kim's house. Both men were alive, Korea was free, and Choi had a second chance. Much of his life had been one long battle against Japan, bullies, his father, and poverty — and he now had a chance to make something of himself, to make good on all the promises and prayers he had whispered in prison. After four decades of oppression, all Koreans had a second chance, and the country blew up into a storm of new-found hope and revenge killings.

Choi's P'yŏngyang Incident was one of the few Korean revolts against Japan during the Second World War, but there was nothing special about Choi's tortures. Most prisoners, especially foreign prisoners of war, endured worse.

However, generations of Koreans had lived through fifty years of Japanese oppression, and the martial artists among them would go on to create Tae Kwon Do, *Tang Soo Do*, *Hapkido*, and other martial arts in their attempts to empower themselves and their nation.

A week after Korea's liberation, an emaciated Choi trudged hundreds of kilometres through chaos and jubilation back to his family in Yongwon, which had transformed in the two years he had been away. His brother found him in an inn outside of the village and helped him back home. To Choi's surprise, a new enemy, communism, hovered like a dark cloud over much of northern Korea, including his village. He was devastated.[35] Korea was free from Japan but now had to contend with communists from the Union of Soviet Socialist Republics (U.S.S.R.), who had staked their Korean territory.

Worse, two American colonels had taken only thirty minutes to decide arbitrarily that the thirty-eighth parallel would divide Korea into north and south, and the U.S.S.R. had agreed to oversee the north.[36] Koreans now added the insult "pro-American" to the popular "pro-Japanese" and "traitor."[37] Overnight, superpowers had created a Cold War between Korean communists (backed by the U.S.S.R. and China) and Korean nationalists (backed by the U.S.) — a conflict that would last more than seventy years and continues to this day.

A couple of months after Choi had arrived in his village in 1945, he wandered to Seoul, the capital of the newly created South Korea. No one was in charge, and people fought in the streets.[38] Like many men, he was uncontrollable and jumped from one gang to another, which were usually organized around a tough tyrant.[39] He stopped using his Japanese name (Yuseki Nishiyama) and acquired a Korean nickname (*chadol*, a small stone difficult to break), and he channelled his strength and anger into a new anti-communist military school in Seoul, following many other young soldiers who had nowhere to go. The Americans had helped the Korean government establish a military academy, the start of a future army, and Choi was one of the first to enroll.[40]

Within a year, he was teaching Karate to a group of constables. Koreans called the art either *Tang Soo Do* (Way of the Chinese Hand) or *Kong Soo Do* (Way of the Empty Hand), the difference in names indicating whose side you were on in the Cold War. They were the same Karate though. The art's Japanese founder, Gichin Funakoshi, had changed "Chinese" to "Empty," which some viewed as insolence, since "Chinese Hand" had been around for centuries,[41] but using *Kong Soo Do* showed your allegiance to Japan. Many Koreans, such as Choi, remained loyal to China, not Japan, and stuck with the old name, *Tang Soo Do*. Amid this division and violence grew a small group of martial arts gyms (or *kwans*), and they contained the instructors and students who would go on to become the pioneers of all future styles of Tae Kwon Do.[42]

Choi and other martial artists used their fists as much as their brains to get what they wanted. Choi's signature move before a fight was to burn one of his knuckles with a lit cigarette — but only the knuckles on his right hand because his left was to remain unscarred in respect of Confucian values. His right fist, however, was toughened with calluses.

In spite of the chaos on Seoul's streets and a South Korean strongman installed by the Americans, Choi felt he could lead an army. At that time, he met Sun-Ha Lim, who had been a student soldier and admired Choi because of the P'yŏngyang Incident. Lim would soon become a general and help to set up Korea's military. In those early days, he noticed that Choi wanted to lead his friends as much as entertain them. During parties, Choi liked to have a good time and loved to see people laugh, so he would jump on a table and dance and sing folk songs, and his friends would laugh their heads off.[43] Lim noticed Choi had to be the centre of attention. On the

In 1948, Choi met his second wife.
They had three children.
PHOTO COURTESY OF CHOI.

streets, Choi would walk in front, not beside or behind, kicking street poles and punching anything he could, until his embarrassed friends would yell at him to stop making a spectacle.[44] Lim wondered what would become of this brash, young soldier from whom his superiors wanted more military art and less martial art.

In 1946, when Choi was a second lieutenant, he became ashamed of teaching Japanese Karate to Korean soldiers.[45] This was during a time when Koreans were rediscovering their culture after decades of war and Japanese oppression. That year, he created his first technique for a supposedly new martial art: it was a "low block," which he stole from Karate.[46] He began thinking about a martial art that would be better than Karate and would strengthen him, his soldiers, and his country because, in his world, Japanese bullies lurked around every corner and superpowers gathered at every border.

Those uncertainties did not stop him, however, from pursuing a woman whom he saw at army headquarters in 1948. He was still in the marriage his parents had arranged when he was a young teen, but that did not stop him either. He carried a large bouquet of flowers to the woman's home every evening, asking her to marry him. When she opened the door for him, all she saw was a bouquet of flowers with legs because he was short and the flowers were huge.[47] She eventually said yes, not seeing the horrors to come.

CHAPTER 3

SUPERNAM

After a couple of years, the Cold War in Asia blew up into the Korean War, known by the North Koreans as the "Fatherland Liberation War."[48] More than two million Koreans died, the majority of them civilians killed by napalm dropped by Americans on 1,000 square miles of North Korea.[49] After the war ended in 1952, people wandered around traumatized. Orphans walked through the streets, and maimed and starving adults begged for food, but Koreans were thankful that American President Harry Truman had not dropped the atomic bombs that he had prepared for North Korea, which would have contaminated the entire peninsula. Most houses and buildings in both Koreas were destroyed nonetheless.

Translator John Koh, who helped me with this book, was ten years old when the war ended and his family returned from refuge to Seoul. He found his house in ashes and, in its place, two dead men tied up. He looked at one of the bodies and saw the face moving in a strange way. Walking closer to the man, he saw that so many maggots were crawling under his skin that the face looked alive.

Those were years of rot and chaos, and the military and martial arts provided ready masters for lost and hungry men. In 1952, Choi was thirty-three years old and already a two-star general.[50] He had survived the war, but his commanding officer, father and calligraphy teacher had all died. Choi married his second wife — the woman who had stared at the bouquet with legs — and they had a daughter, Meeyun. He had left his first wife and first daughter, Song-Jook Choi, and for the rest of his life he would rarely talk about them.[51] In this regard, he seemed much like his father.

While leading his men during the Korean War, Choi had made sure that they learned martial arts to keep them strong, but as he became busier after the war, he realized he needed a full-time martial arts leader for his soldiers — an athlete who could teach hundreds of war-toughened men and perform advanced techniques. He needed a superman. In 1952, he found him: Nam Tae-hi, proficient in *Tang Soo Do* (Korean Karate) and known for using martial arts in a famous, desperate battle.

✕✕✕

Korean poetry and folklore are full of tales of legendary events near impressive mountains, usually involving Korea's great men.[52] Second Lieutenant Nam also had a story. It began — or rather ended — on a cold morning on May 22, 1951, when he woke up with his head on a dead man's thigh.[53] That day, he wondered if he was alive and if his body and mind were intact. He sat up and, in terror, thought that he was in enemy territory, but he saw that his unit was still near the top of Yongmun Mountain, not far from Seoul, South Korea. He had no injuries. It was spring, and a light snow lay on the ground.

Nam and Choi had much in common: they had trained in Shotokan Karate, shot at North Korean communists, and had survived war battles. But Nam and his Third Battalion were near death now, after nearly three days of continuous fighting, much of it involving hand-to-hand combat.[54] Earlier in the week, Chinese and North Korean communists had surrounded Nam's battalion in a nearby township, and the division commander had blamed Nam's regiment for the crisis, even though the communists had outnumbered the South Koreans three to one.[55] As punishment, the commander sent Nam's regiment to a no-man's land on Yongmun

Mountain, a dangerous outpost ten kilometres south of the division's main defensive line, which meant ten kilometres closer to the enemy (China's 187th, 188th, and 189th divisions). Nam's unit set up machine guns on a plateau, but he feared a bloodbath.

On the first night, May 19, he heard the communists attack his compatriots, the Second Battalion, on the next plateau. Chinese soldiers often attacked in waves during the night, overwhelming American and South Korean forces. They had overrun most of the Korean peninsula with this strategy. Nam noticed that the enemy's front lines had guns but that the soldiers behind did not; when enemy soldiers at the front fell, soldiers behind them picked up the dead men's guns and continued fighting.

At daybreak, Nam heard the enemy retreat, which is what they usually did after night attacks. The second day was much the same, but on the third day of fighting, the Chinese army flowed uphill to Nam's plateau. He saw them coming up the mountain and did not fire his gun because it had a firing range of only 500 yards. He waited. To his horror, he realized that there were so many communist soldiers that he would run out of bullets before they ran out of bodies.

As it got darker, the communists flowed within range. He fired, but the enemy destroyed his machine-gun emplacement and shot many of his soldiers. Nam moved into the trenches his unit had dug. It was so dark that he and his soldiers could not use guns, scared they would kill each other. The Chinese soldiers seemed to have the same fears. Who was friend and who foe?

Nam heard a noise, ran into someone, and tried to grab the man's hair. The Chinese soldier was trying to do the same. The only way to distinguish friend from foe was by grabbing at the head because communists had crew cuts and South Koreans had longer hair. In that trench, Nam felt short hair — almost bald — and he struck. His enemy fell.

He heard another soldier. He punched, flailed, ran on. As the two armies fought in the dark, Nam tapped men's heads when he could. Crew cut meant attack; long hair meant pull back. He fought for his life all night, stumbling through the dark, striking, falling, moving.

Near the end of the night, most of his thirty-one men were dead. The communists retreated. Nam had not eaten or slept for three days and nights, and he collapsed from exhaustion.[56]

The next morning, he woke to see that he was using the thigh of an enemy soldier for a pillow; the leg had been more comfortable than a rock. As the sun rose, his regimental commander ordered a retreat, and the American 24th Armoured Division came to their rescue. Nam and the Americans were still hopelessly outnumbered, but, miraculously, the South Korean and American divisions held their own against the communists. Innumerable Chinese bodies lay in a nearby river.

That day, Nam wandered to a spot where he had fought the night before. He found many dead bodies and counted more than two dozen with no bullet or knife wounds. They were the ones he had hit during the night, the ones with broken faces and bones. But there was no time to dwell on these things. Seeing the Chinese divisions weakened, all the South Koreans, including the main line ten kilometres away, counterattacked and chased the communists over Yongmun Mountain. Thanks to Nam and his battalion, the outnumbered Koreans and Americans defeated three communist divisions, and the battle would make its way into Korea's military records as a lesson in how to defend a mountaintop against a 360-degree attack. General Choi Hong-Hi was impressed.

Word spread that Nam was a Korean Karate expert who had killed communists with his bare hands, and Choi wanted him in his division. With men like Nam, he believed that tiny Korea could banish Chinese communists just as it had defeated Japanese fascists. Nam himself was traumatized, however, and in later years would recount his battle mainly through tears. He survived because of his martial arts training and, as he put it, because, "God gave me the strength to survive."[57]

x x x

Nam Tae-hi is in the bottom row, fourth from the left. Choi Hong-Hi sits beside him, fifth from the left. PHOTO COURTESY OF CHOI.

I ask myself how someone can kill two dozen men in hand-to-hand combat. In 2001, long after Nam and Choi had become a formidable duo in Tae Kwon Do, I met Nam in Chicago and asked about the battle. What techniques had he used on Yongmun Mountain? He said he did not remember and, in any case, what a question! It was like asking which way the wind had blown after falling into a pit. He had expected to die during the fighting. Nam had been an expert in Korean Karate, or *Tang Soo Do*, which he and Choi would later rename Tae Kwon Do.

Years before the battle, Nam had studied Korean Karate for the same reason that other Korean children and teenagers had: Japanese bullying. He was born in Seoul on March 22, 1929, in the middle of Japan's occupation of Korea. Like Choi, Nam needed a martial art to defend himself. "When I was in elementary school, I had lots of conflicts with the Japanese boys in the playground," Nam told me. "No matter where I used to go, the boys gave me a hard time, so I always beat them up. Eventually, they told me, 'We can't beat you, but we have a Karate black belt who will.' I didn't know what Karate was. Someone explained that Karate was a martial art, and with one *kihup!* they break everything — and, even, when you do Karate, those who are twenty metres away, their arms break! I wanted to learn."[58]

Nam's bullies may have known about the books that were popular in Asia then, such as *The Complete Illustrated Book of the Secret Lessons of Soft and Hard Gong*, by the Master of Wu Tai Mountain, who wrote about climbing walls, striking your knees with a metal hammer to make them stronger, and throwing your fist to hit a target several metres away.[59] Such fantasies would later leap from books into creation myths about Tae Kwon Do.

At eighteen years old, Nam had begun training after school five days a week at Won-kuk Lee's *Chung Do Kwan* ("gym of the blue way"), the first Karate gym in Korea and the source of many future Tae Kwon Do pioneers.[60] Won-kuk Lee was a pioneer of Korean Karate and was a famous martial arts leader who was likely the only Korean to attain a second-degree black belt in Shotokan Karate before 1945.[61] Born in 1907 (making him older than both Choi and Nam), Lee had studied Karate in the 1920s, long before Choi began.[62] In 1944, during the Second World War and after four decades of Japanese suppression of Korean martial arts, a Japanese governor allowed Lee to open the Chung Do Kwan. As a result of this, the Korean government would later charge Lee with being pro-Japanese. It did not help that, unlike Choi, Nam, and most others, Lee refused to support South Korea's new strongman, who accused Lee of leading a group of assassins. The Karate master and his wife fled to Japan in 1950, but, before that, Nam perfected his techniques. Nam never saw Lee kill anyone, but he said that one kick from him would have been fatal.

The martial art in those days was basic by today's standards. "In the early days, *Chung Do* [Tae Kwon Do] consisted of ten hand and eight kicking techniques all aimed at the vital points of the body," Lee once told a journalist. "The hand techniques were punch, spear-hand, palm, knife-hand, inner ridge-hand (between thumb and forefinger), twin fingers, single finger, back fist and tiger fist. The kicking techniques consisted of front, side, round and back kick and these were aimed at various levels of the body."[63]

A couple of years ago, I asked Nam about one of those hand techniques, a specialized movement called a "straight-fingertip strike," sometimes called a "spear-hand." It is similar to a punch but uses the fingertips, instead of a fist, which are thrust into an opponent's abdomen or solar plexus. To my amazement, one of my instructors said that the strike, with diligent training and properly generated power, was intended to puncture an opponent's skin with the fingers. Choi Hong-Hi elaborated during a 2001 black belt seminar in Toronto: he said that in the instant before striking, you should half-twist the technique, so that the fingertips corkscrew through the skin. In addition, the instructor added that your hand might become embedded in the person's organs after the strike, so immediately withdrawing your hand was essential.

I told Nam all this when I met him and asked if it was possible to perform such a technique. I will never forget his reply because he looked at me calmly, slightly perplexed, and said, "You cannot stay in the opponent's stomach. You have another opponent, maybe. And though you made a hole in the first man's body, it does not mean your opponent will stay still; he will still punch and kick. Pull back and prepare the next action."[64] It was then that I realized the difference between training now and fifty years ago, between my part-time hobby of learning a martial art and his full-time job of teaching a killing art.

Nam and I also talked about the lead-leg side kick, a simple technique in which a fighter lifts the front leg and kicks with the heel or the outside edge of the foot. Because there is little space to build momentum (compared to kicking with the rear leg), the kick is difficult to do with power and speed, and most defenders absorb a weak side kick or grab the attacking leg when sparring. One of my instructors, who had been a student of Nam's, told me that the best fighters mastered the kick so that the edge of the foot became a sword — a "foot sword," as Choi put it — breaking an arm, thigh, foot, rib, or anything else in the way. "The purpose of the attack is to immobilize the opponent," Nam told me. "One punch, one kick, can do a lot of damage: broken bones, skin problems . . . Traditionally speaking, one strike, one kick, can kill.

We trained hard to develop more power, more energy. Instead of punching two or three times, we punched once — for a knock down." Many great fighters who studied *Tang Soo Do* (which relied mainly on arm techniques), such as Bruce Lee, Joe Lewis, and Bill "Superfoot" Wallace, improved their sparring with the lead-leg side kick, becoming as agile with their legs as they were with their arms.

"Tae Kwon Do is different now," Nam told me. "Some people aren't capable, but they're still black belts. Some take it as a recreational activity. I understand . . . But I'm sorry for such a change . . . I want Tae Kwon Do to go back to the traditional way: hard-working — physically and mentally — with total concentration . . . I'm sorry, I wish I could train instructors as before."

Nam was a humble man for a former soldier, and it was surreal to hear him apologize for no longer teaching men how to maim or kill with one blow. Perhaps he had mellowed with age; he was seventy-one when I first spoke to him in 2001. Choi liked to take most of the credit for founding Tae Kwon Do, but, in reality, Nam Tae-hi played a large part and was also a founder.

x x x

On Cheju Island in 1952, General Choi summoned Nam to teach *Tang Soo Do* in the newly created 29th Infantry Division, which would become a Tae Kwon Do incubator. Choi now led 100,000 men on Cheju, and he told regimental commanders to send athletes or martial artists to train eight hours a day under Captain Nam. Fifty soldiers arrived, some from Won-kuk Lee's Chung Do Kwan. These pioneers were part of the first wave of Tae Kwon Do.[65]

The 29th Division would go on to train thousands of martial arts soldiers, including the Black Tigers, an elite unit assigned to espionage and assassination missions in North Korea.[66] Choi took pride in the Black Tigers, whose name echoed the famed Korean "tiger fighters" of 1861, when an American squadron of ships attempted to take over Korean ports at Kanghwa. For hundreds of years, Korea had been known for repelling foreigners. The U.S.

had decided to open the ports by force in 1861, but 650 Koreans repelled them until their weapons were empty, after which they fought to the last man, desperately throwing sand in the Americans' eyes and attacking them with their bare hands.[67] The Americans killed all the Korean fighters, whose bodies lay in bloodied white garments on the beach around a citadel. In the end, after fruitless negotiations with local leaders, the Americans retreated.

Approximately ninety years later, in 1953, the Americans were using more subtle tactics. They supported men such as Choi and Nam, who were part of the Korean military's efforts to rebuild the nation, and the two martial artists made it their mission to empower soldiers, because the streets were dangerous, everyone was traumatized, and the Korean War had only exacerbated the Cold War between the U.S. and the U.S.S.R. and China.

Choi ensured that the training was strict in the 29th Division. Some of Nam's students had trudged for days from North to South Korea, leaving their homes behind to escape communism. They had few belongings and practised on drill grounds of the 29th Division, which had no indoor gym.[68] They trained barefoot in the snow, not because they were trying to be tough but because they did not want to wear out their shoes.

Hee-Il Cho, who later became a well-known Tae Kwon Do expert in the U.S., began martial arts training in those days, when the martial arts were not for exercise but for survival and military training. "Although they were not really gang members, young people used to roam from town to town and beat up kids," Cho told a journalist. "The martial arts facilities were very basic then," he said. "The buildings had a roof, but sometimes they didn't have walls. The floor was dirt. Many children didn't have shoes, so we all walked around barefoot." Hunger was the norm; they ate once a day.[69]

In the early years of Tae Kwon Do, when it was still raw and called *Tang Soo Do*, Choi dreamed and Nam made the dreams physical. Few of Choi's men saw him do much martial arts during the fifty years they worked with him. He did not have to. He was a powerful general who gave orders to lower-ranking athletes, such as Nam, who brought the art to life.[70] Choi ran the show, but Nam *was* the show.

By 1954, Choi and Nam were confident enough in their fifty martial artists to organize a demonstration for South Korean President Syngman Rhee. Choi wanted to show Rhee that the 29th Division had great soldiers.

Nam would never forget the day of the demonstration, which took place on the grass of an outdoor stadium as part of an anniversary celebration for the First Army Corps. President Rhee watched from an elevated platform, along with his generals and thousands of soldiers. Nam and his men sparred and completed self-defence and bayonet-defence techniques. When they finished, President Rhee remained standing, wishing them to continue. (He must have known about Nam's hand-to-hand battle on Yongmun Mountain during the Korean War, as he had awarded special honours to Nam's division.[71]) Nam and his assistant, Han Cha-gyo, had been given only fifteen minutes for a demonstration, so they improvised when the president asked for more, the martial artists exploding in a series of knife-hands and other techniques in a pattern called *Hwa-Rang,* which Nam had created from a Korean Karate pattern. Nam also defended against an attack by two men and then three.

At one point, he walked up to a pile of thirteen clay roof tiles, each three-quarters of an inch thick. Someone with no martial arts training would have found it difficult to break two tiles, and these thirteen rose from the ground more than a foot. Nam exuded power, but he was not a tall man, so as he stood over the tiles and raised his hand, the soldiers must have wondered if breaking them would be possible.

Nam smashed the curved tiles with a single downward punch.

The president was amazed. "What was on his hand?" he asked General Choi, who was nearby.

"Nothing," Choi replied. "He broke them with his fist, his bare hand."

"Is this the part he used?" the president asked, pointing to his first two knuckles.

"Yes, sir," Choi replied.[72]

In 1954, General Choi Hong-Hi shakes hands with South Korean President Syngman Rhee after they watched Colonel Nam Tae-hi break thirteen roof tiles with a punch. Chief of Staff and four-star Gen. Lee Hyung-gun looks on.
PHOTO COURTESY OF CHOI.

Choi explains to Rhee how Nam broke the tiles with the first two knuckles.
PHOTO COURTESY OF CHOI.

The president asked for the martial art's name. Choi had anticipated this and had told Nam to prepare a summary of the demonstration. However, after Choi had read Nam's draft, he struck out the parts about *Tang Soo Do*, or Karate, because the president, who was a hardcore nationalist, loathed the Japanese and would have a fit if he knew South Korean soldiers were practising a Japanese martial art. After all, the president had accused Korea's first Karate master and Nam's teacher, Won-kuk Lee, of being an assassin, and Lee had fled for his life.

Before Choi could reply to the president, someone blurted the truth, that it was *Tang Soo Do*.

The president countered that it was *T'aekkyŏn*, averting a fit but creating a problem for Choi and Nam. The two arts were completely different. *T'aekkyŏn* was a traditional Korean game that required mainly leg techniques, while *Tang Soo Do* was Karate and relied on hand techniques.[73] Rhee probably remembered *T'aekkyŏn* from childhood. Impressed by Nam's demonstration, he ordered Choi to teach this art to more Korean soldiers. The military was now the strongest institution in Korea; it had grown from 100,000 to 600,000 personnel in three years, and every male had to go through military duty: boot camps, disciplinary training, anti-communist speeches, and "an authoritarian practice that chilled even the most hard-bitten American officers," as one historian put it.[74] Martial arts would now be added to the training.

The 1954 demo — the story of it — grew into one of the most memorable moments in Choi's and Nam's lives, and it was followed by extraordinary events. They had gained the admiration of their president but faced a dilemma: they could not teach Karate and call it *T'aekkyŏn*.[75] Although *T'aekkyŏn* contained many hand techniques, it was known for hundreds of years for its soft, rhythmic, foot-fighting game based on powerful leg sweeps, jumps, and pushes.[76] In short, *T'aekkyŏn* was not Karate, and Choi was no fool.

While Choi and Nam meditated on the problem, the 29th Division became well known in the Korean army, and Choi became closer to the president of South Korea, thereby gaining more power.[77] In 1954, Choi ordered the military to build a new martial arts gym inside a military base in Kangwon Province.[78] He called it the *Oh Do Kwan* ("gym of my way" or "gym of our way"). That same year, he became honorary director of Won-kuk Lee's renowned Chung Do Kwan, the civilian gym where Nam had learned Karate at age eighteen.[79] The martial arts leader there, Duk-Sung Son, gave Choi an honorary fourth-degree black belt because he wanted to use Choi's military influence to spread the martial art.[80] Choi transferred martial arts training from the 29th Division to these two gyms, and Nam needed a microphone to train his 300 men in the Oh Do Kwan alone.[81]

Choi's military and civilian gyms were two of the few pioneering gyms (called *kwans*) that South Korea's dictators would force to merge years later. Choi became the administrator at both gyms, but he never taught there. Nam would request something for the Oh Do Kwan, and Choi would order soldiers to jump to it. Together, their vision expanded until it was larger than the South Korean president's ego: every soldier would learn a new martial art — one that would take the best of Karate, add some *T'aekkyŏn*, and grow from there. The spectacular techniques would strengthen their soldiers, bring glory to Korean athletes, and empower a ravaged South Korea.

Moreover, the martial art would make Choi immortal, or so he dreamed. First, he had to rename it, because he could not call it *Tang Soo Do, Kong Soo Do*, or any of the other names that were synonymous with Karate, and they could not name it *T'aekkyŏn*, the South Korean dictator's preference. How could Choi and Nam convince him and martial arts leaders to change the name — and what should the new name be?

There was only one thing to do: arrange a dinner party at Choi's favourite *kisaeng* restaurant, a high-class Korean geisha house where men could buy power along with the best sake, women, and dreams.

CHAPTER 4

TAE KWON DO IS NAMED IN A KOREAN GEISHA HOUSE

It was fitting that on an evening in 1955, Choi hosted a martial arts meeting in a *kisaeng* house, a place of desire and myth, because he was about to sell a few myths of his own. The Kugīlgwan was a Korean geisha house built in the nineteenth century during the *Chosŏn* dynasty.[82] Lounging near a royal shrine and an ancient belfry that gave the street its name, Bell Street, the Kugīlgwan was one of the most famous *kisaeng* houses in Korea, a place where the newly rich opened their hearts along with their wallets. The manager of the Kugīlgwan was the South Korean president's secretary, Yi Ki-bung, an immeasurably useful connection for Choi; Yi was the second-most powerful politician in the country, after the president.[83]

Traditional Koreans with new money and power liked the old rituals of the Kugīlgwan. After the Second World War, a provincial police chief had ordered the *kisaeng* house to Westernize within three days (to add tables and chairs and to switch to Western dishes, such as steak and chicken soup), but the Kugīlgwan gently refused. Venerable families, old money from the *Chosŏn* era, preferred the two other, big *kisaeng* houses, but the Kugīlgwan maintained the *Chosŏn* food and decor. Many Koreans were starving in those days, and, occasionally, angry students would break up the parties, asking how government officials who conducted secret meetings in *kisaeng* houses could represent the people. It was a good question. Corrupt political and military leaders conducted most of the nation's business in *kisaeng* houses — what we in the West would call "backroom politics." *Kisaeng* politics was the only one that mattered in this war-devastated country.[84]

In 1955, on the day of Choi's martial arts meeting in the Kugīlgwan, five candles rested on a low table that overflowed with drinks and appetizers. The room's heat spread beneath them as Choi and his companions sat on the floor. Women whispered into their ears and served rice wine. One could order the *kisaeng* women from a special book and ask for them by flower names — Peoni, Laurel, Chrysanthemum. Men visited *kisaeng* houses not only to drink and deal but to talk to the *kisaengs*. For women of the *Chosŏn* era, becoming a *kisaeng* was an improvement in an era when women ranked low, and men governed their behaviour with a thousand rituals. Confucianism relegated most women to indoors and out of sight, but the *kisaeng* women were elevated. While they were revered, however, they were also reviled. Some became *kisaengs* to escape Confucian society, but in Choi's time most had been sold as young girls to *kisaeng* houses to be brought up as entertainers and mistresses. They lived like Japan's geisha women, and their careers were over by their late twenties.

Occasionally, a wicked truth would emerge from a *kisaeng* house and shatter society's myths about the lifestyle. Once, a *kisaeng* woman from the Kugīlgwan, Kim So-San, was accused of being a North Korean spy. Rather than arrest her, South Korea forced her to become a counter-spy, but the North Koreans suddenly ordered her to kill an anti-communist prosecutor. Caught between the two Koreas, Kim attempted suicide, but the gun malfunctioned.

Usually, such high drama was left to the men as they drank excellent *Ch'ŏngju,* the strained sake that flowed during meetings at the Korean geisha house. Choi liked to drink, but he was not an alcoholic. He believed that when a man wanted to be recognized as great, he had to be good at drinking, gambling, and fighting — and he had to be a playboy, with at least one *kisaeng* woman. In that sense, Choi understood his father's way of living of thirty years earlier. Choi now had two wives and four children:

a daughter with his first wife and a son and two daughters with his second. The three daughters sometimes played together, but everyone behaved as if his first wife did not exist. This was a world where teenage boys married once in their village, a second time in a city (when their social status rose), and a third time in their dreams, with *kisaengs*.

Choi's second wife felt uncomfortable with his visits to the *kisaeng* houses, but she had no say in the matter because, as Choi put it, a man had to show off his wealth and power. Also, meeting in a *kisaeng* house was only natural if you wanted to name a new martial art. This was not the first time that a Karate leader had tried to organize the dominant gyms in the country; the first serious meetings about the topic began in 1951, during the Korean War.[85] Now, however, Choi was powerful enough to succeed at what everyone else had failed to do: he and the South Korean president got along, he ran two of the main gyms, and he had decided to treat his illustrious guests to a good dinner for the first time in his army life.

That night, trench coats hung like bodyguards on the flowered dividers that surrounded their table in the Kugīlgwan. To Choi's right sat Duk-Sung Son, the powerful leader of Choi's civilian gym (the Chung Do Kwan). Choi and Son got along like a fox and a wolf, but they co-operated. Son had brought his head instructor[86] to sit with eight other men sat at the table: Korea's most powerful general, two influential politicians, two businessmen, and three journalists. They were known as the "First Advisory Committee for Duk-Sung Son's Chung Do Kwan." Only later would the meeting become momentous enough for Choi to call it "Tae Kwon Do's Naming Committee," deleting Son in the process.

"We have come here to create a new name unifying the confused and varied terms applied to one martial art," Choi told the others at the table.[87] Choi suggested they vote anonymously to pick the name. Each man scribbled his choice on a piece of paper, and when the ballots were opened, Choi saw that everyone had chosen the venerable name *Tang Soo Do*. Only he had suggested a new one, Tae Kwon Do. Someone wondered where the

A newspaper article about the 1955 meeting in a *kisaeng* house.
Choi Hong-Hi is third from the left and Duk-Sung Son is second from left.
PHOTO COURTESY OF CHOI HONG-HI AND JEONG-SOON CHEON.

odd-sounding *Tae Kwon* had come from. The character "*Kwon*" was well known, but "*Tae*" was unusual, and no one had ever seen the two joined into "*Tae Kwon*."

"Could whoever suggested this name explain the meaning please?" the chairman asked.

"*Tae* means jumping, kicking, or stamping," Choi said. "*Kwon* is, as you all know, a fist. Yet here the fist is not only the clenched palm, but also the various movements of a martial art, such as thrusting, punching, and striking."[88] "*Do*" meant "art" or "way," as in "Karate-Do."

Choi and Nam had made up "*Tae Kwon Do*" using Chinese and Korean dictionaries.[89]

Then Choi, always a gambler, made the astounding claim that *Tae Kwon* could be related to *T'aekkyŏn*, Korea's old art, which South Korea's president wanted to promote.[90] In Korean, the words "*Tae*" and "*Kwon*" were not the same as *T'aek* and *kyŏn*.[91] They were similar in English. More to the point, the physical moves of the two were completely different.

One of the businessmen had immediate reservations and suggested that further research was necessary. Korea's deputy parliamentary speaker, who was also present, suggested that three of them form a subcommittee to find historical proof linking Tae Kwon Do to *T'aekkyŏn*. A deadline of December 31, 1955, was set. The meeting ended and the men departed in their dark trench coats. The "research" later offered by the brash Choi was rooted in three ancient dynasties — connections that were fictional.[92] Choi reported the following:

1. Paintings of warriors in the labyrinthine caves of the *Koguryŏ* tombs that were near P'yŏngyang, North Korea, proved, according to Choi, that Tae Kwon Do's techniques had started in the *Koguryŏ* dynasty (37 BCE to 668 CE).
2. A statue of a Buddhist guardian (*Kumkang Yuksa*) depicted martial arts moves from the *Silla* dynasty (5 BCE to 668 CE).
3. A martial arts manual from 1759 called the *Muyechebo* showed *T'aekkyŏn* practitioners during the *Yi* dynasty.

Martial arts historians later debunked this bogus research (which made little mention of Japanese Karate), but even today, the mythical links still thrive in mainstream martial arts. Perhaps the most popular (and ironic) anecdotes swirl around the *Silla* dynasty's *hwarang* warriors.

It is worth reviewing the realities of the *hwarang* to show how anecdotes about them from 1,500 years ago transformed into militaristic, nationalistic attitudes in the twentieth century. *Hwarang* means "flower boy," and referred to groups of teenage boys picked from the aristocracy who travelled through the *Silla* dynasty wearing beautiful clothes and often singing, dancing and practising shamanism.[93] There is no evidence that they were Korean knights or Buddhist warriors.[94] There is also no proof that they practised martial arts.[95] But in 1952, at the height of Korea rediscovering its culture and creating myths about the *hwarang* being some sort

(*l*) A boy dancer in Korea looks like the *hwarang* of old (1960). (*r*) The ancient *hwarang* were more entertainers than warriors. Here, boy dancers dress as women in 1958. PHOTO COURTESY OF ROYAL ASIATIC SOCIETY-KOREA BRANCH, FROM FATHER RUTT'S "THE FLOWER BOYS OF SILLA (HWARANG)" (1961).

of ancient military cult, Choi named Tae Kwon Do's first pattern after them. Even today, Olympic Tae Kwon Do sites are obsessed with the *hwarang*, and Tae Kwon Do's leaders force black belts to memorize the *hwarang's* so-called five rules:

Loyalty to the king
Filial love toward one's parents
Fidelity in friendship
Bravery in battle
No unnecessary violence

However, there is no evidence that these rules were connected with the *hwarang*. Ironically, old documents and paintings show the *hwarang* dressed in women's clothing as they sing and dance, a far cry from the Korean playboys lounging in *kisaeng* houses of the 1950s.

But the fictions about the *hwarang* must have been as intoxicating as the sake and women. Choi's companions also presumably thought it better to have 1,500-year-old warriors on their side than face the truth that Tae Kwon Do was based on the martial art of Japan, their long-time enemy.

Soon after the *kisaeng* party in 1955, Choi stopped claiming that Tae Kwon Do *could be T'aekkyŏn* and started stating that it *was*. He lied, claiming that it had been prospering since the early *Silla* dynasty, through the *Koguryŏ* dynasty, and into the early part of the *Yi* dynasty. Who could argue with three empires? And who could argue with Choi, one of Korea's most powerful generals?

Even though no one voted for the name Tae Kwon Do, Choi and Nam boldly ordered their soldiers to use it in their military gym, the Oh Do Kwan, and to yell "Tae Kwon!" when they bowed, but Duk-Sung Son at the Chung Do Kwan and the rest of Korea's martial artists stuck with the name *Tang Soo Do*.

Unfortunately for Choi and Nam, South Korea's president also did not agree to call it Tae Kwon Do. "The president would like to write the name as *T'aekkyŏn*," the chief of the presidential guard told Choi a couple of days after the *kisaeng* party.[96] Choi almost fainted. How could he convince the president that the martial art was not their childhood art, *T'aekkyŏn*?

It was time for another party at the luxurious *kisaeng* house, and this time Choi invited the most influential members of the president's entourage, including the president's right-hand man. Choi's superiors might later attack him for handing out favours and bribes, but he thought it was worth the risk. During the party, the *kisaeng* women served *Chosŏn* food and Choi dished out strategic threats.

After the party, someone on behalf of Choi and Nam convinced South Korea's president to accept the name "Tae Kwon Do," which meant Choi and Nam could invoke the president to force martial arts leaders to call the art Tae Kwon Do.

Even fifty years later, Nam would cry when telling the story about how he and Choi had convinced the president to accept the name, insisting also that he, Nam, disliked *kisaengs* and liquor because he had become a devotedly Christian man, unlike Choi.

XXX

In 1956, South Korea's president suddenly ordered the high-flying Choi to quit the military because of corruption charges, which devastated Choi. He began drinking heavily, telling people that he could not support his family — could not even afford a pack of cigarettes on some days. To pass the time, he played Korean poker, *Hwatu*, with Korea's richest men and women, always reserving "some muscle power," as he put it, in case of threats and fist fights.[97] His wife ignored his gambling and abhorred his trips to the *kisaeng* houses. Korea was still in a shambles, as was Choi's life. Despite his best efforts and threats, only two gyms used the name Tae Kwon Do.

Never one to give up, he began writing a Tae Kwon Do book, and after Shotokan Karate founder Gichin Funakoshi died in 1957, Choi plagiarized many of his ideas and words. Choi felt that he was improving Karate. He wanted Korea to have its own art, one that would be superior to anything from Japan, but his lies were becoming outrageous: he accused Japan of taking Korea's *T'aekkyŏn* and renaming it Karate during Japan's occupation of Korea before the Second World War.[98] Choi loathed the Japanese, whose armies and governments had bullied Koreans. He thought nothing of stealing Funakoshi's "elbow," "ball of the foot," "back of the heel," and "sword foot."[99] It was only fair, perhaps, because Funakoshi had originally borrowed the terms from Chinese martial arts.

Choi's book also included the "sword hand," "four-finger spear hand," and "two-finger spear hand," all of which appeared in Funakoshi's 1943 Japanese-language book *Karate-Do Nyumon*. Funakoshi wrote that to strengthen a fist one should punch a tapered wooden post.[100] Choi described exactly the same post for Tae Kwon Do and included Funakoshi's advice to bury it one-third in the ground and wrap it in rice straw at the top.

His five-year-old creation myth became beautifully simple: "Tae Kwon Do is an ancient, Korean martial art," a claim that would be emblazoned on gym walls and in people's minds for the next fifty years.[101] Always the dramatic storyteller, he added 1,500-year-old fictions about *hwarang* warriors. "*T'aekkyŏn* was so advanced that the history books of that period describe martial artists jumping over the high walls and attacking the enemy on the other side," he said. Another tale described martial artists, "kicking a ceiling after jumping from a sitting position."[102]

Plagiarism aside, Choi's book contained an important innovation: the "Theory of Power," which applied physics to martial arts techniques and explained how a human body could generate tremendous power — a priority for Choi, who was only five feet tall and weighed 100 pounds. Karate's founder had taught that power comes from three things during a technique: rotating the hips to put all of one's weight into a punch; pulling the non-punching hand to the waist; and, at the moment of impact, screwing the punch into the target. Choi said the same thing in a 1960 book but added scientific formulas, such as Newton's Third Law of Motion, which states that every action has an equal and opposite reaction — a theory that explains why you have to pull the non-punching hand backwards with a force equal to that of the punching hand.

In later years, Choi summarized his Theory of Power into six parts:

1. Reaction Force (based on Newton's Third Law)
2. Concentration (based on pressure being equal to force divided by area)
3. Equilibrium (maintaining one's centre of gravity)
4. Breath Control
5. Mass
6. Speed (the most essential factor because it unites the other five)

He used a classical mechanics equation to summarize the relationship between mass, speed, and power. Martial artists knew that strengthening one's muscles and throwing all of one's weight into a technique were crucial, but Choi applied the formula $E = \frac{1}{2}\, m \times s^2$ to show why a fast lightweight could generate more power than a relatively slower heavyweight. The formula states that the energy of a moving object (E) equals its mass (m) multiplied by its squared speed (s) divided by two. So if you somehow doubled the mass behind your punch, then your resulting energy, or power, would increase by one unit (half the mass), but if you doubled the speed of your punch, then your power would increase many times more than one unit (speed squared). In short, a speedy lightweight could create more power than a relatively slower but muscular heavyweight.

The physics had implications for training — and for people's egos. Martial artists knew about mass and speed instinctively, but Choi was brilliant at explaining how to increase power. He maximized power in every way he could, which is one reason that board-breaking later became an impressive aspect of Tae Kwon Do — with Choi adding board after board. Alongside his obsession with martial arts power was his ambition for military and political power, which was one reason that he was soon back in the military.

In 1959, after beginning a job as acting commander of an army corps, Choi moved quickly to promote Tae Kwon Do. He published the book that he had worked on during his low period, and in 1960, after the now-unpopular South Korean president fled to exile in Hawaii, Choi issued a second edition of his book *Introductory Tutorial to Tae Kwon Do*. Moreover, the two gyms that he oversaw, the Oh Do Kwan and Chung Do Kwan, ran successful satellite schools, sending their advanced black belts to a special instructors academy that, among other things, prepared them for culture shock when they taught overseas.

Also in 1959, Choi and other martial arts leaders finally unified within the Korean Tae Kwon Do Association.[103] The KTA would later be implicated in violent espionage missions in the U.S., but in 1959 it was an empowering force for the military and for civilians. Choi elbowed his way past other martial arts leaders to become president, later claiming to be Tae Kwon Do's sole founder when, in fact, he was only one of the founding members. Still, many big men challenged the puny Choi in those years, and few people called the martial art Tae Kwon Do.

In 1961, as Choi and a couple of generals sat drinking in a high-class *kisaeng* house in Nonsan Training Camp, in Taegun,

Leaders in the Korean Tae Kwon Do Association met in 1959 to try to unify the martial arts in Korea. Bottom row, from left to right: Hwang Kee (from the Moo Duk Kwan); Yoon Kwei-byung (owner of the Jidokwan); Choi Hong-Hi (wearing uniform); Ro Byung-jik (Song Moo Kwan); an unknown Korean Athletic Association representative; Lee Nam-suk (Chang Moo Kwan); Uhm Woon-kyu (Chung Do Kwan); and Hyun Jong-myung (Chung and Oh Do kwans). Top row, from left: Kim Soon-bae (Chang Moo Kwan); Ko Jae-chun (Chung and Oh Do kwans); Nam Tae-hi (Chung Do Kwan); Lee Houng-sup; and unknown.
PHOTO COURTESY OF CHOI HONG-HI.

they complained about the state of South Korea now that their dictatorial president had fled to Hawaii. [104] The opined that recent elections had resulted in a weak government, student protests, and more chaos. Democracy did not work for them, so they decided to support a few generals and take over the country.

CHAPTER 5

ENTER THE DRAGON AND HIS DICTATOR

Choi sounded like a megalomaniac as he helped pull off a *coup d'état* on May 16, 1961, against South Korea's first democratically elected government.[105] The coup began in Seoul at 3 a.m. — an easy, bloodless takeover that was backed by the U.S. Twelve hours later, while Choi and his soldiers were celebrating in Taegun, Major Nam Tae-hi called from Seoul.

"How is it?" Choi asked.

"Not good, sir," Nam replied in a shaky voice.

"What on earth is happening?" Choi asked.

"Right now, fully armoured troops have gathered in the square of Army Headquarters," Nam explained.[106]

Choi was shocked. Their general ran that headquarters. Their superior, who was leading the coup, was completely surrounded. That could mean only one thing: the coup had failed.

Nam called back to announce that the coup had not failed. The military had taken over Seoul, but a little-known general named Park Chung-hee was leading the coup, not their general. Choi was astonished. Park was leading? The Japanese collaborator during the Second World War? The man whom Choi once wanted to execute for communist activities? Yes, that Park.

Choi was in deep trouble. Park had specialized in political assassinations and repression for the Japanese during the Second World War, and now he had been cunning enough to seize power during the coup. Would Park forgive him for having helped issue an execution sentence thirteen years ago? Supporting the coup looked like one of the most reckless gambles of Choi's life — in the same sphere as losing his mother's education savings during a poker game.

The world's newest dictator, General Park Chung-hee, soon led an ominous campaign to "purify" South Korea. He banned 4,300 politicians from politics, arrested nearly 30,000 opponents within a year of seizing power,[107] and, with the help of the American CIA, created a terror network with the Korean Central Intelligence Agency (KCIA).[108] Choi refused to address him as "Honourable President Park" and criticized him behind his back.

A group of powerful, vicious men had helped Park during the coup, men who would build and use many Tae Kwon Do executives and instructors for spy missions over the next few decades.[109] Kim Un-yong was one of them, yet another Kim who would torment Choi. A former lieutenant colonel, Kim worked for Park after the coup and became a high-ranking KCIA agent known as "Mickey Kim."

Born on March 19, 1931, the Year of the Ram,[110] Kim's last name means "gold" and his first name means "cloud dragon." When he was three, his father worked as a journalist for a Japanese newspaper and introduced his son to a provincial premier who wore a gold-embroidered uniform. Kim later vowed to wear such a uniform. His family was rich in the 1930s, a time when many Koreans went hungry; the Kims owned a mine, land, and buildings in Seoul and Taegu. Although both Kim and Choi were in the military, they could not have been more different: Kim came from privilege, the aristocracy, and Japanese collaboration; Choi emerged from poverty, peasant stock, and a hatred for Japanese collaborators.

In 1961, the dictatorship's prime minister hired Kim as a protocol secretary, and one of the architects of the coup soon recruited Kim to the KCIA.[111] All of them lined up against Choi and his martial artists, some of whom had senior positions within the KCIA. And so began a horrific era in the history of Tae Kwon

Kim Un-yong (centre) with my ITF instructor, Jong-Soo Park (second from left) and my WTF instructor Yoon Yeo-bong (second from right). At far left is Chung Oh and at far right is Myung-Soo Son. PHOTO COURTESY OF PARK.

Do. Martial artists worked for KCIA branches in charge of assassinations, abductions, sabotage, and spy networks in Korea and overseas.[112] (Even Nam would join the KCIA, from 1965 to 1972.)

A KCIA director would later admit, "I had extensive powers at my disposal — more power than you can imagine — covering every aspect of my country."[113]

For most of the 1960s, the KCIA's power extended deep into economic, cultural, religious, and sports activities, including Tae Kwon Do. Kim worked as a "project officer for cultural activities" at the South Korean Embassy in Washington, DC, but he was really senior spy "Mickey Kim," working in multiple countries and within the United Nations.[114] He spoke perfect English, funded Tae Kwon Do gyms and events in the U.S. and England, and helped to run spy missions from 1963 to 1971, perhaps longer. Overall, the KCIA missions involved tormenting Korean-Americans and bribing American politicians who did not support the South Korean dictatorship.

In 1961, Choi (in uniform on the far left) partied with Park Chung-hee (standing in the middle of the shot, wearing civilian clothes). PHOTO COURTESY OF CHOI.

With men like Kim in the regime, Choi knew he was in trouble, but he was still powerful; he had his own connections within the KCIA, commanded 100,000 soldiers in five divisions, and partied at influential *kisaeng* houses. The South Korean dictator did not frequent the same *kisaeng* establishments as his generals — and certainly not Choi's hangout — because the dictator had opened his own *kisaeng* house, called *An-ga* and operated by the KCIA.

In the autumn of 1961, martial arts leaders asked the new dictator to help reunify the martial arts in South Korea. He agreed, authorizing a name change from the "Korean Tae Kwon Do Association" to the "Korean Tae Soo Do Association," effectively killing the name Tae Kwon Do after its two short years of existence.[115] The group's acronym was still the KTA, and its dozen leaders were still a who's who of martial arts leaders in the country.[116]

The personal vendetta between Choi and the dictator worsened, and the dictator eventually banished Choi to an ambassadorship in Malaysia while Kim was in the U.S. The posting seemed like a cozy one, but the blunt-talking Choi found being away from South Korea excruciating, and forcing him to become an ambassador was like putting a fox in a chicken coop.

To "celebrate" Choi's posting, the dictator hosted a farewell party at Korea's best restaurant. At one point, he sat beside Choi.

"Elder General Choi, I feel sad," the dictator said, pouring Choi another drink.

"There is nothing to be sad about," Choi lied. "I think it is a pity that you will be surrounded by corrupt advisors after I, who have always given you honest advice, leave you."[117]

The president soon walked away. Choi sat there, meditating on dusty aphorisms from Chinese philosophy, such as "Pay a malignant person back with a virtuous deed." Could Choi show such virtue? No. Bitter feelings haunted his better instincts, and revenge peered behind pride.

After the party, Choi and Nam Tae-hi bid farewell to each other. They had worked together for ten years, training Korean soldiers and struggling to create a new martial art. In 1962, while Choi flew to Malaysia as "Ambassador Extraordinaire and Plenipotentiary," Nam parachuted into the Vietnam War, where he began teaching soldiers how to do what he had done on a mountaintop during the Korean War: kill communists with bare hands.[118]

After Choi and his family settled in Malaysia, he became obsessed with Tae Kwon Do, setting up an outdoor gym for himself in the front yard of the Korean Embassy, not caring what anyone thought of an ambassador jumping around like a country boy. He hated the official duties of an ambassador, especially the formal events. At dinners, he would be mortified when he accidentally ate the bread of a guest sitting beside him or when he showed up in top hat and tuxedo when everybody was dressed casually.

In 1962, he decreased his responsibilities as ambassador and devoted more time to translating his 1960 book from Korean into English. During formal events, he would talk about Tae Kwon Do every chance he could. He used the embassy's typists and squirreled away every spare hour from his diplomatic duties to create new patterns (*hyungs* or *tuls*), dancelike movements that show off martial arts techniques. Unbeknown to Choi, one of the Korean councillors at the embassy noted his obsession and told the KCIA that Choi was abusing his position.[119]

A few months later, Choi found a white envelope on his desk that contained a letter from his elder brother, whom he had assumed was dead in North Korea because he had not heard from him in fifteen years. Choi was elated but suspicious. Could this really be his brother's handwriting, or had somebody imitated the handwriting to entice him to become a communist? North and South Korea were still technically at war, with covert operations replacing outright battle, and any contact with a North Korean, even a family member, was a crime punishable by death in South Korea. Scared that someone would tip off the South Korean CIA, Choi read the letter and then ripped it up.

Soon after, he met the man who had snuck the envelope into the embassy, and Choi obtained another letter and a photo from his brother. And so began Ambassador Choi's treasonous relationship with North Korea. He began communicating with North Koreans and forwarded his brother's letters to his mother, who lived in South Korea with Choi's first wife and first daughter. When his mother saw the photo, she wept for many days because she had not seen her eldest son since the Second World War. She died within a year of seeing the photo, and Choi, stuck in Malaysia, was unable to visit her. He was devastated and haunted by memories of her, his brother, and their childhood in North Korea.

As usual, Choi fled to his martial art. He built Tae Kwon Do's foundations from 1962 to 1964, starting associations in Malaysia and Singapore (only the third and fourth associations in the world at the time, after Korea's and Vietnam's), and he created most of the martial art's patterns — his second major innovation. (His first innovation, in the late 1950s, had been his Theory of Power.) Tae Kwon Do still looked like Korean Karate, and Choi still practised the Karate patterns, but he was creating twenty-four patterns of his own with the help of some of Tae Kwon Do's pioneers.[120] He treated the athletes like surrogate sons, and none of them knew he was communicating with the enemy in North Korea. He dreamed

Chang Keun (C. K.) Choi demonstrates a jumping front kick.
He was one of the pioneers who developed Tae Kwon Do in the early 1960s.
PHOTO COURTESY OF C. K. CHOI.

up and stole techniques for Tae Kwon Do, and his chosen men transformed the techniques into reality. "He wrote the moves and we physically demonstrated them until they looked good," said C. K. Choi, one of the pioneer instructors.[121]

Ambassador Choi called the twenty-four patterns *Ch'ang Hon*, his name for calligraphy and books. He said that he stopped at twenty-four to acknowledge the hours in a day, which was a symbol of our short life on earth.[122]

In 1964, Choi may have thought that his time on earth would be short. He suddenly left Malaysia — people accused him of embezzlement — and his return to Korea shocked martial arts leaders who thought they had forever jettisoned the name Tae Kwon Do. Choi rounded up his athletes from the Oh Do Kwan and Chung Do Kwan for a new mission: to promote Tae Kwon Do and to publish a new book. They altered Karate hand techniques, encouraged more dodging, and experimented with flying and jumping versions of Karate kicks.

Jong-Soo Park, for example, had just won a national sparring championship in Korea and told Choi about a difficult kick that he liked to use when sparring: the reverse turning kick. Choi forced him to demonstrate it at least a thousand times that week.[123] Tae Kwon Do already had a "turning kick" from Karate, but Park's kick required a 180-degree spin, so Choi added the term "reverse" to Karate's "turning kick." This was not a new technique; it had been developed by Park's senior, Woo Jong-Lim, who had developed many of Tae Kwon Do's reverse kicks in the 1950s.[124] Athletes such as Park, however, were applying the techniques during competitions, taking risks in the air with basic punches and kicks, and gambling with 180-degree versions. None of the basics were new — a kick was a kick — but an airborne or 180-degree development was new and impressive, especially when it regularly knocked out opponents during sparring tournaments. Choi had never seen such techniques in action, and he inserted them into his book one by one. This is how some of Choi's champions (who displayed the techniques), such as Park, made it into the footnotes and some instructors (who developed the techniques), such

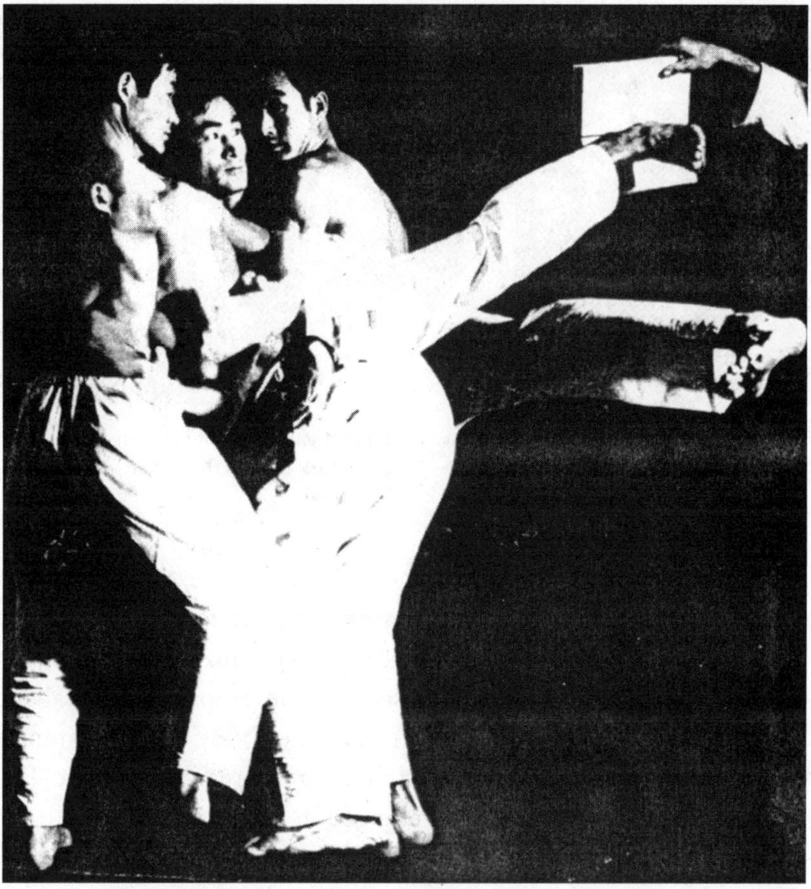

Choi overlapped four photos into one to show Jong-Soo Park executing a reverse turning kick. PHOTO COURTESY OF CHOI.

as Woo Jong-Lim, did not. This is also how Choi came to regard himself as the creator of the techniques, crediting almost no one in the process.

But Choi was a master at renaming old techniques, brilliant at organizing and pushing his athletes to do impossible-looking techniques, and an expert at explaining and naming the movements. Park said that Choi often had eureka moments for Tae Kwon Do names. "Sitting stance" (*annun sogi*) came from a demonstration in Lebanon, when Choi saw a circus act in which a clown remained sitting when someone pulled away his chair.[125] In West Germany, Choi saw a traffic-light pedestrian symbol and "walking stance"

Choi's books were full of strobe-like photos to highlight the in-between moves of jumping kicks. This one shows Jong-Soo Park doing a flying side kick.
PHOTO COURTESY OF PARK.

(*gunnun sogi*) popped into his head for a Karate stance that he wanted to rename. Choi avoided animal names for Tae Kwon Do — there is no "horse stance" or "cat stance," no crouching tigers or hidden dragons. He was obsessed with developing a martial art based on scientific principles for the human body. A horse stance was a "sitting stance" and a cat stance was a "rear-foot stance." A tiger was a tiger, and dragons belonged in parades.

In 1965, one of Choi's prison mates from the Second World War, now a smuggler, financed the publication of Choi's new Tae Kwon Do book, which showcased complicated jumping, spinning, and flying kicks. For the average person, the near-impossible kicks would be hard to conceive without the book's step-by-step photos, which Choi laid out as if a strobe light was capturing the moves. The flying kicks, in particular, were astounding. For example, around 1954, Nam Tae-hi had been one of the first to demonstrate the flying side kick. As eleven men crouched in a row, Nam jumped over them and broke a board on the other side. A photo of that kick landed in Choi's book. At the time, martial artists were focused on perfecting ground techniques — on fundamentals such as front and side kicks — yet there hung Nam in mid-air, and there sprung an athlete named Jong-Soo Park on the 1965 book cover, floating at head level.

Choi had continued to plagiarize, and after he published his book in 1965, he was accused of copying a Karate book,[126] but his text clearly pointed in a new direction, usually up. That same year Nam Tae-hi joined the Korean CIA, which posted him to the South Korean embassy in Malaysia until 1970. In later years, I asked him what he did there, and he refused to tell me, saying that it had no relationship to Tae Kwon Do. Nam did, however, continue to teach the martial art in Malaysia, one of many KCIA agents involved in Tae Kwon Do.

So as the world teemed with secret-service agents pretending to be martial artists (such as Kim Un-yong in the U.S.) and martial artists pretending not to be agents (such as Nam in Malaysia), Choi and his pioneer instructors continued to build a martial art that would empower them, their soldiers, and their nation. But they seemed ill prepared or did not care how much the art would be used for illegal and violent purposes.

CHAPTER 6

THE VIETNAM WAR POPULARIZES TAE KWON DO

Nam Tae-hi trained soldiers in Vietnam during the war for a year or so before the Korean CIA sent him to Malaysia.[127] Just as Karate had grown popular during the Second World War, Tae Kwon Do exploded in Vietnam's jungles and gyms.[128] Nam did not fight on the front lines but trained those who did, picking sixty martial artists and athletes from the Korean army, training them for six months, and sending them out to teach others. This was only the start. Korea would eventually post 647 Tae Kwon Do instructors in Vietnam.[129] Funded by the Americans, South Korea would send approximately 300,000 personnel to fight communists there.[130] The U.S. had been backing South Korea against North Korea for twenty years, and South Korea would return the favour in Vietnam for the next ten. Korea sent the Blue Dragon Division, Tiger Division, and the fanatically anti-communist White Horse Division, which was supposedly full of third-degree black belts.

The Blue Dragon marine corps was the first group of Korean soldiers to fight in the Vietnam War. They were tough mercenaries, bought by the Americans to fight the Viet Cong, but the communists massacred the Koreans, who had not been trained to fight in the jungle; every night, military planes full of Korean bodies flew back home. In response, the Korean government set up a special boot camp that simulated Vietnam's jungles, and they provided better uniforms, boots, and martial arts training for the soldiers.

The Korean marines learned more than self-defence however; they learned a killing art.

Among the first experts to train soldiers after Nam left was a Vietnamese officer, Nguyen Van Binh, who hated communists as much as Choi and Nam did. He began teaching martial arts in his Oh Do Kwan in Saigon in 1962. He told me that he trained approximately 60,000 students (2,000 of them black belts) in his gyms, the first in Vietnam, from 1962 to 1975.[131] He estimated that a million civilians and soldiers studied Tae Kwon Do during that time. Soldiers kept fit and learned specific skills.

"In close combat, or even far away, it was better when they knew a martial art," Van Binh told me.

The soldiers who trained had more confidence, moved faster, and had better reflexes, even after only six months of Tae Kwon Do training. Those who trained longer could kill with their bare hands. I asked Van Binh how someone could do that because it seemed impossible.

"If you punch to the temple, you can break the skull," he said. "You cannot kill a man with a punch to the forehead, but if you punch the nose or mouth, for example, you can break the face easily."

Many stories circulated about how Koreans used Tae Kwon Do in combat during the Vietnam War. In 1966, a *Time* magazine reporter wrote:

> To Westerners, the process sometimes seems as brutal as it is effective. Suspects [the Viet Cong] are encouraged to talk by a rifle fired just past the ear from behind while they are sitting on the edge of an open grave, or by a swift, cheekbone-shattering flick of a Korean's bare hand. (Every Korean soldier from Commanding General Chae Myung Shin on down practices for 30 minutes each day Tae Kwon Do, the Korean version of Karate.) Once, when the mutilated body of a Korean soldier was found in a Viet Cong–sympathizing village, the Koreans tracked down a Viet Cong soldier, skinned him and hung him in the village.[132]

An American officer in Vietnam, A.S. Bolcar, read the *Time* article and sent a letter to the publication:

> Sir: We of the special liaison group have lived and worked daily with the Korean Tigers since their arrival in Viet Nam. They rank professionally with any fighting unit we've known. We find them 'brutally efficient,' but nowhere have we seen any grave sitting, Tae Kwon Do cheekbone splitting, or mutilation by skinning. Had the Tigers done these things, 695 Viet Cong would never have surrendered.[133]

Still, a rumour began that the Viet Cong had orders to move as close as possible to American ground forces and avoid close combat with the Koreans.[134] One reason was a night battle in 1967, on Valentine's Day, when 1,500 Viet Cong soldiers attacked approximately 250 Korean marines in the Blue Dragon's 11th Company. The Koreans were entrenched in a heart-shaped camp studded with barbed wire and concrete barriers in a communist stronghold near Tra Binh Dong village in Quang Ngai Province. With flame-throwers and cannons, including 120-millimetre mortars that elephants had carried down the mountains, one Vietnamese battalion blasted into the Korean camp from the southeast, beating drums, blowing whistles, and screaming "*Tai Han ra di, ra di!*" ("Come out, Koreans!") while a second Vietnamese battalion burst through the wire from the north, overwhelming the trenches in waves and attacking so fast that the Koreans were often unable to shoot.[135]

As the communists overran them, many Korean soldiers fought like ambushed tigers as bodies piled up in the trenches. One Korean rushed into a hole and lobbed out grenades as Vietnamese soldiers chased him. A second ran through fire to attack a Viet Cong fighter holding a flame-thrower. A third Korean exploded a last grenade while jumping on a group of the enemy, committing suicide in the process. After the hand grenades ran out, the Koreans had no choice but to lash out with rifle butts and Tae Kwon Do. In the trenches, it was hand-to-hand and knife-to-knife combat, with the Vietnamese soldiers pushing and pulling the trapped Koreans deeper into the camp.

Two hours after the start of the attack, the communists controlled about one-third of the camp, and the Koreans faced annihilation as fog and rain prevented Americans from flying to their aid, but two of the few things going right were Korean artillery fire and the Korean soldiers' fighting spirit. When the Vietnamese faltered in the middle of the battle, Captain Jung Kyong-gin ordered a daring move that would decide the battle: he counterattacked. One of his platoon leaders led a courageous charge into a breach that the Vietnamese had made earlier in the battle. The commander shot five enemy soldiers with a pistol after which his squad pushed the Vietnamese back into the breach, trapping the Viet Cong within the wire. A second group of marines saw the counterattack and joined the fight, so that the Koreans soon surrounded their surrounders. Now the Koreans shouted, "*Ra di, ra di!*" ("Come out, come out!").

When the fog finally cleared, four American Skyhawks flew in to attack the remaining Vietnamese force. After the battle, the traumatized Koreans counted 15 dead companions and 104 dead Viet Cong inside the heart-shaped perimeter and another 140 dead Viet Cong outside of it, near the concertina wire.

Captain Jung Kyong-gin's general flew to the site to congratulate him, and details of the battle flew into headlines of Korean- and English-language newspapers. South Korea awarded Jung and one of his officers, Shin Won Bae, the *Tae Geuk* (Korea's Medal of Honour), and all the Korean soldiers in the 11th Company received a full-rank promotion. Jung's exceptional leadership in ordering a counterattack, along with his soldiers' bravery and their Tae Kwon Do training, had contributed to the communist defeat. Shin Won Bae, who later commanded that same Blue Dragon unit (then called the 2nd Marine Division) told a Marine Corps publication in 2004:

> Even though tactics call for fixing bayonets to rifles during close quarters to neutralize the enemy, our weapon at the

> time, the M1 rifle, was not a weapon that could be wielded quickly. In urgent situations, the Marine in the front would fiercely strike the enemy's face and vital parts using Tae Kwon Do, causing him to momentarily lose his will to fight. Then a second Marine would finish off the enemy with the rifle. Additionally, striking the enemy with an entrenching tool was highly effective in destroying the will to fight among the enemy's lead elements. While Tae Kwon Do demonstrated its practical effectiveness on the battlefield, more importantly, martial arts training instilled the confidence to defeat the enemy . . . I think this is the greater significance of Tae Kwon Do training.[136]

In 1968, Korean marine headquarters included Tae Kwon Do training and tests in combat training. "The Marine Education Base, which oversaw initial training for noncommissioned officers, and enlisted Marines, initially established an objective of 85 percent of Marines earning the highest Tae Kwon Do certification," a Marine Corps publication noted.[137]

Vietnam showcased Korean martial arts and popularized the art. As word spread of Korean soldiers' fighting abilities, many Americans learned that the name of the art was *Tang Soo Do*,[138] and some, such as American CIA official Robert Walson, began regular training in the 1960s.[139] Only a handful of Koreans called the art Tae Kwon Do, but American officers, such as platoon commander James L. Jones, were so impressed with the Valentine's Day win that they enrolled more American soldiers in martial arts and began their own programs. Jones later became U.S. Supreme Allied Commander in Europe and the Commandant of the Marine Corps, where he helped to create the Marine Corps Martial Arts Program, which still exists. He said that his marines had envied the skills of Captain Jung's soldiers.

Meanwhile, American soldiers and officials such as Walson invited Korean instructors to teach in the U.S., which soon hosted more Korean gyms than any country in the world.[140] One journalist estimated that there were twenty-five Korean instructors in the U.S. in the early to mid-1960s, at the beginning of the Vietnam War. By the late 1960s, there were 800. As a result, the U.S. became a pillar of Choi's Tae Kwon Do in the 1960s, along with Vietnam, West Germany, Malaysia, and five other countries.

Few people, however, were calling it Tae Kwon Do, not even senior spy Kim Un-yong, the man who would create Olympic Tae Kwon Do and try to destroy Choi Hong-Hi and traditional Tae Kwon Do in the process. None of that stopped Choi and his men.

CHAPTER 7

THE ACES, CULTS, AND SPIES IN TAE KWON DO

In 1965, as the Vietnam War raged and South Korea terrorized its own citizens, Choi Hong-Hi and his athletes ran martial arts demonstrations around the world. A tour in Europe astounded foreigners, even as a Korean mission to kidnap, torture, and murder South Koreans around the world hit the front pages of newspapers. South Korea's ambassador to West Germany, one of Choi's close friends, found himself at the centre of a terrifying spy mission at that time. He had been promoting Choi's Tae Kwon Do for years and had invited Choi and an "Ace demo team" to conduct the tour.[141]

On the first day of the tour, Han Cha-gyo, one of the Ace team's four members, jumped over two standing soldiers and broke two wooden boards on the other side. The audience, most of whom were Italian soldiers, yelled and clapped — and kept clapping, nonstop. Choi was startled. He assumed they were protesting.

"How on earth can they go on clapping for such a long time?" Choi asked South Korea's ambassador to Italy.

"That means encore," the ambassador replied. "I think you had better demonstrate it again."[142]

Choi motioned for Han to repeat the manoeuvre. After Han sailed over the soldiers' shoulders and broke more boards, the audience went wild. The jump was not a trick. This was the same Han Cha-gyo who, along with Nam Tae-hi, had amazed the South Korean president with a martial arts demonstration in 1954.

The Ace team in 1965 stands in front of the Trevi Fountain in Rome, Italy.
PHOTO COURTESY OF CHOI.

During the 1965 tour, Han and his Ace teammates (Jong-Soo Park, Joong-keun Kim, and Jae-hwa Kwon) flabbergasted audiences in Turkey, Malaysia, Singapore, and West Germany. Choi had chosen his best fighters because the demonstrations included sparring with audience members who taunted them, especially Karate experts who would publicly challenge them to fights.[143] None of the Ace team members lost or, if they did, no one publicized the losses.

In Egypt, however, audience members were not as impressed by the Ace team. The four Koreans had conditioned their hands and feet to break bricks, but during the demo at the headquarters of Egypt's ranger corps, an audience member yelled, "I can do that!" as Joong-keun Kim was preparing to strike a brick. Choi immediately ordered Kim to add another brick because some of the men in the audience looked as big as Hercules and probably could crack a brick in half.

"We can do that," yelled another man.

Choi directed Kim to add a third brick. Finally, no one yelled anything, and Kim smashed all three bricks. Some audience members were impressed, but others tried to replicate what Kim had done. None succeeded.

After the demonstration, though, an Egyptian soldier asked his Egyptian commander, who was with Choi, if he could show him a breaking technique. The commander agreed. The soldier removed an oblong stone from his pocket and broke it with one Karate chop. The commander was astonished, and the proud soldier looked as if he had knocked out a tiger. Something had to be done, Choi thought, because everyone knew that a stone was harder to break than a brick. Choi summoned the Egyptian host of the demonstration to find a stone ten times bigger than the one the soldier had broken, and Ace team member Jae-hwa Kwon smashed it to pieces.

News about the challenging Egyptian demo spread through the country's military forces, and Choi took advantage of the goodwill to boldly announce that Tae Kwon Do was Korea's national sport.[144] This was a lie as bold as Choi's claim that Tae Kwon Do was hundreds of years old. Martial arts leaders in Korea could not decide on a name to unify their various martial arts, let alone pick a national sport, but that did not stop Choi from turning Karate experts into Tae Kwon Do black belts and setting up Tae Kwon Do associations in Egypt, West Germany, Italy, and Turkey during the tour.

Many people wondered how Tae Kwon Do could suddenly have whole "associations" in multiple countries overnight, but Choi was more than an opportunist; he was a showman, a poet, and a public-relations man before PR became a household term. In the 1960s, the demo teams showed off spectacular flying front kicks, flying side kicks, and the impossible-looking flying twin-foot kick.

In 1965, Choi Hong-Hi (in shades) stands beside an official as the Ace demonstration team prepares to leap into action. In uniform, from left to right: Jong-Soo Park, Jae-hwa Kwon, Kim Joong-keun, and Han Cha-gyo (off camera). PHOTO COURTESY OF CHOI.

One variation of this last technique involved one foot kicking the face while the other kicked the chest. Two other devastating kicks were the mid-air spin kick (jumping and spinning 360 degrees or 540 degrees to kick the face). People had grown accustomed the overwhelming power and speed of Karate, but Tae Kwon Do's jumping kicks impressed many.

The tours wore out the elite martial artists and wrecked their limbs over the years, especially their joints, but Choi took care of them and ensured they did not get out of control at night. He would even peek into their bedrooms, making sure they were indeed sleeping.[145] Sometimes the martial artists would pretend to sleep and sneak out to party after Choi left.[146] The problem with performing day after day while being jetlagged and drinking at night was that Choi would force them to wake around 6 a.m. no matter what. Choi rose at that time every day of his life, no matter what time zone he was in and no matter how hard he himself had drunk, gambled, and partied the night before.[147]

Typically, Choi would rouse the exhausted, hungover Ace demo members with his morning meditation, which involved knocking a callused fist against a hotel wall. He conditioned only the right fist, keeping the left sacred because of Confucian values.[148] His son-in-law, Michael Cormack, a black belt who later joined the international demo team, said, "We'd be sleeping and we'd hear the wall: he'd be tapping his knuckles, thinking about what he's going to do, and the whole hotel would shake." Boom. "He was very focused." Boom. "We didn't need alarm clocks." Ba-boom.[149] It's no wonder that the tired supermen sometimes dozed during demonstrations, in which case Choi would wake them with a punch to the stomach.

And not all went well between the men during the international tours. On the first day of the Ace demo tour in 1965, for example, Choi looked into a bag that Jong-Soo Park was holding and noticed that it contained a package of hot pepper that was leaking onto Choi's newly printed Tae Kwon Do books. Choi barked at Park for carrying the pepper with the books. Pepper stains were impossible to remove. But Choi's wife had given the pepper to Park's teammate, who had placed it in the bag for Choi and the team. They loved spicy food. Still, Choi was angry at Park, not the teammate.

Later that day they were all walking into an elevator, and Park slowed down to allow a woman to enter before him. Choi threatened to send him back to Korea for walking too slowly. This was too much for Park. He had carried the heavy bag as a favour and had let the woman pass out of courtesy, but the enraged Choi did not seem to understand. Park put down the bag and glared at Choi, and the rest of the team said nothing as the elevator hummed. This was day one.

Park announced he was going back to Korea and asked for his passport.

Choi was surprised and turned his head away, which is what he usually did when someone displeased him. He looked at the wall, as if Park had not spoken. Choi caused many conflicts in his life, but he rarely resolved them in a straightforward manner, face to face, unless he was certain of a victory. The two men treated each other with more care after the Hot Pepper Incident, and Park figured out a secret about Choi, his surrogate father: you had to stand up to him, no matter how scary the consequences seemed.

On the last day of the tour, after the stress of the demonstrations — the sparring, taunts, and constant travel — they were eating in a Hong Kong restaurant just before returning home. The team was worn out. After more than a month of travelling together, the Korean macho men were aching, irritable, and dangerous. A waiter placed two eggs on the table in front of Choi, even though he had ordered only one. He offered the extra egg to Joong-keun Kim, one of the team members, who in turn offered it to Jong-Soo Park because Park was much "younger," Kim said. This was an insult, in Park's view, because Park was only one or two years younger. Kim was once again throwing his weight around, pulling rank, trying to make Park feel inferior. Park slid into a quiet rage and ordered Kim to leave the room.

Kim began to shake. He and Park had been avoiding a fight during much of the tour, and Park wanted to settle it. In hindsight, challenging Kim was not a good idea, as he was a key member of South Korea's elite presidential guard and, in some ways, was even Choi's superior. As with Kim Un-yong, he was yet another Kim connected to the dictatorship, and he liked to torment his Ace teammates. As Park and Kim walked upstairs, Park seethed and Kim foamed at the mouth. Park could see the white spit on Kim's lips. At that moment, Choi interrupted with a stern lecture: "We've lasted one and a half months together!" he said. "Why fight now?"

Kim apologized to Park and stuck out his hand. Park refused to shake it.[150]

* * *

The international tour failed to impress other martial arts leaders in Korea, but Choi still had connections within parts of the government and the Korean CIA, and he hoped to consolidate his martial arts power. The South Korean dictator ignored him, busy with the Vietnam War, a potential famine, and an escalating covert war with North Korea, but Choi needed the dictator to help him unify Korea's main martial arts gyms under the name Tae Kwon Do.

The KTA was still the Korean Tae Soo Do Association, and nearly every martial arts leader wanted to be KTA president. They planned *coup d'états* and counter-coups inside the KTA as often as their political friends planned them against South Korea's president. In this context, Choi bullied his way to the position of KTA president once again.

Even though he and the South Korean dictator hated each other, Choi continued to threaten powerful men and manoeuvre politically as deftly as his Ace team did physically. Somehow, he convinced the dictator to accept the name Tae Kwon Do, and, under Choi, the KTA became the Korean Tae Kwon Do Association again — but few martial arts leaders got along with the loud-mouthed Choi, especially one of the most famous in the country, Hwang Kee.[151] And everyone continued teaching Karate patterns, avoiding the Tae Kwon Do patterns that Choi and his men had developed.[152]

Soon after, martial arts leaders ousted Choi, calling him a "permanent troublemaker."[153] Choi could not care less. He resigned from the KTA and, in 1966, created the International Taekwon-Do Federation (ITF),[154] which contained nine founding associations, mainly the ones that Choi had conjured during the tour the year before. The ITF grew overseas, thanks to Choi's diplomatic connections, Nam Tae-hi's students, and a wave of pioneers who started their own gyms.

Jhoon Rhee was one of those pioneers. Partly by using money and influence from the Korean CIA and a Korean cult, he popularized the art in the United States. Rhee was friends with Bruce Lee,

(*top*) Many martial arts leaders partied as hard as they trained. Here, in 1965, Choi sticks a cigarette in the mouth of Hwang Kee, Choi's beloved enemy and head of the powerful Moo Duk Kwan. Han Cha-gyo, member of the Ace team, is second from the right. (*bottom*) Hwang Kee and Choi Hong-Hi, 1965. PHOTOS COURTESY OF CHOI.

nurtured many champions, and became known as the "Father of American Tae Kwon Do," but he had also befriended senior KCIA agent Kim Un-yong (Olympic Tae Kwon Do's future leader) and other secret-service agents, and he was a member of a cult that sometimes supported Tae Kwon Do events.[155]

The KCIA had modernized Korea's Confucian values, replacing dynastic worship with modern secrecy, and it had become a state within a state, launching hundreds of espionage missions against North Korea while terrorizing its own citizens at home and abroad, with martial artists involved from top to bottom.[156] While the KCIA used martial artists to help plan kidnappings and murders, it also extorted its millionaires and ran businesses, sports associations, and other legitimate groups.[157] The KCIA also helped many martial artists in those days, especially in West Germany and the U.S.

In turn, some Tae Kwon Do leaders were KCIA spies. Nam Tae-hi was on the KCIA payroll from 1965 to 1972.[158] Jhoon Rhee denied being a secret-service agent and claimed not to know that he was involved in operations run by the KCIA, but both the KCIA and the cult supported him and Tae Kwon Do, helping him to open his Karate Institute in Washington, DC, one of the first Tae Kwon Do gyms in the U.S.[159]

The cult, called the Holy Spirit Association for the Unification of World Christianity, or Unification Church, was a wealthy, loopy operation that co-operated with the KCIA on many illegal missions. The members of the cult were called "Moonies" and believed that the Reverend Sun-Myung Moon, their leader, was the second coming of Jesus Christ. Jhoon Rhee was a Moonie and a leader in some of the cult's major activities.

At the time, Kim Un-yong worked in South Korea's embassy in the U.S., which basically had two purposes: improving Korea's image and receiving economic and military aid from the U.S.[160] Rhee helped one of Kim's secret-service colleagues at the embassy to establish fronts for espionage missions that shut down criticism of South Korea's regime and tricked Americans into donating money.[161] Both Rhee and the colleague were ardent followers of the cult.[162] Rhee joined its board of trustees and its radio station, which raised money for espionage work.[163] He later said that he was surprised that Kim and other intelligence officials helped with these and other KCIA missions.[164]

In spite of the intrigue — or perhaps because of it — Tae Kwon Do continued to do well, and in the mid-1960s, Rhee's Karate Institute became the hottest thing since the *Seven Samurai*. He had started the institute in 1962, after a martial arts open house during which he had jumped eight feet in the air and broken three wooden boards.[165] In 1964, Rhee's first black belt in Washington, Pat Burleson, won Rhee's first national karate championship. Rhee also knew powerful people in Washington: one of the cult's vice-presidents sent a note to the South Korean embassy to remind the ambassador of the championship.[166]

In those days, the Karate sparring on the open circuit was as tough as the Cold War politics. Pat Burleson, for example, had studied Shotokan Karate in 1957 while stationed with the American military in Japan and was already a strong fighter when he met Rhee.[167] "We got the fundamentals from Rhee, and he improved my kicks five hundred per cent," Burleson said. "The Japanese had poor kicks compared to the Koreans. We kicked to hurt: short, sharp kicks." The kicking was the main reason for the Korean art's rising popularity. "We called it Karate," Burleson said. "I coined it 'American Karate,' because Tae Kwon Do was the least known martial art in the U.S. Chuck Norris called it *Tang Soo Do*."[168] Only later would Choi Hong-Hi convince Rhee and others to rename it Tae Kwon Do.

No matter what it was called, the bare-knuckled sparring was tough, with no safety gear. "It was supposed to be non-contact, but we sent each other to the hospital right and left," Burleson said. He lost most of his teeth while sparring in those years, which was similar to the fights in the mixed martial arts today, minus the ground fighting. "Do you remember the Jean-Claude Van Damme movie *Bloodsport*? The movie was not a true story — a Hollywood lie — but those were the types of matches we had."

Long before the martial arts craze, Rhee, a good businessman, had predicted the high entertainment value of his competitions and had persuaded NBC's *Sports in Action* to cover his second national championship in April 1965, the first tournament to receive such coverage. In the semifinal, Burleson lost to Mike Stone in what Burleson described as a "grudge fight." He explained, "I had beaten his teacher in 1964. It was a tough fight. Afterwards, Mike and I remained good friends."

No one was hurt badly, but Stone, who had learned Karate when he was a soldier in the U.S., knocked out Burleson with

In later years, Choi awarded a ninth-degree black belt to Chuck Norris, making Norris a Tae Kwon Do grandmaster.
PHOTO COURTESY OF CHOI.

a ridge-hand to the head. Afterwards, Stone faced Walt Worthy in the final. Sitting in the audience were the Korean ambassador, the U.S. White House chief of secret police, leaders from the cult's foundation, and the cult's leader, Rev. Moon.[169] NBC's producers, surprised by the aggression during the fight, especially the bloody final showdown, broadcast only excerpts.

"The public didn't understand Karate," Burleson said, "not like today, with Tae Kwon Do in every neighbourhood and mixed martial arts around the world. Americans thought it was a mythical, spiritual thing. I can't tell you how many times I was challenged by men walking into my gym to fight. Our shortcoming in those days was that we didn't go into the character-building as much as we should have; we were too busy showing that it worked, and our goal was to make a national champion out of anyone who walked through the door." Burleson's experience was typical in Tae Kwon Do gyms in North America.

Burleson, Rhee, and others eventually toned down the aggression. "The rules softened in 1969 or 1970, and I moved to California to train with Chuck Norris," Burleson explained. Norris had learned Korean Karate in the early 1960s while stationed as a soldier in South Korea, winning many championships. He later appeared in the 1972 Bruce Lee movie *Way of the Dragon* in a scene that ranks as one of the best in martial arts movie history. It's no wonder that Burleson and others joined Norris in California: "There, we played the same game but added rules to protect the face. And I went to see [Allen] Steen and told him that we were all going to jail sooner or later because someone was going to die. We used safety equipment after that, and added a point system."

Ironically, Rhee's televised 1965 competition contributed to Americans discovering the truth about his links to the cult. (Rhee's connections to the Korean CIA, however, would only arise in later years.) In 1965, a well-known supporter, Robert Roland, ordered the cult to remove his name from the structure of the organization because he could not support a "fanatical pseudo-religious group." He wrote to the U.S. government to advise that the group "proclaims through its teachings, Divine Principles, that their 'leader' is the fulfilment of the Biblical prophecy concerning the coming of the Messiah . . . To substantiate my position you will find attached excerpts from the official publication of the Holy Spirit Association, *The New Age Frontiers*, published in San Francisco. These will show the apparent affiliation of the Korean Cultural Foundation with the Holy Spirit Association and its affiliates; the Karate Institute of Washington, DC [Jhoon Rhee's gym], and the 'Little Angels' of Seoul, Korea."[170]

Korean CIA agent and future Tae Kwon Do leader Kim Un-yong had also helped with the Little Angels, a group of Korean children who pretended they were orphans while raising money for the South Korean dictatorship.[171] Some of the activities of the cult and the KCIA went underground after people discovered the lies. Meanwhile, Rhee taught his friend Kim, how to drive a car in Washington, DC.[172]

It is unclear how much Choi Hong-Hi knew about the KCIA-cult connections back then, but he needed leaders like Rhee. In 1966, he invited Rhee to help negotiate a merger between the newly created International Taekwon-Do Federation and other martial arts associations in Korea.[173] At the time, a former KCIA director served as both the honorary president of Choi's ITF and honorary chairman of a cult foundation that Rhee supported. The merger talks failed, but three years later Choi helped Rhee and other pioneers in America start a Tae Kwon Do association in the U.S.[174]

Soon after, Rhee visited Choi's home for dinner and, during the meal, could not believe when Choi began crunching pheasant bones in a soup.[175] Everything was a battle or a contest for Choi, even eating. He ate things that few people could touch: roasted grasshoppers, pig's feet and tails, even an entire pig's head half-crushed with hot stones to squeeze out the fat. Choi would eat these "delicacies," as he called them, while his daughters screeched in horror.[176]

During the pheasant dinner, Rhee watched him destroy the bones. "How can you eat that?" he asked, finding the bones nearly impossible to swallow.

"There's nothing to it," Choi replied, and continued crunching.

Rhee turned to Choi's wife. "For sure, he is a special person," Rhee told her.[177] The former general was five inches shorter than Rhee, who was five-foot-five, but he thought Choi was very tough. Choi had to be tough — to face dragons like Kim Un-yong.

Choi would one day ask Rhee to replace him as ITF president, and Rhee would politely decline.[178] "Why should I take over a headache?" Rhee said.[179] He had watched the ITF mess up the ranking system, especially in Europe, where Choi had randomly bestowed high black belt ranks to men who had not trained enough. Or perhaps Rhee was too preoccupied with avoiding cults and spy missions.

Choi split the ITF from the Korean Athletic Association[180] (which was or would soon become a front for a KCIA global terror mission), and he connected the ITF directly to the KCIA, appointing the KCIA's creator as the ITF's honorary president and including secret-service agents in the federation's leadership.

The KCIA continued to harass and torture its own citizens — its interrogators clubbed innocent people with metal pipes, suffocated them with wet towels, and imprisoned thousands of them in 1966[181] — but Choi needed the KCIA to protect and expand Tae Kwon Do, and he did not mind when a former KCIA director hosted a drinking party for Choi at a *kisaeng* house.

In 1967, though, even Choi was jolted when he discovered that two of his German-based Tae Kwon Do executives, Kim Kwang-il and Lee Gye-hoon, were KCIA operatives involved in a mission to abduct hundreds of Koreans. The cruel mission in West Germany, referred to as the East Berlin Incident, was as surreal as it was illegal and was a warm-up for a larger KCIA global terror mission in the U.S. in the 1970s that involved Jhoon Rhee, Kim Un-yong, and other Tae Kwon Do leaders.[182]

Jhoon Rhee and Choi Hong-Hi in the early seventies.
PHOTO COURTESY OF CHOI.

CHAPTER 8

KAFKA WOULD HAVE CRIED: THE EAST BERLIN INCIDENT

Early on June 17, 1967, in West Germany, an official telephoned well-known Korean composer Isang Yun at his home in West Berlin and asked him to visit the South Korean embassy. Yun travelled to Bonn, and once he was inside the embassy, officials grabbed him, stuck him in an attic, and for two days accused him of being a spy for North Korea. The composer denied the charges, but officials transported him to a Hamburg airport and slipped him onto a Japanese Airlines plane bound for Seoul — even though he had no passport or plane ticket.[183]

Meanwhile, in Heidelberg, rumours of missing South Koreans trickled into a German police station after a letter arrived from a student studying at the University of Heidelberg. The letter explained that the student had found himself "in the situation of K," the man in Franz Kafka's *The Trial*, a book that follows a man who is arrested and tried in court but never finds out the reasons why. When Korean agents arrived to detain the student, he tried to escape and discovered that they knew Tae Kwon Do, judging by the way they roughed him up. By this time, Choi's brand of Tae Kwon Do was well known in West Germany and had spread to thirty countries.[184] The agents hustled the student onto a plane and deposited him in Seoul, where South Korea put him on trial on trumped-up charges of treason.[185]

(*left*) Kim Kwang-il in 1971. PHOTO COURTESY OF THOMAS KUKLINSKI-RHEE.
(*right*) In 1967, people around the world protested the torture and imprisonment of composer Isang Yun after the Korean CIA kidnapped him in West Germany and flew him to South Korea. PHOTO COURTESY OF FELICITAS TIMPE.

In West Germany, officials heard more stories: a Korean student in Heidelberg was invited to dinner and kidnapped; a lecturer vanished from a Frankfurt university; a doctor, painter, poet, and several newspaper reporters had gone missing — all of them Korean-Germans. In total, more than forty-five Koreans were missing from Germany, eight from France, and 143 from Austria, the U.S., the U.K., Australia, and South Korea. What was going on?[186]

A Korean spy chief in Germany knew. Yang Doo-wan was hiding undercover as an embassy official and leading the German part of an operation to arrest students and artists that the South Korean dictatorship disliked.[187] To help with the operation, he imported fifty extra agents and recruited Korean Tae Kwon Do instructors and Korean miners. The miners had been introducing Tae Kwon Do to Europe since 1964.[188]

This was the turbulent 1960s: anti–Vietnam War students were demonstrating, the Cold War was peaking, and the KCIA had made up allegations that students in Europe were moonlighting as North Korean spies.[189] The KCIA flew the abductees from Germany to

South Korea, where agents deposited them in Namsan, a wooded hill in the centre of Seoul that contained the KCIA's headquarters, the basement of which was equipped with torture devices.[190]

Choi eventually discovered that two of his men were involved in the mass abductions. During the week of the kidnappings, thirty-one-year-old Kim Kwang-il, a KCIA operative and Tae Kwon Do pioneer and instructor who had lived in Stuttgart for many years, had travelled 600 miles from city to city, showing Korean officials where students lived.[191] Lee Gye-hoon, a second Tae Kwon Do pioneer who was involved, was a KCIA agent at the end of 1966 and an executive of Choi's International Taekwon-Do Federation.[192]

In Dusseldorf, West Germany, one student managed to escape on the way to the airport and stumble into a police station, where he filed a desperate report. The German police were baffled. Mass kidnappings? Women luring students to abductions? Martial artists forcing people into cars? The police were not aware that the German and American secret services had allowed the Koreans to carry out the mission. However, escapees and media coverage forced Germany to issue an official protest, calling the operation "a grave breach of international law" and offering police protection to the remaining 4,200 South Koreans in the country.

The kidnappings were dubbed the East Berlin Incident because the South Korean government had made up lies about students visiting North Korean agents for espionage training in East Berlin, which was communist at the time. As news of the international scandal spread around the world, South Korean dictator Park Chung-hee faced a barrage of criticism, and he was livid; the KCIA was supposed to quietly "encourage" suspected communists to fly to Seoul, but the world now saw thuggishness usually only associated with North Korea. As the scandal grew, Germany expelled three South Korean diplomats and suspended aid to South Korea.[193] Police arrested a Korean miner and Tae Kwon Do instructor Kim Kwang-il, and France formally protested to South Korea, where an uproar had begun, partly because of the kidnapping of composer Isang Yun.

Agents in Seoul treated Yun as badly as they had treated the other abductees. They bound his feet and hands, covered his head with a wet towel, suspended him from a pole, and kicked and beat him with wooden sticks, insisting that he confess to being a spy. He fainted repeatedly and finally agreed to sign the confession because he was afraid his torturers would murder him.[194] Under Korea's National Security Law and the Anti-Communist Law, he and his cellmates faced death sentences.

The composer had been through this before, during the Second World War, when Japanese agents had arrested and tortured him for resisting the Japanese occupation, something Choi Hong-Hi would have understood. Choi had rebelled and devoted his life to empowering his country's soldiers with Tae Kwon Do; Yun had rebelled and devoted his life to writing music about justice and humanitarian concerns.

The KCIA had kidnapped Yun because he had visited an ancient tomb in North Korea in 1963, when he was looking for a possible setting for a new composition. A worldwide petition led by famed composers Igor Stravinsky and Herbert von Karajan was presented to the South Korean government; the KCIA responded by allowing Yun to compose an opera on the floor of his cell.

Choi heard about Yun's incarceration and learned that the mastermind of the global operation was the Korean CIA director himself, the notorious Kim Hyung-wook, an officer during the Korean War whose unbearable arrogance was surpassed only by his appetite for bribes. Just that spring, Choi had asked for his help in convincing the South Korean president to build a Tae Kwon Do centre in Seoul, but the lobbying had failed.[195] Kim's nickname was "Wild Boar," and he held an unimaginable amount of power: he swayed elections, stole tens of millions of dollars, and could launch espionage missions anywhere on the planet.

After the German kidnappings, the Wild Boar laughed that James Bond could not have arranged a better abduction of the 203 people who had ended up in Korean jails. "Our people," he told *Der Spiegel*, "were already home by the time the story first appeared

In Seoul in 1967, innocent South Koreans await trail during the dictatorship's East Berlin Incident. PHOTO COURTESY OF CHOI HONG-HI.

in the press." The operation was "impeccably unobservable," he said.[196] His arrogance may have been fuelled by the support of the West German government and American CIA, which had also "encouraged" three South Koreans in the U.S. to return to Seoul.[197]

Choi thought the operation made his people deserve to be called savages.[198] He suspected that the story was worse than the publicized version, that the KCIA had tried to force the South Koreans into becoming spies (or counter-spies), and he did not like that Tae Kwon Do instructors were involved. Two of Tae Kwon Do's tenets were Integrity ("able to define right and wrong") and Courtesy ("a sense of justice"), but now the world was reading about the art's link to a violent mission.

It is likely that Choi was mad not only about the mission's brazenness but at the KCIA for failing to notify him — and in West Germany of all places! He was close friends with Korea's ambassador there. Why had he kept Choi in the dark? As it turned out, the Korean government had not notified its own ambassador about the abductions, and the KCIA had supposedly tortured *him* as well.[199] Afterwards, the ambassador asked his government to relieve him of his duties and became a religious hermit.

Choi Hong-Hi (on the left) shares a gift with Oyama as Lee Gye-hoon (second from left) looks on. PHOTO COURTESY OF CHOI.

Worldwide protests and diplomatic pressure helped the 203 victims in South Korea; the vast majority of abductees were released — including the Kafka student — but not composer Isang Yun and two others, whom the dictatorship executed. Yun was charged with spying and, in spite of an international campaign to release him, languished in jail for two more years.[200]

Back in Germany, police released Tae Kwon Do instructor and Korean CIA operative Kim Kwang-il. A year later, in 1968, he was back in Choi's International Taekwon-Do Federation, promoting the martial art and building a West German ITF organization where he would play a leading role until 1971.[201] Meanwhile, the other KCIA agent involved in the mission, Lee Gye-hoon, went back to work for Choi's ITF a couple of months later. In Tokyo, he introduced Choi to the renowned Karate master Masutatsu Oyama, a Korean who had become Japanese and was famous for punching out bulls. Choi tried to convince Oyama to switch his citizenship from Japanese back to Korean and to jump from Karate to Tae Kwon Do, but to no avail. Lee helped them to become blood brothers anyway and later rose to become the KCIA's deputy director.[202]

Choi was a pragmatist, putting Tae Kwon Do before everything, even human rights, but soon after the East Berlin Incident, he was financially broke and politically weak and began negotiating for C$2 million from a North Korean agent. This was treason, a crime punishable by death in South Korea. Nothing came of the talks, but the risks were enormous.

Afterwards, Choi found out that the South Korean president had approved for senior spy Kim Un-yong to take control of Tae Kwon Do.[203] In 1968, Kim moved from the U.S. to South Korea to merge the martial arts gyms and, along the way, to deal with Choi.

CHAPTER 9

AS IF IN A BRUCE LEE MOVIE

By 1968, Choi and his Tae Kwon Do were in trouble. It was a violent time politically, and Kim Un-yong had become assistant to the head of the Presidential Security Force (PSF), which was the South Korean president's personal bodyguard.[204] That January, more than thirty North Koreans dressed in South Korean army uniforms had rushed thirty miles from the border and had almost assassinated South Korea's president. Two days later, North Koreans seized an American spy ship, the USS *Pueblo,* and the Americans' first reaction was to consider dropping a small nuclear bomb on North Korea.[205]

In the PSF, Kim was now at the centre of power. Former American CIA officer Philip Liechty explained the PSF to a journalist this way: "You have to understand what kind of people were recruited to the Presidential Security Force . . . It was a time when there were several carefully planned paramilitary assassination attempts on the president, attempts by teams dispatched from North Korea, and so he surrounded himself with proven killers. The important thing is that the man who protects the president in a country like that has to have demonstrated that he is willing to kill without hesitation for his boss, to do anything the president asked him to do."[206]

Kim was now the number-two man in that security force of proven killers, and in 1970, he became president of the Korean Tae Kwon Do Association (KTA).[207] South Korea's dictator told Choi that he should move to an honorary position in Tae Kwon

Do and let others, like Kim, take over.[208] Choi did not appreciate that sort of "honour," but he had no choice. One of Kim's primary responsibilities was to raise huge sums of money for a new Tae Kwon Do centre and a world championship. Meanwhile, Kim maintained his ties to the Korean CIA and cult leaders in the U.S., both of which funded Tae Kwon Do gyms and events.

In 1971, when Kim officially became head of the KTA, he accused Choi of allying the ITF with North Korea, and the South Korean president announced that "Tae Kwon Do" was *Kukki* (which rhymes with "spooky" and means "national sport" in Korean).[209] Tae Kwon Do was now officially part of the Cold War.

Back then, Kim claimed, "Tae Kwon Do was like a pearl in the mud. Depending on how it is led, it will shine or stay in the mud."[210] This insulted Choi, Nam, and the pioneers who had turned Tae Kwon Do into one of the hottest martial arts on the planet, with membership in the millions.[211] The ITF contained more than thirty national associations, and it had become as popular as Japanese Karate in the U.S. and Canada and was part of a martial arts craze led by Bruce Lee, Chuck Norris, and Kim Un-yong's friend Jhoon Rhee in North America. Surely all this was the "pearl" part. The "mud" was in the South Korean regime, despite the extraordinary economic boom there.

Without a trace of irony, Kim claimed he would clean the dirt from Tae Kwon Do. He also claimed that he had funded Tae Kwon Do gyms in the U.S. and England in the 1960s (during a time when he was also helping to run KCIA missions to bribe politicians and torment Koreans living overseas). "I busied myself when there was a tournament, and I financially helped instructors to open martial arts gyms," he wrote in one of his memoirs.[212] He said that he had paid rent for instructors and helped them negotiate bank loans and organize competitions in the mid-1960s in the U.S. and that he had helped establish a Tae Kwon Do association in England.[213] It's likely he did actually do all this because martial artists were involved in KCIA missions overseas.

In 1970 and 1971, for example, when Kim promised to put together a World Tae Kwon Do Championship in Seoul, he and his

Tae Kwon Do association accepted cheques from the KCIA and a foundation run by the Unification Church, a cult. Naturally, when the story leaked to the media, people wondered why the agency and a cult would channel money to a martial art. It looked like an odd financial relationship. In later years, U.S. government investigator Howard T. Anderson would ask one of the cult's leaders, Pak Bo-Hi, about money flowing from the cult's foundation to Kim. Anderson asked about three cheques to "Mickey Kim" and a number of other cheques to Kim's Korean Tae Kwon Do Association:

MR. ANDERSON: Do you recall what these payments were for?

MR. PAK: I think this was a payment, an assistance to his publication known as the *Korean Observer*.

[Pause]

MR. PAK: The indication we have here is, scholarship and research. We classified that [as] scholarship and research.

MR. ANDERSON: Scholarship and research?

MR. PAK: Yes, scholarship research, a grant, probably.

MR. ANDERSON: To Mickey Kim?

MR. PAK: Yes.

MR. ANDERSON: But he was a Korean government official at that time, was he not?

MR. PAK: At that time? What was it, 1971? I don't know . . . I remember one or two times we gave a research grant to the *Korean Observer*. This may be granted for that purpose.

MR. ANDERSON: There are also — I won't show them to you,

> but the inspection of some of the records show that there were checks to the Korean Tae Kwon Do Association. Does that have any connection to Mickey Kim?
>
> **MR. PAK:** I think so, because he was president of the Korean Tae Kwon Do Association. This is a giant cultural and sports organization, nonprofit, that the Koreans are very proud of, and apparently they had some international event. They needed some funds contributed by various organizations. I think we contributed to that because the same cultural [sic] and field of workers. It is fitting into our purpose of the foundation.[214]

The implication was that the South Korean regime had paid martial arts leaders to be part of a large, secret mission run by the KCIA and a right-wing cult. The Tae Kwon Do association and so-called *Korean Observer* were fronts, two of many in a mission dubbed the "Plan" by the American government. One of Kim's bosses led the Plan.[215]

This mission resembled the East Berlin Incident of 1967 — only much bigger, with South Korea's president overseeing it directly.[216] The Plan's overall goal was to reverse the U.S.'s decision to drastically reduce American aid and troops in South Korea. Documents about it outlined how to bribe, seduce, and influence more than a hundred members of the U.S. Congress, how to infiltrate the American Joint Chiefs of Staff, how to bribe and intimidate American academics and the press, and, along the way, how to buy off, harass, and threaten Korean-Americans who were criticizing the South Korean dictatorship.[217] It was as vile as it was detailed.

Kim's Korean Tae Kwon Do Association (KTA), for example, was part of an umbrella group called the Korean Athletic Association, which included agents for the Plan. Under his guidance, the KTA moved quickly to stymie opposition from Choi's group. In 1971, South Korea's president announced that 360 martial arts gyms in Seoul, Korea, needed permits. Most of the gyms were part of the ITF, and the rules for obtaining the permit were so strict that eighty per cent of the gyms failed to get it. Afterwards, the president decreed a new, large tax on businesses, including a tax on gyms.[218] This was a country where millions in bribes flowed to the South Korean regime then into Swiss bank accounts or into a cabinet behind the president's desk.[219]

While he was part of the Plan, Kim promised to use Tae Kwon Do to improve Korea's international image. He tapped his connections within the Presidential Security Force to raise 200 million Won (U.S.$1 million in today's currency) for a Tae Kwon Do building, the Kukkiwon. He was also part of a mission to "collect" donations from American companies for a South Korean election in 1971. For example, the KCIA wanted U.S.$100,000 to U.S.$150,000 from Colt Industries, maker of the M-16 machine gun. In the mid-1960s, Kim had set up an important meeting between a Colt official and the South Korean president, who had wanted to build a gun factory in Korea.[220] In 1971, Kim asked Colt for a campaign contribution for that same president, for the election in a few months.[221]

Colt officials authorized a cheque for U.S.$100,000, payable to Kim Un-yong, but on the advice of lawyers withdrew it because they discovered that such donations were illegal in South Korea. Still, the KCIA deftly raised at least U.S.$8.5 million in "loans," "pre-paid fees," and "commissions" from American firms, which were all sent to President Park Chung-hee for his dubious 1971 election. The dictator defeated his rival, Kim Dae-jung, by a small margin. A U.S. Congressional report would later conclude: "Given the fact that Kim Dae-jung lost the 1971 presidential election by less than 8 per cent of the vote . . . the possibility exists the $8.5 million, when co-mingled with funds from other [American] sources, accounted for the difference in votes."[222] And so began another round of dictatorship.

Following the election, the South Korean president announced an emergency decree that resulted in more torture and torment. For the average Korean, the consequence of the "fees," "loans," and a rigged election was the most politically repressive period under President Park Chung-hee, who ruled for nearly twenty years.

Meanwhile, Kim also sent instructors to countries that already had thriving ITF schools,[223] and he told a reporter that he'd take care of Choi and the ITF "through the efforts of people who are quietly looking into the matter."[224]

As I list the adversaries of Choi and his men in the early 1970s — the KCIA, Kim Un-yong, and the other special Ks — I marvel at Choi's ego and his limitless desire to control Tae Kwon Do. His ITF was thriving, but Choi had entered a game, the Plan, that promised to annihilate him.

The Plan contained nine points, the ninth of which was "To intimidate 'unco-operative' Korean residents in the U.S. through their families, relatives, and close friends in Korea."[225] In the 1970s, KCIA collaborators seemed to be watching everyone in Korea, and families survived by not talking to anyone, including each other, about anything.[226] The KCIA exported this attitude to North America, partly through martial arts groups: under the heading "Operations Relating to Korean Residents," the Plan highlighted the "U.S. Branch of the Korean Athletic Association" because the branch was an "Anti-Communist Organization."[227]

This was the same KAA that contained Kim Un-yong's Korean Tae Kwon Do Association, the group that was accepting money from the KCIA and a cult. The Plan provided details to South Korea's diplomats and secret-service agents about what to do with the KAA: they should formulate "an organizational network of anti-communist fronts" that involved an unnamed ex-marine association based in Los Angeles and eighty collaborators in five U.S. cities.

For years, Choi Hong-Hi had been warning about such activities. Between 1970 and 1976, the Korean secret service budgeted U.S.$50 a month to ten KAA collaborators in San Francisco, ten in Chicago, twenty in Los Angeles, twenty in Washington, and twenty in New York City.[228] As with the 1967 kidnappings in West Germany, KCIA agents and collaborators, including Tae Kwon Do instructors, threatened and kidnapped Korean-Americans who criticized the South Korean regime.

By 1973, American officials were hearing complaints from terrified Korean-Americans. KCIA officials were ordering people to stop criticizing South Korea, were threatening them on the phone at night, and were spreading rumours about family and friends interrogated in South Korea.[229] An editor of a Korean-American newspaper, someone known to be against the regime, was on his way to give a public speech when he was kidnapped.[230] A professor committed suicide in South Korea during KCIA interrogations.[231]

As the years went on, the reports became worse: anonymous phone callers threatened to kill children in the U.S. and Korea, and family members were tortured and imprisoned in South Korea because they were related to the regime's critics in the U.S.[232] At first, the American CIA and FBI largely ignored the complaints (and the two agencies likely helped out, too); Korea was a U.S. ally in the still-raging Vietnam War, but a small number of American politicians in Washington and Seoul, including the U.S. ambassador in South Korea, were appalled. Korean-Americans turned to them for help.

Korean communities also relied on courageous publishers, such as Song Sun-keun, a newspaperman who published the *Korea Journal*, a small community paper in San Francisco. Song was a friend of Kim Dae-jung, the democrat who had nearly defeated the South Korean dictator in the presidential election of 1971. Song and his newspaper had been criticizing dictator Park Chung-hee for more than a year when KCIA agents tried to buy the paper. Song refused. KCIA operatives then forced Korean-American businesses to stop advertising in the *Korea Journal*, thereby draining the paper of its revenue. Song kept the paper going anyway, a voice of dissent during a time when journalists were bribed or threatened into supporting the dictatorship.[233]

Then, on a Tuesday in 1974, Song received a phone call: a sinister Korean voice told him he would be killed on Sunday. The caller claimed to be a reader of the *Korea Journal* and accused Song of being a communist.

"You don't read my paper," Song replied. "We are strongly against Communism, just as we are against Park's dictatorship."[234]

The caller hung up, but Song had recognized the voice based on the man's accent, which was from a southern province of South Korea; the man was both the consul for the San Francisco area and a KCIA agent.[235] Song reported the threat to the police and to the FBI, which responded with only a few interviews of suspects.

The consul did not kill the journalist, but the KCIA tormented Song with death threats. He published a story in which he described the consul's threat, and he named him as the culprit, which turned the political conflict into a personal vendetta. Soon after, Song discovered that the KCIA were planning to send a thug from Los Angeles to run him over with a car. Then in 1976, one of Song's friends overheard the consul arrange for a Seattle-area martial arts master to kill him. The friend also overheard a martial arts instructor discuss another option, one involving kidnapping Song and taking him back to Korea. That year, Song said that the consul himself had attempted to ram him with a car and that he had moved out of the way just in time.[236]

If these situations had not been so terrifying, they would have been farcical, like scenes from the movie *Kill Bill*, but this was reality. I find the story unnerving, not only because it obliterated everything good for which my martial art stood, but because it was typical of what was happening in those days and was one of the few publicized stories.

Relentless KCIA campaigns, such as the one against Song, kept Koreans around the world silent and fearful throughout the 1970s, but not Choi Hong-Hi. True, Choi had once used the KCIA to help Tae Kwon Do, but the crucial difference was that he put Tae Kwon Do first and South Korea second. For him, the KCIA had been a tool to expand and protect his martial art. For his enemies, Tae Kwon Do became a repressive tool of the state.

Few people believed Choi's warnings about the regime, calling him paranoid, jealous, and a troublemaker. From a martial arts perspective, one of the most disturbing parts of the Plan was that the names Kim Un-yong (KCIA agent and president of the Korean Tae Kwon Do Association) and his boss (chief of the Presidential Security Force) kept popping up in accounts of the Plan's missions.[237]

The KCIA not only required huge amounts of cash and martial arts manpower, it also needed more unconventional items, such as poisons. The KCIA station chief in Washington smuggled much of the illegal money in and out of the U.S. in Korea's diplomatic pouch.[238] American intelligence once discovered a secret shopping list from the pouch, a list that included "electronic surveillance equipment" and "poison," which the regime needed in South Korea.[239] Choi Hong-Hi had heard that a preferred method of murdering political opponents was to poison their liquor during social engagements.[240] Since hearing that, he had always checked his drinks at the *kisaeng* houses. Often, a rival would drink first to show that the liquor was not spiked.

In 1971, Choi must have known how insane things were getting with the KCIA and Tae Kwon Do, as he still had many connections within the secret service. He knew the two instructors who had been involved in the 1967 kidnappings, for example, and he continued working with Jhoon Rhee, who was a friend of Kim Un-yong's and collaborated with KCIA agents.

At the same time, a martial arts movie craze was sweeping the world. In 1971, the movie *Billy Jack* featured Karate and Hapkido sequences and soon became a hit, followed by *Red Sun*, starring Charles Bronson and Japanese acting legend Toshiro Mifune. Then Bruce Lee, who learned a lead-leg side kick from Jhoon Rhee, released *The Big Boss* in 1971, *Fist of Fury* and *Way of the Dragon* in 1972, and *Enter the Dragon* in 1973, all of which turned him into a household name in Asia and the West.[241]

The show I remember, however, is the television hit *Kung Fu*, starring David Carradine, which merged marital arts mayhem with Eastern philosophy in the American Wild West. A recurring theme in the show related to maintaining a just and peaceful attitude amid violence, crime, and people who regularly insulted the Kung Fu master. It was a great fantasy — something to strive for.

Tae Kwon Do's pioneers faced the same dilemmas but without commercial breaks. In South Korea, the secret police were more powerful than the Prime Minister's Office, and in North America, the KCIA's station chiefs had more influence than Korea's ambassadors.

In 1970, Choi and Nam Tae-hi learned this the hard way after starting yet another Tae Kwon Do tour, this time of Asia, Europe, and the Middle East.[242] They were dignitaries, so everywhere they went, South Korea's embassy officials would invite them to banquets — and at every banquet lurked a KCIA agent. Nam himself was on the KCIA payroll. Choi would badmouth the South Korean president at events, and KCIA agents would report the details to the president himself. Nam was stuck between the KCIA and the trash-talking Choi. There were many juicy details to report to South Korea, Nam told me. He wished Choi had not badmouthed the president so much.

When Choi returned home after the 1970 tour, he realized that he was no longer safe in his own country. Finally, in 1972, after South Korea's dictator declared himself president for life, two KCIA men visited Choi at home for a friendly chat.[243] At first, Choi treated them like friends because they were subordinates. He complained that the South Korean president was abusing the situation in Tae Kwon Do by pitting Kim Un-yong's organization against Choi's. The two agents agreed with Choi and, in that moment, he suddenly remembered a passage from Han Fei, a philosopher in the third century BCE: "Watch for the enemy within your group."

One of the men, a former KCIA branch director, patted Choi on the back and said, "Sir, wouldn't it be better for you to do your best from abroad, considering the current situation?"

"Never!" said Choi, realizing that they were fishing for information. "Why would I live abroad? I need to straighten what is going on in the field of Tae Kwon Do."[244]

With that statement the KCIA relaxed its surveillance of Choi, and within a week he met his right-hand man, Nam, in Hong Kong, and they flew to Canada from there. While Choi settled in Toronto, Nam flew to Chicago to start his own gym, as he was no longer in the KCIA and wanted to start a new life teaching Tae Kwon Do in the U.S. His situation would only get harder, however, starting with Choi spreading a rumour that the KCIA had given Nam an enormous sum of money to buy a Cadillac and start a gym. Nam told me that he never received a penny for a car.[245]

Still, as with so many other exiles, both men faced ruin, and they prepared for yet another series of conflicts.

CHAPTER 10

EXILES AND HEROES

Choi transferred the headquarters of his International Taekwon-Do Federation to Toronto, but left his family behind. He arrived in Canada with no money, no reputation, and not a Korean geisha house in sight. Why Canada? It was located between Europe and South America, where Choi wanted Tae Kwon Do to expand, and Jong-Soo Park, one of his best pioneers, lived there and ran a growing network of gyms that were generating sparring world champions. But more importantly, Canada was a relatively neutral country politically: a Canadian passport would give him access to both communist and non-communist countries. Choi had well-hidden hopes to introduce Tae Kwon Do to communist nations.

But first he had to adapt to a culture where money meant more than position (and honour had a low exchange rate). He told people that he used two names ("Choi Hong-Hi," given by his father, and "Tae Kwon Do," given by heaven), but how could he become immortal while living in a Canadian suburb, a cultural wasteland by his standards?

His martial art empowered him once again. On the way to Canada, Choi and Nam had picked up Choi's newly published Tae Kwon Do book in Hong Kong — yet another book. It contained 518 pages of old and new techniques. It featured Nam Tae-hi and Jong-Soo Park on the cover and finally proved that Choi and his men had developed techniques that were different from Karate's.

Nam Tae-hi (on the left) with student Dennis Callanan in Chicago in 1979. Nam was on the payroll of the Korean CIA until 1972 or so, and had respect for it, but he disagreed with the KCIA plan to threaten Korean-Americans and bribe American politicians.
PHOTO COURTESY OF DENNIS CALLANAN.

An example of Choi's obsessive detailing was "Finger Belly," which referred to the inside part of one's hand, between the palm and the fingertips, which is used to support a back fist in certain strikes. He had plucked the name "Finger Belly" from a dream.[246]

A more dramatic addition was Choi's section about *T'aekkyŏn*, a series of kicking techniques that distinguished Tae Kwon Do from Karate. He had continued to claim that Tae Kwon Do rested on Korea's ancient art of *T'aekkyŏn*, a lie repeated so many times that most people believed that Tae Kwon Do was indeed thousands of years old. It was only natural that Choi finally got around to adding *T'aekkyŏn* techniques to Tae Kwon Do. He entitled them "Foot Technique Sparring" (*Jokgi Daeryon*) in the 1972 book and, in later books, simply "Foot Sparring" (*Bal Matsogi*). Most of the *T'aekkyŏn* techniques required extraordinary leg agility and power. One of the easier moves involved a defender kicking the ankle of an attacking leg in mid-air and immediately kicking the attacker's head with the same leg, a one-two move that forces the leg to be as fast as a punch.[247] Choi's *T'aekkyŏn* techniques mimicked those from ancient times, promoting dodges and circular attacks that were unlike Karate's linear strikes, blocks, and counterattacks.[248]

Even though Nam Tae-hi dominated the martial art and the cover of Choi's book, the two men did not get along, mainly because of

Choi's narcissism and verbal abuse. Nam had been a KCIA agent from 1965 to 1972, but he now had to start a new life and earn an income in Chicago. Nam's former star assistant, Han Cha-gyo, was running a successful gym there, and Nam and Han began a new martial arts organization, the U.S.A. Taekwon-Do Federation.[249]

To make matters worse, Choi and Nam had landed in the heart of the KCIA's terror mission to bribe U.S. congressmen and threaten Korean-Americans. Nam was loyal to the KCIA and had respect for it, but he disagreed with the mission, dubbed the "Plan" and "Koreagate" by Americans.[250] He and Choi had heard stories about the KCIA harassing their Tae Kwon Do instructors in North America. For example, after the KCIA transferred one of its agents from Washington to Toronto to pressure the Korean Consulate to take "action" against activists, a Korean consul in Toronto applied for refugee status.[251] Years later, a colonel would tell Choi that this same consul had previously directed Jong-Soo Park, Choi's disciple, to kidnap Choi in Toronto.[252] Park denied the charge.

The Plan also involved kidnapping and killing another man in exile, Kim Dae-jung, the democrat who would likely have beaten Park Chung-hee in the 1971 South Korean presidential election had it been less corrupt.[253] Park was overseeing one of the hottest economies and most brutal regimes in the world, and he began a new wave of repression, partly because of Kim Dae-jung's mass support in 1971.[254] Travelling around the world, Kim was denouncing the dictatorship and becoming a hero, just as Choi was (but without the hero part). Koreans love their philosopher-kings, and Kim embodied Korea's resistance to decades of military dictatorship.[255] Moreover, he was a Confucian gentleman toughened by years of harassment, and he courageously stood for the many Koreans who had never wanted to collaborate with dictators and thugs.

In 1973, President Park found Kim's overseas activities intolerable. Kim was to begin a fellowship at Harvard University in the U.S., where he would regularly visit high-level American officials. Part of the KCIA's Plan was to assign martial artists to follow him everywhere he went — anywhere in the world.[256] In South Korea in 1971, Kim had survived a house bombing and had also been severely wounded when a truck almost ran over him.[257] Now, in 1973, the KCIA was looking for an opportunity to quietly kidnap and kill him.

Tae Kwon Do black belts became involved whether they knew about the Plan or not. One of the few episodes that landed in the local media occurred in 1973, as Kim Dae-jung prepared to speak in San Francisco about his idea to reunite North and South Korea. The South Korean Consul in San Francisco directed the Plan in the area, overseen by a KCIA chief in Washington, DC. They focused on the Organization of Korean Studies in Berkeley, California, where Kim was booked to speak at 7:30 on the evening of May 18, 1973.[258]

That evening, the hall was extremely tense, mainly because a dozen dubious characters were wandering in and out of the lobby. Who were they? Washington's KCIA chief knew. Yang Doo-wan, the same man who had led the kidnappings and tortures in Germany in the 1960s (the East Berlin Incident) had sent a high-ranking thug, Bae Young-shik, from Los Angeles to the San Francisco hall. Bae was both vice-consul of the Korean Consulate in L.A. and a KCIA agent. (It was normal practice for South Korea to secretly assign KCIA agents to government positions overseas.) KCIA chief Yang himself was not in the hall, but he directed the operation from the Hilton hotel where he was staying — the same hotel where Kim had checked in.

A Korean journalist and family friend of Kim Dae-jung's, Song Sun-keun, was in the Berkeley hall and later wrote an article in his *Korea Journal* about the events that followed. He noted that ten martial artists were in the room.[259] At 8 p.m., a security guard was keeping an eye on them as they stood in front of the hall and discouraged people from entering. The guard followed them upstairs, where he confiscated a large shopping bag that contained ten ketchup bottles and a dozen eggs, and returned downstairs to hand the bag to the event's director. The master of ceremonies stood at the podium and held the ketchup and eggs before the audience. "Someone with these things tried to disrupt our orderly meeting tonight," he said.[260] The audience booed.

They livened up when Kim Dae-jung entered the hall, accompanied by four bodyguards. Also in the hall was Rhee Min-hi, a Tae Kwon Do instructor who had trained in *Kong Soo Do* at the Jidokwan, one of the important martial arts gyms (or *kwans*) in South Korea. Rhee was a powerful man in the San Francisco area, especially after South Korea awarded him one of its highest medals for his services in the Korean community in the U.S. in the early 1970s. In San Francisco, he oversaw a martial arts gym on Polk Street, ran a travel agency, and was head of a broadcasters' association. Some people suspected that he was a KCIA operative. He did not like Kim Dae-jung's criticism of South Korea, and he hated Kim's proposal of reuniting north and south, an idea that smacked of communism. Also, Kim had been claiming that the South Korean government was out to murder him — a ridiculous allegation, in Rhee's view, because if Korea had wanted to kill Kim, why had it allowed him to leave South Korea?

Rhee later claimed that he did not know there were ten other martial artists in the hall — a dubious claim. He installed himself at the back while Kim Dae-jung walked up to the microphone and the crowd clapped heartily. As Kim began speaking, Rhee interrupted him. "Why do you criticize the head of our nation?" Rhee yelled, marching to the front. "You should fight in Korea! Don't stir up good compatriots here!" Rhee climbed onto the stage, making it to the podium. Bodyguards pushed him away as the hall erupted into yells.

Scarier than the melee was the fact that there was a man taking photos and filming the audience with a camera. People knew that KCIA agents in the U.S. routinely filmed controversial public events. Agents would note the names of Korean audience members and mail the lists and the films to Seoul, where the KCIA would threaten the families of those who had been at the events.[261] The man taking photos in the hall was a KCIA agent.

The master of ceremonies, who was near Kim, pointed at Rhee and said, "Whoever this man may be, he is definitely disrupting our meeting, which is being conducted in a democratic manner.

Therefore, all those who are in favour of dismissing him from this room, may you please clap your hands." The audience cheered and clapped.

"All those who don't wish to hear this speech, follow me," Rhee suddenly announced. No one rose, and Rhee once again dashed at Kim near the podium.

"Please be excused," Kim told him. Rhee stood there.

"Get lost!" yelled someone from the audience.

At that point, San Francisco police officers with guns and clubs entered the hall and arrested Rhee. As police were escorting him out, Bae Young-shik, the KCIA agent from Los Angeles, walked up to the officers and flashed an identity card: "I am an official of the Korean government," he told them. "This is a Korean meeting. We will manage our own affairs." The police ignored him.

As police drove Rhee away, he said that he was simply expressing his opinions to Kim. In South Korea, communists were not liked, Rhee explained, and people could not walk around holding a North Korean flag. Police advised Rhee not to return to the meeting and released him.

Meanwhile, one of Bae's compatriots was on the phone to the KCIA chief at the Hilton, telling him what was happening. This level of organization is impressive, and I suspect Yang then quickly updated someone in Seoul. Viewed from a vantage point from outer space somewhere between San Francisco and Seoul, the scene would have looked like this: as martial artists harassed Kim Dae-jung and police arrested Rhee, an agent was reporting the blow-by-blow to the KCIA chief at the Hilton hotel, who, in turn, was reporting to Seoul. Why such organization? Because the South Korean government wanted to silence Kim and the KCIA was looking for an opportunity to kidnap and kill him.

Back in the hall, Kim continued his speech, explaining that the unfortunate incident with Rhee had taken place as if everyone in the hall lived in South Korea. They had just witnessed the kind of politics that was typical in Korea, he said, adding, "This incident tonight, however unfortunate, can prove a point I've been making all along." Kim went on to explain his point: that political disagreement should not degrade into physical conflict and terror.

A year and a half later, in 1974, when FBI agents finally got around to speaking to Rhee Min-hi about the incident, he admitted to disrupting the speech but denied being a KCIA agent — and claimed that the KCIA had never approached him. The Americans let him go.

More than thirty years later, I looked up Rhee and discovered that his sons, Simon and Phillip Rhee, had become martial arts movie stars, known for *The Best of the Best* movie series in the U.S. (1989 to 1998). Their father had advised them on the films, which featured Tae Kwon Do techniques. Simon Rhee told me that the brothers had never been involved in their father's political work and that the Rhee–Kim confrontation ended up in a thirty-second spot on a well-known Korean television series, *Hourglass*, in which an actor playing his father confronts an actor playing Kim.[262]

"I later apologized to Mr. Kim," Rhee Min-hi told me on the phone. "I said I wasn't against him as a person, but I didn't like his policies."[263] Rhee claimed that only after the 1973 confrontation did he learn that Korean consulate members and KCIA agents had attended the talk in the hall. Three people reported to the FBI that Rhee had probably been a KCIA agent, but Rhee denied it.[264] "I was maligned for so many years," Rhee told me. He also claimed that, long after the incident, he and Song Sun-keun, the journalist who had written about the confrontation, met at a party in Seoul and patched things up. And Rhee met Kim Dae-jung many times, too, both men working out their past differences, Rhee told me.

In spite of the actions of Rhee and other martial artists, the KCIA failed to stop Kim Dae-jung in the U.S., but agents constantly shadowed him, looking for the right place and time to kidnap him. Meanwhile, Koreans in North American cities felt like they were living in surreal South Koreas, with consulates, not the U.S. government, running communities, and KCIA agents, not American police, enforcing laws. But kidnapping Kim in the U.S. became less feasible as American intelligence services increased their vigilance.

Kim Dae-jung and Rhee Min-hi in 1998, 25 years after their famous confrontation.
PHOTO COURTESY OF RHEE.

For years, the Americans had been tracking the KCIA and were becoming more annoyed with Koreans' boldness and blunders on U.S. soil.[265] Most American intelligence leaders and government officials did not seem concerned that the KCIA was harassing and threatening Korean-Americans, but a high-octane kidnapping of the famous Kim Dae-jung involving martial artists would lead to bad publicity in Asia, where American leaders needed the Koreans onside in the Vietnam and Cold wars. In the early 1970s, the Americans were constantly telling the KCIA and South Korean government to control themselves and get their agents in order in the U.S., especially the collaborators who were not officially listed as KCIA agents. In short, the KCIA would have to kidnap their man in another country.[266]

The KCIA finalized that plan in July 1973 and picked Tokyo, Japan, as the place.[267] One of Kim Dae-jung's people would later tell the FBI that, just before the kidnapping, Rhee Min-hi flew out of San Francisco to Asia,[268] but Rhee laughed when I asked him if he had flown to Tokyo for this mission. "I never knew about a KCIA plan to kidnap Kim Dae-jung," he spluttered. "It's all nonsense."[269]

The FBI heard that an assistant instructor at a martial arts school and a martial artist from the Wha Rang Karate Institute flew out of San Francisco just before the kidnapping. In addition, KCIA operatives flew from the U.S. to Tokyo: one from San Francisco, two from New York City, and two or three accompanying Washington-based KCIA chief Yang Doo-wan. Twenty-four KCIA personnel were on the kidnapping team — from South Korea, Japan, and the U.S. — all of them coordinated by the sixth branch of the KCIA, the one in charge of assassinations.[270]

On August 8, 1973, Kim Dae-jung was staying at Tokyo's Grand Palace Hotel, which was spiked with KCIA agents. After lunch with a Korean official, who turned out to be part of the plot, Kim stepped out of his hotel room and agents grabbed, drugged, and stuffed him into a car trunk and raced to Osaka. An uproar immediately followed in Japan, where police, who had been tipped off about the plot, had been following the KCIA agents in the days before the kidnapping.

The day after the abduction, agents transferred Kim to a speedboat that zipped back to South Korea. During the explosive international reaction, the Seoul station chief for the American CIA tipped off the American ambassador in South Korea that the KCIA was behind the kidnapping. The ambassador jumped into a car, drove to the Blue House (the president's residence), and demanded that the South Korean president release Kim.[271]

Meanwhile, on the boat, agents tied Kim down with weights and were preparing to pitch him into the Sea of Japan. Suddenly, aircraft buzzed overhead with a message to release him, saving his life.

A couple of days later, the KCIA let him go in Seoul, only to kidnap and deposit him in prison the following week. The debacle refused to die down, especially after Japan downplayed the operation and South Korea denied that the KCIA was involved.

By 1974, the American government had had enough of the James Bond scenes. From the start, the FBI, the U.S. Department of Justice, and the American CIA, which had been tracking KCIA agents and had supposedly bugged the South Korean president's meeting room in Seoul, had thought that the Plan was a nuisance. Koreans who were neither diplomats nor KCIA agents were handing cash to baffled U.S. congressmen, assigning agents to infiltrate the U.S. government, and offering prostitutes to politicians. Meanwhile, rogue martial artists jumped in and out of various surreal and scary scenes. Some U.S. politicians accepted the bribes, and the stories began crawling across newspaper front pages. For American intelligence leaders, the entire operation had grown embarrassing, but to honest Tae Kwon Do instructors and other Koreans around the world, the whole thing was terrifying. It did not help to hear that, at the time, the American CIA was busy training torturers in Chile, Brazil, Uruguay, and Argentina.[272]

Still, the Americans quietly kicked Washington KCIA station chief Yang Doo-wan out of the country in 1974 because the U.S. State Department considered him responsible for harassment in the U.S. and because his Plan had become an embarrassment.[273] When Yang returned to Seoul, the South Korean dictator promoted him and expanded the Plan covertly. This meant that day-to-day, non-diplomatic officials had more work to do; the KCIA became nearly invisible but continued to threaten Koreans in North America.

Choi Hong-Hi was talking himself hoarse, warning people about South Korea.[274] He said that the South Korean government was harassing his martial arts pioneers, and he became more fearful for his own life. Many thought he was exaggerating, but he knew the truth. Newspaper stories about tortures in basements and calls at night were intimate reminders of the larger repression in South Korea and in other American CIA–backed dictatorships. Choi knew the game; after all, he was still part of it.

One day, when he was organizing a tour of Europe and the Middle East — and planning to get on a plane the next day — a Tae Kwon Do instructor called to say that he had flown from South Korea to the U.S. with a message: "In Korea, I was able to sense that they are planning some scheme against you," he told Choi. "As you know, they kidnapped the opposition leader, Kim Dae-jung. They would not leave you alone. I am calling because I care about you, so please consider and delay your schedule instead of leaving tomorrow."[275]

The next day, Choi ignored him and got on a plane for an international tour with the latest Ace team, all of them seventh-degree masters.[276] It was unlikely anyone would mess with them, but they had some muscle behind this tour: the American CIA was financing the trip and providing protection, thanks to Choi's friend, Robert Walson, a CIA officer and sixth-degree black belt in Tae Kwon Do.[277]

Walson had known Choi before the American joined the CIA, and Walson had sponsored Korean Karate instructors to move to the U.S.[278] In fact, many American CIA agents practised Korean Karate and Tae Kwon Do during the martial art's heyday in the 1960s and 1970s. The CIA had stationed Walson in Ethiopia in the 1970s, where he had introduced Tae Kwon Do in his spare time, and he had spent three years in Laos during the Vietnam War, during which he survived a helicopter crash, thanks to his Tae Kwon Do training. With multiple wounds and a report that the Viet Cong were on their way, he side-kicked the helicopter door and helped to carry a Laotian general from the crash site. Choi surrounded himself with such black belts and proven warriors, and Walson's friendship with Choi grew over the years, including when Walson later opened a Tae Kwon Do gym for dozens of agents in Washington, DC.

Also, thanks to Walson, Choi met CIA officer Gary C. Schroen, one of Walson's Tae Kwon Do students (a first-degree black) and a close friend of Walson's since 1961.[279] Schroen taught basic Tae Kwon Do to U.S. marines while working for the CIA in Pakistan, and had switched from *Tang Soo Do* around 1966, when Walson had made a connection with Choi. Schroen said that Tae Kwon Do had been popular in the CIA. "The agency always stressed fitness, and the guys and gals that we hired usually wanted to be in shape — and Tae Kwon Do was popular," he told me.

Schroen was assigned to work in the U.S. embassy in Iran in 1972 and liked training in Tae Kwon Do. "I got a little use out of it in Iran, because it generated contacts, and that's what you need," he said. That year, he met the head of the Korean CIA in Iran, and Schroen asked him if he knew anyone to train with. The fellow introduced Schroen to a World Taekwondo Federation instructor from South Korea who was training the Iranian Special Forces — a program between South Korea and Iran. The instructor taught Schroen, who in turn, helped him to set up a Tae Kwon Do gym for Americans in Tehran. "At one point, we had forty students, and I ran the club for a while, but it got to be too much work," Schroen said. "I did a lot of night work." It was a dangerous time for Americans in Iran, especially after one of Schroen's Iranian colleagues was murdered.

Schroen helped Choi and Walson to organize a 1973 ITF tournament in Iran. Ironically, Schroen enlisted the help of the KCIA head and the WTF instructor, both of whom knew about General Choi Hong-Hi but did not want to meet him. The ITF tournament was televised in an Iranian police sports stadium, with a large showing from the Iranian military. The WTF instructor, Schroen's instructor, did not attend, telling Schroen, "Oh, I can't meet Choi. I'd get in trouble."

Choi was elated by the success of the Iran demonstration and awarded Schroen a second-degree black belt after testing him in a tiny hotel room. Schroen was more amused than awed by the Ace team. "Their egos were as big as their skills," he told me. "They strutted around and competed with each other in everything from eating hot peppers to breaking wooden boards."[280] And most of them wanted to drink Scotch and look for women when they were finished the demonstrations, Schroen said.

He did not need to protect Choi and the Ace team from KCIA officials in Iran, but he did provide protection from an Iranian terrorist group that was kidnapping and killing foreigners at the time. Without Schroen and Walson, the Tae Kwon Do team would not have been able to travel easily. This sort of local threat was an anomaly, though. Elsewhere, South Korean officials, not local terrorist groups, bugged them much more.[281]

Unfortunately, things got spookier after 1973.

(*top*) Walson was as adept at flipping opponents as he was in getting American CIA financing for Choi Hong-Hi's international Tae Kwon Do. (*bottom*) Walson demonstrates a release from a grab. He trained with Tae Kwon Do's pioneers in the early 1960s and helped a few of them to settle in the U.S.
PHOTOS COURTESY OF WALSON.

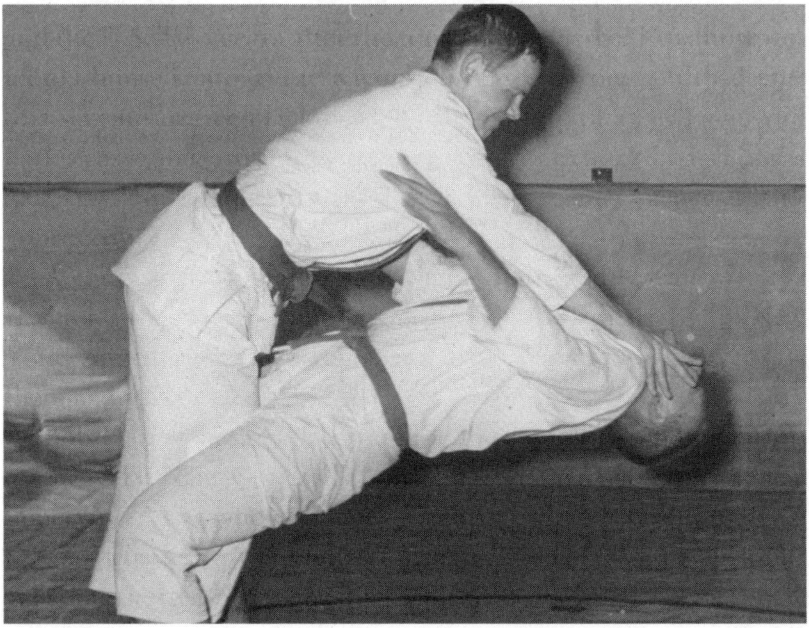

In 1965, Robert Walson was a case officer with the American CIA and a black belt in Tae Kwon Do. He spent three years in Laos during the Vietnam War. The CIA stationed him in Ethiopia, where he introduced Tae Kwon Do. PHOTO COURTESY OF WALSON.

Tae Kwon Do's jumping side kick was popular in the 1960s. Walson trained dozens of other American CIA agents in Tae Kwon Do then and in the 1970s.
PHOTO COURTESY OF WALSON.

CHAPTER 11

FROM SPOOKY KUKKI TO WTF

I now know that whenever a martial artist looks into the history of his art, it is time to reach for the Scotch. From the beginning, Tae Kwon Do has had high ideals and fought violence with violence (and sometimes fought justice with violence, too), but the history of the martial art has always hidden its painful truths. Millions of people, including Koreans, do not realize that the tall tale about Tae Kwon Do being an ancient martial art is more than a neat story: the creation myth sells the serenity while hiding the brutality and points to heaven while ignoring the blood. In the 1950s and 1960s, Tae Kwon Do needed ancient mumbo-jumbo to hide its Karate roots, and in the 1970s, it needed ancient, invisible warriors to promote a wicked regime.

Choi's myth about 1,500-year-old dynasties and *hwarang* warriors had a deep and practical purpose in the early 1970s: the sketchy "research" that embedded Tae Kwon Do in Korea's old culture grew into a legend as hardy as an ancient gingko. It came as no surprise, then, that the Korean Overseas Information Service published a booklet, *Taekwondo*, that opened with "Taekwondo is a martial art unique to Korea developed about 2,000 years ago."[282] But the dictatorship borrowed more than Choi's creation myth. To his amazement, it stole the name of his martial art, Tae Kwon Do, and it assigned super-spy Kim Un-yong to unify the martial arts gyms (*kwans*) under one Tae Kwon Do umbrella.

One of Kim's most important projects was raising money for a world Tae Kwon Do headquarters, the Kukkiwon. In fact, political and martial arts leaders chose him as a leader in 1970 partly because he could raise huge amounts of money.[283]

At Kim's first press conference, a journalist asked him if he would indeed build the Kukkiwon as promised.

"Yes," Kim replied.

"How much will it cost?" the journalist asked.

Kim froze. He turned and whispered to Lee Chong-woo, a martial arts leader who sat nearby.

"Say that three hundred million Won will do," Lee whispered back. In those days, that was an enormous sum, equivalent to U.S.$1.5 million today.

"I think we need no more than two hundred million Won," Kim said, not wanting to alarm people with the larger number. Korean newspapers reported the amount.[284]

Kim wanted the Kukkiwon built in the old style to, as he said, "give the impression of tradition, like the Korean palaces, for instance, or the magnificent homes of the Confucian high officials."

For its roof, he chose a traditional Korean tile, the blue *kiwa*, the same type of *kiwa* that was on the Blue House, the country's presidential mansion. In the old days, the making of blue *kiwa* was a respected, secret art passed from father to son. There is a saying in Korea: he is as secretive as a *kiwa* merchant.

Kim could not find land in Seoul for the Kukkiwon, so he approached a friend, the mayor of Seoul, who offered him a flat patch.

"I need the highest ground in Yeoksam-dong," Kim countered.

"You can have lower ground," the mayor insisted. "I don't understand why you need a place on the top of the mountain."

"This martial arts gym will have a monumental meaning," Kim said. "I also have a feeling that a Tae Kwon Do miracle might occur if we build it at the summit."

Kim received his mountaintop miracle, and construction began in November 1971, "financed with my personal property," Kim wrote, "and donations from my acquaintances — large companies like Samsung."[285]

One year later, the Kukkiwon was inaugurated by Kim Chŏng-p'il, Kim Un-yong's former KCIA boss, who was now the country's prime minister.[286] The beautiful, three-storey building rested on a two-acre lot and contained studios, an auditorium, a dormitory, a recreation room, and the distinct aura of ancient history around its blue *kiwa* roof. The Kukkiwon would unite rival martial arts factions by forcing them to conduct black belt promotions and Tae Kwon Do business in the Kukkiwon itself.[287] Gangsters would take over the Kukkiwon in later years, but in the early days the building would be more market than monastery.

Many martial arts leaders refused to unite, but they soon had no choice. With the iron support of the Korean regime, Kim transformed part of the Korean Tae Kwon Do Association into the World Taekwondo Federation, which sounded nearly identical to Choi's International Taekwon-Do Federation.[288] Also, the acronym "WTF" sounded like "ITF" in English. Choi, in a rage, warned them not to use the term "Tae Kwon Do," but everyone ignored him, and South Korea severed all ties with the ITF in Canada.[289] The war between Choi and Kim entered a new phase.

The timing of the WTF's birth seemed inauspicious — it was created between the month of May (when the KCIA was targeting Kim Dae-jung in the U.S.) and the month of August (when martial artists tried to kill him in Japan) — but creating a global Tae Kwon Do group was a smart move for the dictatorship, which needed Tae Kwon Do to improve the nation's image overseas. At the time, South Korea was an economic powerhouse, generating self-confidence along with self-reliance; this was an achievement for a tiny country overshadowed by Japan and China for much of its modern history. Promoting Tae Kwon Do was a physical manifestation of Korea's confidence. Kim Un-yong wrote: "By practising Tae Kwon Do, one can build up the spirit of self-denial and perseverance, gaining confidence in tackling whatever difficulties one may face."[290]

After the Kukkiwon was constructed and the WTF launched,

Kim focused on the "tackling" part: globalizing a new brand of Tae Kwon Do.[291] Choi was appalled at the bluntness of Kim's campaign. He worried that people around the world would confuse his Tae Kwon Do with the new one: "Wild panic grass, easily mistaken for wheat or rice, can actually prevent the growth of the genuine article," he later wrote.[292]

In May 1973, Kim hosted a world championship for thirty countries at the Kukkiwon, "the first official universal match of the art held 20 or 23 centuries after Tae Kwon Do began to be practised," Kim lied.[293] Choi and others had been organizing championships since 1962 (and Tae Kwon Do was nowhere near 20 or 23 centuries old). South Korea ranked first at Kim's tournament, and the U.S., stocked with Korean Karate champions, ranked second.

Choi responded with a 1974 ITF world championship in Montreal, which Nam Tae-hi and Dong-Ja Yang helped run. Choi insulted Nam (for the last time, as it turned out), accusing him of orchestrating a Korean CIA plot. Paranoia and threat hung around Choi like a dark cloud, so Nam, a former KCIA agent, was not surprised by the accusation: "We were very close in the army," Nam told me, "but he thought I was doing things against him."[294] In Nam's view, Choi's relationships with his pioneers followed the same pattern: "What I found was that, when he started, he said very good things about a person. In the end, he always disparaged that person."

Meanwhile, Choi's family lived at the whim of the KCIA's fifth branch, which was in charge of finalizing passports. In Canada, he was in the middle of a process to obtain Canadian citizenship when he heard that Korea would not issue a passport to his adult son, Jung-Hwa, and daughter Sunny.[295] Choi's wife and a second daughter, Meeyun, had already joined him in Canada, thanks to Jhoon Rhee, who had helped Choi's wife sneak into the Dominican Republic.[296] She flew to Canada from there. But Sunny and Jung-Hwa were still stuck in South Korea, and Choi believed they were hostages.

Many stories were circulating about the KCIA hustling people to the dreaded Namsan torture chambers in Seoul. Choi knew the

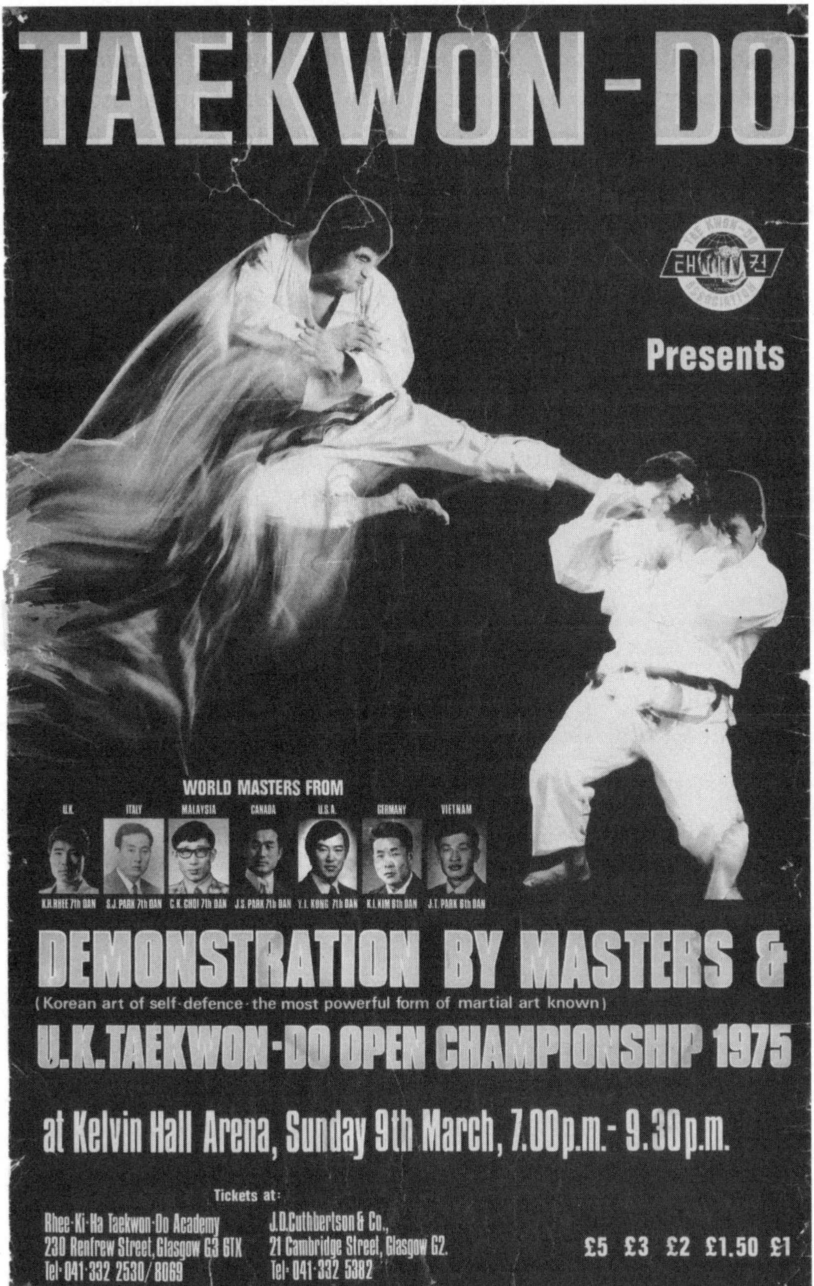

Iconic Tae Kwon Do photos in the 1970s and 1980s often depicted martial artists jumping at face level, with a flame-like special effect behind the kicker. Rhee Ki-ha, a pioneer instructor in the U.K., is the jumper in this poster.

PHOTO COURTESY OF CHOI HONG-HI.

stories and worried about his children, but he refused to fly to Seoul. He was sacrificing them for Tae Kwon Do, as he saw it, but he fell into a bottomless agony. He had miscalculated how fast his power would wane while in exile. Night after night, he cried in bed, facing a wall. He feared that one wrong move might end his children's lives. He tried to muffle his sobs so that his wife would not hear.[297]

But a year later, in 1974, South Korea allowed his two children to leave. They arrived at Toronto's airport, where their father stood waiting for them. The Choi family did not show much emotion in public, because Koreans of Choi's generation were like that, restricted by a hundred rules. In private, Choi could be funny and talkative, but at the airport, he greeted his children in the manner he usually did in public, as if nothing dramatic had occurred.

He simply looked at his son and daughter and said, "Good."[298]

x x x

The World Taekwondo Federation (WTF) was already writing Choi out of Tae Kwon Do history and elevating former KCIA agent Nam Tae-hi as founder of the now-famous Oh Do Kwan, the only military gym in the mid-1950s that had practised Tae Kwon Do.[299] The statuses of other martial artists also rose as Choi's fell. Uhm Woon-kyu and Lee Chong-woo, for example, helped to create and lead the WTF and the Kukkiwon, which is still the WTF's governing organization today, and their stars rose. These WTF leaders claimed that no one had written down the rules of Tae Kwon Do, ignoring Choi's five books from 1959 to 1972.[300] Lee, with Uhm's help, wrote the WTF's first book of techniques, *Taekwondo Textbook*, which was published in 1975.[301]

Uhm, Lee, and a pioneer named Hyun Jong-myung (who had attended Tae Kwon Do's "Naming Committee" meeting in a *kisaeng* house in 1955) also helped to develop the WTF's patterns, which contained techniques similar to those in Karate and the ITF. For example, *Taegeuk Il Jang*, the WTF pattern for beginners, used the same punch and two blocks that Choi had inserted into his first pattern, *Chon-Ji*, which, in turn, was based on the *kihon* pattern from Karate.

A new rule in the WTF surprised everyone however: punching an opponent in the face was no longer allowed during sparring. Martial artists laughed because it made no sense; how could you spar and not hit the face? A punch was fundamental in the fighting arts.

None of this stopped Choi's men from deserting him and joining the WTF. A common criticism of Choi is that his martial arts instructors, most of them anti-communist soldiers, left him because he co-operated with North Korean communists, which, in those days, hit the same triggers as the term "terrorist" does today. In reality, his instructors began leaving him long before he formally co-operated with North Korea. They left him partly because South Korea had increased the pressure on ITF pioneers and instructors, a pressure that became unbearable for many in the 1970s, and partly because Choi was difficult to work with.

The first major defection occurred in 1971 in West Germany, where conflicts exploded between the German Tae Kwon Do leader Heinz Marx and Kim Kwang-il (the Tae Kwon Do pioneer and KCIA operative who had been involved in the East Berlin Incident of 1967). Choi backed Kim Kwang-il, and Marx and the entire German association left the ITF and joined Kim Un-yong's WTF two years later.[302]

The second loss occurred in 1974, when the organization in Turkey also jumped to the WTF, mainly because Choi had failed to solve an alleged corruption problem. After those two defections — two pillars of the ITF gone — the losses came hard and fast, and Kim Un-yong continued to globalize the South Korean regime's martial art. In 1974, the dictatorship forced thousands of gyms, ITF or not, to line up behind Kim's WTF. Also, the Amateur Athletic Union in the U.S. accepted the WTF, not the ITF, as a member. Choi lost high-calibre instructors such as Jae-Hun Kim (who ran gyms in Boston and whose father was in the South Korean government) and Dong-Ja Yang (a brilliant sports administrator who later helped usher the WTF into the Olympics).[303]

Kim Kwang-il with Heinz Marx in 1971. Marx led much of the International Taekwon-Do Federation but broke away from it and Kim in 1973 to join the enemy (the World Taekwondo Federation). PHOTO COURTESY OF THOMAS KUKLINSKI-RHEE.

Meanwhile, everyone was riding the martial arts film craze started by Bruce Lee and others. Even boxer Muhammad Ali learned Tae Kwon Do: Jhoon Rhee taught him the "accupunch" that Ali apparently used to knock out Richard Dunn in 1975.[304] But political forces pushed Rhee around despite his successes. He did not join Kim Un-yong's WTF, but a Korean newspaper reporter told U.S. officials that Rhee had received money from the Korean CIA to open martial arts schools (which was true if you consider that the money flowed through a cult). However, the Internal Revenue Service investigated and cleared Rhee of wrongdoing.

In 1975, Tae Kwon Do was booming in South Korea, and Kim Un-yong had awarded himself an eighth-dan black belt, which placed him one level above a master and meant that in only four years he had done what other martial artists usually took decades to accomplish. Kim noted that 721 Tae Kwon Do experts taught in forty-eight countries, with more than two-thirds of the instructors teaching in the U.S., Canada, and West Germany. In South Korea, three million students, including 300,000 black belts, were training in Tae Kwon Do.[305]

In Canada, Choi announced that twenty million students were members of the ITF around the world.[306] South Korea had one of the hottest economies on the planet and, building on Choi's and Nam's twenty years of sweat and yells, now boasted one of the hottest martial arts.

But Choi's ITF ran out of money once again, and he realized that Kim had obtained too much, too fast, irreparably damaging the ITF. Meanwhile, Kim lobbied for the WTF's inclusion in three international events: the Asian Games, the South American Pan-Am Games, and an international military sports competition.[307] A cunning strategist, Kim was registering Tae Kwon Do with these big-name organizations so that in one swoop he could marginalize Choi, raise the value of Korea's martial art, and gain access to bigger budgets. In North America, the KCIA continued bribing and threatening Koreans, including Choi's martial arts pioneers, who then drifted from Choi to Kim's federation.

It did not help that Choi was homesick. Canada allowed him to travel everywhere — it was his new home — but he recalled a saying from Lao-Tzu: the ideal society is where one can live comfortably in one's hometown from birth to death. He envied his friends in Korea, who woke up to the crowing of roosters and went to sleep to the barking of dogs. Choi loved rural areas, but in Canadian cities, roosters were illegal and dogs were not supposed to bark at night — and people kept to themselves. Choi said that he had not laughed in a long time.

South Korean officials harassed Choi and his Tae Kwon Do bodyguards at airports, trying to stop them from travelling and occasionally threatening them, according to Choi. One of his pioneer instructors, C. K. Choi, told me, "The South Korean government was backing the WTF. Because of that, the ITF was dissolved in Seoul, Korea . . . Most of the time, these diplomats abroad went after the Tae Kwon Do pioneering instructors."[308]

Choi could not turn to the Americans for help. A couple of American CIA agents who were black belts had helped the ITF, but other than that, American intelligence agencies and politicians were ambivalent when it came to criticizing their South Korean allies. And Choi had reason to be scared. The U.S. Justice Department, the American CIA, and the FBI knew about the KCIA missions in North America, but they investigated as little as possible.[309]

By this time, thanks to news reports, the world knew that South Korea was a criminal enterprise and that its agents threw human-rights advocates off bridges and ran them over with cars, but in the Americans' view, South Korea was an important ally in the Cold War. In 1973, the U.S. had promised it would "not interfere" in Korean internal affairs, but it had, in fact, committed U.S.$1.5 billion for a modern militarization program. U.S. Secretary of State Henry Kissinger knew about the bribery, threats, and illegal activities in the U.S., and in 1974, after a particularly violent crackdown in South Korea, the U.S. ambassador in Seoul suggested to Kissinger that the U.S. should counsel moderation.

The ambassador would not forget Kissinger's reply: "Why counsel moderation?"

"If you were where I am, you would want to do so," the ambassador replied.

"No, I wouldn't," Kissinger said. "I don't think we should be involved. So why counsel?"

In Korea, the ambassador expressed concern anyway, privately. Kissinger ordered that a cable be sent to him to "tell him to get off their backs."[310]

Understandably, the South Korean president interpreted this American attitude as support, and the Korean regime became stronger.

With that strong backing, Kim Un-yong became an indomitable force against Choi and his ITF pioneers, and Choi discovered that the KCIA had approached a black belt with an assignment to kidnap him. Another time, in the hours before flying to a Tae

Kwon Do event in Chicago in 1975, he heard that demonstrators were gathering at a church of Reverend Sun-Myung Moon, a cult that was involved with the KCIA and nefarious missions. A U.S. CIA agent tipped off Choi, but he flew to the event anyway, and there was no demonstration.[311]

✗✗✗

How does one fight an indomitable force? With indomitable spirit. In Washington, DC, on June 10, 1975, a former Korean Embassy attaché, Lee Jai-Hyon, sat at a witness table in a large hearing room of the House International Relations Committee and became the first of many Korean officials to expose South Korea's secret Plan in the U.S. and Canada. The Plan was dubbed "Koreagate" by the North American press. That same year, a journalist reported that the Los Angeles president of the KAA — of which the Korean Tae Kwon Do Association was a member — beat up Koreans, raided their businesses, and threatened to massacre their families. "The pampering attitude of Korean government authorities encourage and condone a long record of violent activities of the officers of the Korea Amateur Association [KAA] of America," the journalist wrote.[312]

Angry and scared, Lee told U.S. Congressional investigators: "I will testify on other aspects that have not yet been touched upon."[313] Out poured details during five years of hearings, but it was too late for Choi, too late for Tae Kwon Do, and too late for the Koreans already in prison. In Choi's view, it was time for drastic retaliation.

He began negotiating with South Korea's and the U.S.'s longtime enemy, North Korea, in the gamble of his life. For thirteen years, off and on, he had been talking to agents from the Hermit Kingdom, flirting with the idea of visiting and accepting money. Now, he published an open letter to the South Korean president, listing reasons why "Choi Hong-Hi is the one who would cut his throat."[314] His list included the regime's violation of human rights and its role in turning Tae Kwon Do students into gangsters. Choi sounded like a martial arts hero — or a vigilante.

95th Congress } COMMITTEE PRINT
2d Session }

INVESTIGATION OF KOREAN-AMERICAN RELATIONS

REPORT

OF THE

SUBCOMMITTEE ON INTERNATIONAL ORGANIZATIONS

OF THE

COMMITTEE ON INTERNATIONAL RELATIONS
U.S. HOUSE OF REPRESENTATIVES

OCTOBER 31, 1978

Printed for the use of the
Committee on International Relations

U.S. GOVERNMENT PRINTING OFFICE
35-508 O WASHINGTON : 1978

In 1975, the U.S. government began hearings about the Plan (or "Koreagate"), a mission to seduce and influence more than a hundred U.S. Congress members and to bribe, threaten, and kill Koreans who criticized the South Korean dictatorship.

One month later, a North Korean advised him that he could meet his North Korean brother, whom Choi had not seen in thirty years.[315] Choi and the North Korean picked a date and a place — Sweden, which was politically neutral during the Cold War. On the day when Choi finally met his brother, the elderly man was sitting in a car with North Korean agents. Choi climbed in. Overcome by emotion, neither Choi was able to say anything, so they simply clenched hands and allowed themselves to be overwhelmed by all the grey hair and wrinkles.

At the North Korean embassy, with agents hovering nearby, they talked about their parents, who were dead, their younger sister, friends, and relatives — a conversation that spread bitterness through their hearts like bad liquor. The North Koreans brought out the real stuff, and the North Korean ambassador to Sweden joined them in drink after drink, with the conversation inevitably veering into politics. Choi announced that the two Koreas should unite, and he listened to an eager explanation about the superiority of communism, but all he craved was to be left alone with his brother. The ambassador picked up the cues and left the room, and Choi and his brother talked all night and all day and all night again, with North Koreans popping in to invite him to his hometown, discuss Korean unification, and meditate on the possibility that Choi could expand Tae Kwon Do in North Korea.

On the third day, his brother asked him to visit Yongwon village, their hometown in North Korea, right then and there, because relatives and friends were waiting for them. Choi refused. He did not want to fly from Sweden to North Korea and risk being labelled a communist, which would jeopardize his chances of becoming a Canadian citizen. Not knowing whether they would see each other again, Choi and his brother embraced, lamented, cried — and everyone in the room cried with them.

Emotionally exhausted and sleep deprived, and numb with drink, Choi lost track of how he ended up at his hotel. He stumbled to an airport, where officials did not allow him on the plane, and he settled into a waiting area to sleep off his grief. His luggage departed without him.[316]

CHAPTER 12

WHAAA!

In 1977, Cold War politics thrived in Tae Kwon Do like a disease, and the martial art burned in Choi like a fever. Since the *coup d'état* of 1961, he had succeeded in working against the South Korean dictator, devoting his life to saving his martial art from him and Kim Un-yong, as he saw it. He turned to his long-time enemy, North Korea, with an ambitious campaign to expand Tae Kwon Do around the world and challenge South Korea and Kim in every arena he could. North Korea had been giving Choi money to publish a Tae Kwon Do encyclopedia set, but the volumes were not complete.[317] The books — fifteen volumes eventually — contained more technical details than all Choi's past books put together and were being published one or two at a time, but Choi needed more money and power.

For easy money, he turned to an old enemy, Kim Hyung-wook, the former leader of the Korean CIA who had organized the mass abductions and tortures of the East Berlin Incident. Because of the international outcry generated by that operation, the South Korean president had fired Kim, who had fled to the U.S. in 1973 and taken with him at least U.S.$15 million along with details about the KCIA's Plan, which he leaked to U.S. officials and the media.[318]

In the summer of 1978, Choi engineered a meeting with Kim to ask for funds for South Korea's democracy movement (and for Tae Kwon Do, of course). In return, Choi would supply him with

Tae Kwon Do bodyguards and possibly a post in his Tae Kwon Do organization. But Choi and the former KCIA director ran out of time. As the American investigation into Koreagate petered into nothingness (probably because Koreagate scampered too close to Congressional Democrats), Choi met Kim only once before the KCIA in France abducted him in 1979. The story goes that someone cut off Kim's head and sent it to the South Korean president in a diplomatic pouch or that the KCIA secretly shipped Kim back to Seoul where the president shot him twice in the head.[319] Kim's body was never found, and since then, no high-ranking Korean official has ever testified about Korean wrongdoing in the U.S.

Around that time, Choi unveiled an impossible-sounding campaign to North Korea, an operation that seemed more reckless than the poker game where he had lost his mother's savings almost forty years before. The KCIA's Plan had continued expanding in North America, in spite of investigations and press coverage, and Choi's men had continued switching to Kim Un-yong's organization. Choi's mission promised to counter this. He had applied military tactics to Tae Kwon Do sparring, and he seemed to now be applying them to martial arts politics: "You must create opportunity, assess your opponent and his weapons, assess his techniques and habits, and press them to your advantage," he once explained.[320]

His new mission would take him to North Korea to train large numbers of new instructors and post them around the world, countering and cornering Kim's World Taekwondo Federation everywhere. Very few instructors accepted the political mission, but some defended him: "General Choi had to go to North Korea, because the South Korean dictatorship was taking over all the ITF," explained Michael Cormack, who was Choi's son-in-law and an official in the International Taekwon-Do Federation at the time. "ITF instructors were getting knocked off the master's list so fast . . . you need to have some funds to propagate Tae Kwon Do. It was a bad situation for him."[321]

Still, ITF masters and instructors worldwide did not like Choi's operation because South Korea was technically at war with North Korea. Choi ignored their pleas. Everything was a mission for him,

Choi Hong-Hi clinks glasses with North Korean leader Kim Il Sung during a 1980 Tae Kwon Do tour. PHOTO COURTESY OF CHOI.

including trying to marry off his daughters to Tae Kwon Do instructors.[322] Once he set his mind on a mission such as this North Korean operation, he would not give up; he would order his best pioneers to North Korea because he needed resources and power. But what would he give to the North Korean dictatorship in return?

He and the North Korean dictator, Kim Il Sung, shared several things in common: both had been born in northern Korea long before the Americans and Russians split the nation; both had survived the Second World War and Japanese colonialism and would never forget the scars; and both hated and respected Japan and the United States. For a Westerner, it is difficult to comprehend the bitterness within these men's hearts, where history was measured in centuries, not decades. Most Koreans of their generation had considered Japanese rule not only illegitimate but humiliating.[323] For centuries, the two nations had been equal in terms of geography, Chinese influence, and economic development, so Japan's dominance in the nineteenth and twentieth centuries had been galling. North Korea's leader demonstrated his infinite loathing in 1977 by running a covert mission in which agents abducted children and couples from Japan's beaches and whizzed them on speedboats to

North Korea, where they were forced to teach Japanese culture, mannerisms, and language to North Korean agents.[324]

Choi would soon be co-operating with such agents because he wanted all North Koreans to practise Tae Kwon Do, especially in the military. The nation's soldiers trained informally in a martial art called *Kuksul*, but martial arts were not popular, and there was no Karate or Tae Kwon Do.[325]

Few of Choi's men could fathom the General's mission. His son-in-law, Michael Cormack, agreed to go, as did Choi's son, Jung-Hwa, but most of Choi's pioneer instructors were shocked that he wanted them to visit communist Korea at the height of the Cold War. One story demonstrates how psychotic tensions could get between the two nations. The Tree Cutting Incident, or Axe Murder Incident, in 1976 involved twenty or thirty unarmed North Korean guards attacking twenty or so American and South Korean soldiers who were pruning a tree in the demilitarized zone (DMZ), which lies on the thirty-eighth parallel between North and South Korea. Trimming this tree was supposed to be a routine event, and neither side carried guns in the DMZ, which was a no-man's land. However, after an argument about the sacredness of the tree, the North Koreans used axes and clubs to beat to death two Americans, which was all filmed by a corporal on the South Korean side. Three days later, in retaliation, the Americans and South Koreans rounded up approximately sixty Tae Kwon Do experts and special-forces soldiers to cut down the sacred tree in front of hundreds of North Korean guards. The South Korean black belts provided protection on the ground while bombers flew overhead, but the North Koreans did not attack.[326]

Stories like this made Tae Kwon Do masters, most of whom had been soldiers, wonder if the General was losing his mind. Was he really planning a mission to North Korea? In South Korea, criticizing the country to a foreigner was punishable by seven years in jail, and talking to a North Korean was punishable by death.[327]

Among the first masters whom Choi contacted was Kong Young-il. Kong was running a gym in the U.S. and was one of Tae Kwon Do's finest masters. He had begun studying martial arts in

1952, had trained soldiers for the Vietnam War, and had demonstrated Choi's art in 127 countries.[328]

Acting like a general, Choi called Kong and got right to the point: "You have to come with me to North Korea."

Kong listened to the mission's goals and replied, "I cannot go." It was the first time he had refused one of the General's orders.

"You have to go!" Choi yelled.

"Think about my family; think about my school," Kong said.

"Whaaa!" Choi yelled and slammed down the phone.

He called back immediately. "You have to go!"

"No, sir," Kong said.

"Whaaa!" and the receiver hit the phone again.[329]

Kong picked up the ringing phone two more times, refusing again and again. Saying no to the General — his mentor, leader, and father figure of more than a decade — was one of the most painful experiences of his life. Choi was a generous man, but if you did not follow his orders he became angry, cut you off, and considered you a nobody. Kong and Choi stopped speaking to each other for many years.

Nam Tae-hi, Choi's right-hand man in the U.S., had had serious personal problems with Choi in the past, but the final split between them was due to Choi's involvement with North Korea. Nam, a former South Korean colonel and secret-service agent, viewed the mission as a colossal betrayal: "General Choi didn't do bad things, but he always betrayed other people," Nam said. "I fought the North Koreans and Chinese," Nam said. "I killed many of them."[330]

Nam never spoke to Choi again. It did not help that Nam had been a member of the Korean CIA from 1965 to 1972 and that Kim Un-yong's World Taekwondo Federation awarded Nam a ninth-degree black belt and turned him into a grandmaster equal to Choi. From 1970 to 1972 especially, the KCIA's and Kim's pressure on Choi increased so much that Choi feared for his life and his martial art. To find out that Nam, his SuperNam, was collaborating with both must have been maddening.

In Canada, Jong-Soo Park, a pioneer instructor who had helped Choi and Nam with books and world tours, also refused

The good old days: Choi Hong-Hi (standing in the middle) and Nam Tae-hi (standing beside Choi) visited Jong-Soo Park's first Tae Kwon Do class in Toronto, Canada, in the early 1970s. Park stands on the far left. PHOTO COURTESY OF CHOI.

to go to North Korea. He had been one of the few to find out that Choi had visited his brother with the help of North Korean agents in 1975, and he did not like the current mission. Park's relatives lived in South Korea, so KCIA threats were possible. Park also joined Kim's WTF,[331] which angered Choi. Choi was trying to get the Canadian government to recognize the ITF, and here was his Canadian pioneer joining the enemy. He did not talk to Park for the next twenty years.

As more South Koreans learned of Choi's mission to North Korea, the KCIA increased the pressure. The agency's tactics had become subtler over the years — less physical torture and more covert pressure and infiltration.[332] Choi heard that the consul general of Los Angeles, who was part of the KCIA's notorious mission in the U.S., had told Master Choi Sunduk that his relatives would face trouble in South Korea. In another story, someone visited the mother of Han Sam-soo, one of Choi's pioneers, and told her that Han might be kidnapped.[333]

"There were scenarios where the KCIA approached many instructors or non-Koreans, first-degree to third-degree black belts," said Michael Cormack, who overheard phone calls and private conversations with masters. "If your brother was in the army or air force, he'd lose his commission; he'd be out of the army." There were other penalties. "This was heavy-duty pressure," Cormack told me. By 1980, out of hundreds of top-notch Korean instructors, only about a dozen had remained with Choi.[334]

It was the ITF's worst crisis. Choi felt like he was losing his sons. In his view, how could so many of them worry about their own families and jobs after Choi's sacrifices? He continued with the mission anyway, wearing judgments like military badges and threats like medals.

Choi taught techniques to new supermen, such as the agile Park Jung-tae, who could complete five kicks in mid-air and jump over a car.[335] Park also represented a calmer, more dignified approach to the art. Choi taught him for six months in the basement of the Chois' house and gathered a team of fifteen martial artists who were brave enough to visit North Korea: seven Korean instructors from the U.S., England, Greece, and Yugoslavia; seven instructors from Canada; one American master; and a photographer to record the event.[336] If Choi was obsessed before, he was possessed now.

And he was sixty-four years old. Time had flown like an arrow, and now he had to start over, produce hundreds of instructors, and disperse them around the world to compete with Kim Un-yong and the South Korean regime, especially in Sweden, the U.S.S.R., and the communist countries that South Korea had been avoiding during the Cold War. "He felt he was making history," Cormack explained. "He felt he was doing something that would profoundly change Tae Kwon Do for the better. There would be problems, there would be adversaries from it, but with General Choi, you know, he always liked attention. There's a book called *Thriving on Chaos* — but he thrived on chaos. It gave him momentum and energy to take Tae Kwon Do further."

"He was an extremely energetic, driven man — extremely focused: Tae Kwon Do was his life," Cormack added. "I mean, there are not many human beings like him anymore. You have to understand that for a son like James [Jung-Hwa] and a son-in-law like Michael Cormack, he was very difficult. We'd be watching a movie at home on Sunday night, after dinner, and we'd be into the plot, and we'd be right at the point where the action's starting, and the whole family is there. We'd look in the corner and see General Choi going, "Is it W-shaped block going 'into' or going 'towards'?" He would be doing his seminar and asking us to wordsmith for him! So, we would laugh and chuckle, but General Choi couldn't even get into a movie, although he did like comedy once in a while."[337]

To others, however, he seemed drawn to tragedy. Would the North Koreans accept Choi and his Tae Kwon Do? Would they forgive all his hateful words spilled about communists? Would they even allow him to return to Canada?

What few people knew was that Choi had been planning this mission for years; he took calculated risks and knew the outcome of this one would be good.[338] North Korean leader Kim Il Sung had been funding Choi's Tae Kwon Do encyclopedia writing for years and he summoned Choi for a visit in 1979, before the mission.[339] The route from Canada to North Korea, then, had been as convoluted as Choi's life: a plane from Toronto to Vienna, then to Hong Kong, then a ship to Macao, where he had met a North Korean agent, then both flew to Beijing, where a private airplane flew them to North Korea's capital city.

On the day of the meeting with North Korea's leader, Choi's car crept around a lake surrounded by low hills. The car stopped in front of a summer house, where Kim Il Sung waited in a doorway. The gesture touched Choi, who had met many presidents and prime ministers; here was a leader waiting on his front step, even though Choi had possibly shot at him during the Korean War. Inside, the two men settled into a meeting room, where they smoked and talked as if they were friends. They discussed the Cold War and Kim's wish to unify North and South Korea, and they clinked glasses.

That same year, 1979, after yet another round of tortures and murders of striking workers, South Korea exploded in protests, and its president, Park Chung-hee, went to a safe house with his Korean CIA chief. During dinner, an argument erupted between the chief and the president's bodyguard, a man known for his ability to kill with his bare hands.[340] The KCIA chief shot the bodyguard and then, for some reason, shot the president, too.

Many Koreans celebrated. Choi and his men heard about the assassination while on a Tae Kwon Do tour in Argentina and raised a glass of champagne, but the party mood did not last long because a new general took over South Korea and sentenced to death the man who could have been president: human-rights activist Kim Dae-jung. South Koreans took to the streets, and Generalissimo Chun Doo-hwan, the new leader of South Korea, declared martial law. In May 1980, he ordered a crackdown in Kwangju city that resulted in the slaughter of hundreds of people (some reported thousands). The Kwangju Massacre became a new low in South Korea's modern history.[341]

In 1980, in the Year of the Monkey (a year of erratic geniuses and cheery opportunists), South Korea's newest dictator received good news: the International Olympic Committee had officially recognized the World Taekwondo Federation (WTF), which was another step toward Tae Kwon Do becoming an Olympic sport. The news, coming two months after the Kwangju Massacre, focused the regime on the Olympics and Tae Kwon Do, and the South Korean government continued using martial arts and sports to improve its image.

Olympic hopes also focused the martial arts gyms (*kwans*) that had been in turmoil since 1978, when the Korean Tae Kwon Do Association (KTA) had abolished the traditional *kwan* system, merged all gyms under the WTF, and demanded that gyms send black belt test fees directly to the KTA and WTF's Kukkiwon. Various martial arts leaders delicately wondered why they should give away most of their money and power, but the KTA was unsympathetic: "Even though you sacrificed much for Tae Kwon Do, it is wrong for the *kwans* to ask for compensation for their sacrifices. We need to give up the old idea of *kwans* in favor of the new system, for standardization purposes."[342]

So much for ancient tradition. How could one argue with gangsters and KCIA leaders in a country that had perfected the arts of threat and extortion?

XXX

In September 1980, as Kim Un-yong and the WTF began their unlikely climb up the Olympic ladder, Choi and his team climbed off a plane for what seemed to be a suicide mission in North Korea. A historian once described the nation as "the most astounding garrison state in the world," which meant that specialists in violence were the most powerful group in the country.[343] North Korea had a history of fighting Japanese colonialism for half a century and fighting the U.S. and South Korea for another thirty-five years. Every North Korean man completed eight years of military service. The North Koreans were more than ready to learn Tae Kwon Do. At the airport, a brass band and a thousand people greeted Choi and his team, who had long hair and were wearing bright suits with bell-bottomed pants and collars as wide as kites, because Choi had instructed the team to show off Western trends.

The speeches were followed by martial arts demonstrations. Did Choi mention that North Korea was running one of the world's most sophisticated prison gulags? No, but he noted that North Korea was self-sufficient in agriculture, and during a Tae Kwon Do demonstration he watched Park Jung-tae jump over a man on a motorcycle.

Did he notice that North Koreans called their leader *urŏrŏ patta*, which means "to look up to and receive," the way Christians look to Christ?[344] No, but he did give an obsequious speech to Kim Il Sung, who said he was proud of Choi and that Tae Kwon Do would be taught in North Korea.

Did Choi mention North Korean human-rights atrocities? No, but he was gratified to see that, in the north, the custom of respecting ancestors remained intact and that Kim Il Sung had covered the entire cost of the trip — and offered Choi millions of dollars.[345] Nearly 30,000 people watched the team's demonstration.

Choi's speech contained a clear message: you are our friends. He told his North Korean hosts that Tae Kwon Do avoided violence, especially against communists, reassuring them that "Tae Kwon Do is not meant to kill or harm people, but is a defensive art and a people's martial art, which endows people with spirit and encourages a healthy body and a sound mind."[346]

"They thought Tae Kwon Do was anti-communist," explained Michael Cormack, who was there for Choi's speech in North Korea. "They saw Tae Kwon Do instructors in Vietnam killing communists with it. General Choi, probably after a few Scotches, had written in a newspaper or had said, 'We will kill communists with Tae Kwon Do,' whatever. So, whether that was stated or not, they still had this nervousness . . . James [Jung-Hwa Choi] and the Koreans were extremely nervous, because they had been brainwashed that the North Koreans were the devil, the evil empire of the North."[347]

Had General Choi sold his soul to the devil? No. He was accustomed to terror and, more to the point, he was in the middle of a wicked game with Kim Un-yong and the South Korean dictatorship.

While in North Korea, General Choi, his son, and his son-in-law left the rest of the team to visit Choi's birthplace. He had last visited after the Second World War, when he had trudged into town to discover communists in control. The three men visited Choi's brother, sister, friends, and the house where he had helped his mother grind tofu. The wrestler was no longer in the village. Everything was blue pine trees and Russian helicopters.

In return, Choi later gave the North Koreans a new pattern of moves that he called *Ju-Che*, which was the name of North Korea's ideology. He did this to jettison the *Ko-Dang* pattern, which had been the pseudonym of one of Choi's heroes, Cho Man-sik, a Christian educator and an early North Korean leader until communists imprisoned him in 1946.[348] Now that Choi's friends were those same communists, *Ko-Dang* had to go. Expunging it and creating *Ju-Che* was a sellout to the communists, even though Choi argued that the change was not political. The term *Ju-Che* is nearly untranslatable into English: it means self-reliance and independence and, deeper, everything that makes Koreans Korean.[349]

As if to highlight this, Choi designed the *Ju-Che* pattern to be the most difficult out of the twenty-four, demanding a jumping split kick and two techniques that were supposed to stop momentarily in mid-air, as if the attacker was floating. Today, in gyms and championships around the world, we yell "*Ju-Che*" after the final technique of this pattern, saluting North Korea's ideology whether we like it or not.

A more important gift to the communists, however, was a change to "sine wave," a series of subtle movements that applied to all techniques. Good martial artists had always slightly bent their knees and rotated their hips before launching a technique (thereby creating more power), but Choi now wanted everyone to lower and then raise their entire body, with no hip rotation, so they could use gravity while driving downwards with a punch, for example. Everyone had been practising a small sine wave (requiring a small knee spring and snapping of the hips), but Choi's gift was a big sine wave (requiring a big knee spring).[350] The differences sound subtle, but when put into action, they gave Choi's Tae Kwon Do patterns a distinct style — a slower, more rhythmic, bobbing-on-the-sea look that dramatically distinguished it from Karate and Kim Un-yong's Tae Kwon Do. Sine wave also meant that every ITF martial artist on the planet had to relearn basic techniques, starting with the first pattern.

Just as dramatic were Choi's announcements that North Koreans were practising "pure Tae Kwon Do" (because they were doing a big sine wave) and that all the other instructors in the world were "fakes." The majority of Choi's pioneer instructors had disassociated themselves from him and his mission to North Korea, and Choi's reaction was swift. As one of my instructors once explained to me, Choi inserted a three-dimensional signature on the martial art (sine wave), handed it to the North Koreans, and, in one move, disowned his wayward disciples, men whom Choi viewed as disobedient and unfilial. In fact, disowning those surrogate sons was perhaps Choi's chief goal with the sine wave. (Also, as everyone scrambled to adapt, Kim Un-yong's group continued to rely more on leg techniques and less on hand techniques during sparring, distancing the two types of Tae Kwon Do even more.)

What else did the North Koreans want? Power and access to the rest of the world — and the occasional martial arts assassin. "Believe me, Tae Kwon Do is a very powerful instrument, not just kicking," Michael Cormack told me. "They wanted access to the diplomatic tools, to be close to all those countries. They also saw Tae Kwon Do as part of their culture, and wanted to be involved with it."[351] They wanted to do what South Korea was already doing: use Tae Kwon Do for sports, culture, politics, espionage, and propaganda. Choi had disagreed with much of that in South Korea, but he was fine with it in North Korea because he was in charge of the martial art there. Choi was politicizing what was supposed to be an apolitical martial art, or, to put it more accurately, he was hyper-politicizing a martial art that had always been political.

Choi's son, Jung-Hwa, co-operated in the venture to the north, even though he discovered that North Korean agents were becoming involved. "I had an inkling, because I saw that the ones who we trained were not going out as instructors, and strange guys who we'd never met were coming out as instructors instead." He saw a sophisticated motive in North Korea's involvement, especially when his father moved the International Taekwon-Do Federation headquarters from Toronto to Vienna, Austria: "Tae Kwon Do, to them, was a godsend, a present to them, because the *Ju-Che* idea was already dead; this was a way of getting into common people's minds, and they needed something that could replace *Ju-Che* philosophy. Tae Kwon Do, you can say, is a philosophy, and when they found how close the relationship between the instructor and practitioner was, they laughed and said, 'This is it!'"[352]

That relationship was a special bond — part militaristic, part fatherly — that agents could exploit. As Jung-Hwa explained, "They thought if the agent would be an instructor or the instructor would be an agent, then it would be a very easy way to control many people and infuse Korea-ism in their minds. Another thing is that Vienna is a way station for many agents and many activities."[353]

Within a year of Choi's 1980 visit to North Korea, the twenty-six-year-old Jung-Hwa was co-operating with some of those North Korean agents to plot the assassination of South Korea's newest dictator.[354] It began when he met North Koreans who claimed to be the families of those killed in the Kwangju Massacre in South

Korea. They apparently wanted to avenge the deaths, and someone proposed an assassination plot. Jung-Hwa knew a couple of gang members in Toronto and agreed to find an assassin, deliver the funds, and act as a middleman between the agents and the assassins. The young martial artist thought it was cool to use gang connections for a worthy mission, but, more than that, he wanted to make his father proud. He wanted to put his father's teachings into action — to protect the weak from the strong — and to rid the world of a sadistic president.

CHAPTER 13

OLYMPIC MANIA AND NORTH KOREAN MAYHEM

On September 18, 1981, Korean Airlines Flight 901, scheduled to fly to Frankfurt, West Germany, sat for thirty minutes on the runway of Gimpo Airport in Seoul, South Korea, as the crew waited for an important, last-minute passenger, Park Chong-kyu, also known as "Pistol Park" because he carried a pistol everywhere he went.[355] South Korea's dictator, Chun Doo-hwan, had assigned him and his men to an important mission, Operation Thunderbird. Pistol Park was a martial artist who had helped organize South Korea's military *coup d'état* in 1961, was lobbying to become a member of the International Olympic Committee (IOC), and had steered secret-service agent Kim Un-yong to take over Tae Kwon Do in 1970. Now, Park and Kim were leading Operation Thunderbird, a mission to convince the most powerful people in international sports that South Korea should host the 1988 Summer Olympics and that Tae Kwon Do should be an Olympic sport in the process. Once again, sports, and Tae Kwon Do in particular, would hide human-rights atrocities and government-organized corruption in South Korea.[356]

Wearing dark sunglasses, Park finally walked onto the plane. He and Kim had gathered a team of 107 elite Koreans from Tae Kwon Do, sports, business, government, and the secret service, including the Korean CIA's deputy director. Flying from various countries, they were to meet in Baden-Baden, West Germany, for a crucial Olympic Congress, where the IOC would vote on which country

Around 1963, Park recruited Kim Un-yong into the Korean CIA. In 1970, Park Chong-kyu (crouched) and South Korea's dictator (sitting in the chair) gave the okay for Kim to steal the name "Tae Kwon Do" and take over its operations. PHOTO COURTESY OF JEONG SOON-CHEON.

would host the 1988 Games. Along the way, Operation Thunderbird would provide security against plots by Choi Hong-Hi and his North Korean friends. Choi had threatened to disrupt the Baden-Baden meeting, and his son was still plotting to assassinate the South Korean president.

Pistol Park and Kim had launched the top-secret Operation Thunderbird in June 1981, when South Korea had been in chaos. After the Kwangju Massacre, President Chun had continued his predecessor's policy of using martial artists to do some of the government's dirty work, which consisted mainly of smashing unions. One-third of political prisoners were workers, and the rest of the workforce took turns going on strike and protesting. Martial arts experts and plainclothes police officers, called the White Skull (*paekkol*) strike-breakers, would pad themselves from head to foot and race on motorcycles to protests, where they would wade into crowds, breaking heads as they went.[357]

The new regime concluded that the fastest and most effective way to diffuse conflict, unite Koreans, and improve the country's image overseas was by hosting an Olympics. It was such a far-fetched idea that few people inside or outside the tiny nation took it seriously, especially because Korea had no Olympic-sized facilities and, as Kim soberly acknowledged, did not even have colour television. But perhaps sports would redeem their nation and, in the process, cover up the massacres and corruption.

Korea was the underdog in the Olympic process, and the objective of Operation Thunderbird was to entice and bribe powerful international sports officials to support the Korean Olympic bid. That was the easy part, because many IOC officials were corrupt.

The hard part involved Korea's two opponents: Nagoya, Japan, the front-runner that had begun the "enticements" long before Korea; and Choi Hong-Hi, who wanted to disrupt the Baden-Baden vote. Nagoya in particular was a worry. Korea's martial arts leaders (and not only Choi) tend to become unhinged when comparing their martial arts to Japan's. Kim did not want Japan to win. He recalled his days being bullied in Japanese schools.

Pistol Park was "to take all available steps to win the support of IOC members," Kim said.[358] Park and others contacted Horst Dassler (the president of Adidas, a company that made a lot of Tae Kwon Do gear) as well as the Mexican president of the Association of National Olympic Committees and many other influential officials. Park worked backstage, gaining support from IOC members in South America and Africa. The Korean CIA also lent a helping hand, and overseas Tae Kwon Do instructors lobbied thirteen IOC members in Europe and North America.[359] Pistol Park and Mickey Kim knew what they were doing. From 1967 to 1972, Kim had been Park's aide, and they had worked with the Korean CIA and a Korean cult in forcing millions of dollars and many favours from foreign companies to South Korea's dictator. That mission had been part of the Plan, as the U.S. had dubbed it, to bribe, threaten, and kill Koreans overseas who criticized the South Korean dictatorship. The Plan had also aimed to seduce and influence more than a hundred members of U.S. Congress.[360] Park and Kim were experts at running huge, covert missions to influence people.

However, rumour had it that Choi Hong-Hi planned an anti-Olympic demonstration for Baden-Baden. This news rattled the Korean Olympic Committee, which is surprising when you realize who was in that group — some of South Korea's most powerful politicians, millionaires, martial artists, and spies. Kim did not believe the rumours but concluded that he needed bodyguards at the meeting, so he "called five Tae Kwon Do instructors in Europe to stand by the entire time," including Kim Kwang-il, the Korean CIA operative who had been one of Choi's pioneer instructors and who had once been arrested in connection with a KCIA kidnapping plot in West Germany.[361]

When the Operation Thunderbird team arrived in Baden-Baden with its 107 personnel and deep pockets, Kim Un-yong switched hotels, staying with IOC delegates instead of the team. That way, he could eavesdrop on what delegates were saying about Korea's chances before the crucial vote and report back to the team, who were meeting illustrious guests at French and Chinese restaurants in Baden-Baden.

In 1982, Park Chong-kyu (second from right) invited the President of the International Olympic Committee, Juan Antonio Samaranch (second from left), to a Korean geisha house. Samaranch, a former card-carrying Fascist but still an avid churchgoer, left after thirty minutes. In 1984, Park became a member of the IOC. He died of liver cancer at the age of fifty-eight, in 1985. PHOTO COURTESY OF JEONG SOON-CHEON.

No one believed that the Koreans offered only ginseng tea and jade trinkets to IOC members, as Kim later explained. "Compared to us, Japan invited IOC executive members to Nagoya and gave Seiko watches as gifts," he said. Still, accusations of bribery would fly.[362] A *New York Times* reporter heard that someone had slipped "first-class airline tickets under the hotel room doors of I.O.C. members, expecting them to cash the tickets in, in order to curry their vote for the South Korean city."[363]

Tae Kwon Do pioneer and KCIA operative Kim Kwang-il and other Tae Kwon Do experts stood guard in Baden-Baden. One instructor, Park Soo-nam, drove to the team's hotel with a carload of Korean food because he knew that the members of Operation Thunderbird were craving Korean home-cooking. Unfortunately, Prince Philip, the husband of Queen Elizabeth II, was staying at the same hotel, and, security being tight, Park was kicked out of the hotel as a suspected terrorist. He was only able to re-enter after explanations about all the Korean food in his car.

Finally, on the day of the vote, Kim Un-yong entered the Baden-Baden meeting, sat down, and fielded questions as if fighting in a war zone. Delegates carpet-bombed the Korean team with requests and criticisms, and Kim deftly handled them all.

After the vote, when IOC President Juan Antonio Samaranch announced in French that the winner was "Seoul, Korea," the words rang in Kim's ears. Korea had soundly beaten Japan by fifty-two votes to twenty-seven, which amazed even the Koreans.

"I wonder if the count was wrong," Samaranch said. It was not. The South American and African IOC members had tilted the vote in favour of the Koreans. Small Korea, the rabbit trying to be a tiger, had defeated Japan, and everyone forgot about the terror and torture under the South Korean dictatorship. Korea would host the 1988 Summer Olympics. Operation Thunderbird had been a success.

Just as sweet was the IOC's decision to include Tae Kwon Do as one of two demonstration sports at the 1988 Games. Seoul had little experience organizing world-level championships, but Korea had accomplished a so-called economic miracle, leaping from Third World country to industrialized nation in only two decades, and it would perhaps pull off a sports miracle. "The Olympic Games were a turning point for Korea to move into the ranks of the world's advanced nations," Kim later wrote.[364]

Tae Kwon Do would show that Korea was not only powerful economically but also physically and culturally. Olympic glory, power, and billions of dollars spread before Kim Un-yong and Korea, as the nation's strongman picked "Harmony and Progress" as Seoul's Olympic slogan, a cunning cover for a dictator who was busy massacring his own people and hoarding nearly U.S.$1 billion in "slush funds."[365]

Choi's men and the North Koreans did not disrupt the IOC meetings.[366] However, his son and North Korean agents continued to plot the assassination of South Korea's dictator. And, after his visit to North Korea, Choi began calling himself the "founder" of Tae Kwon Do more frequently. Before that, he had used "founding member."[367] If South Korea was going to steal a martial art that he had named, then it was better for people to know that the "founder" was not happy.

✕✕✕

In Canada, many people mocked Choi after his 1980 North Korea trip, calling him a communist.[368] Even Choi's American CIA friend, sixth-degree black belt Robert Walson, worried, but Choi thrived within an aura of chaos and worry. And he continued co-operating with North Koreans.[369] He did not publicize what he and the North Korean dictator had discussed, but within a year, he was training the North Koreans in hand-to-hand combat, and his son, Jung-Hwa Choi, was plotting with Michael Gerol and Charles "Chuck the Bike" Yanover to assassinate South Korean President Chun Doo-hwan. Jung-Hwa idolized secret agents, and he would party with tough men at Cooper's, a club in downtown Toronto, befriending them in case he needed his back covered or his family protected.[370]

At first, General Choi thought the plot sounded childish. He told the North Koreans that he did not want his son involved because it was a risky and dangerous mission.[371] General Choi cared about his son, who was one of his best Tae Kwon Do assets and his favourite in the family. When Jung-Hwa and his two sisters had been children, Choi would come home after a night of drinking and, thinking the boy was asleep, would lovingly stroke his head. He would slip money under Jung-Hwa's pillow and whisper, "Don't tell anybody I gave you this, because I love you the best." Choi would do the same with his daughters, but they knew that Jung-Hwa, his only son, was the favourite.

In 1981, on a plane trip to Switzerland, father and son discussed the assassination plot, and the elder Choi gave his son the okay, Jung-Hwa was in charge of the money and interpretation for the plot, and Yanover was supposed to assassinate the South Korean dictator, possibly during a visit with Prime Minister Pierre Trudeau in Canada. Yanover was an international arms dealer once convicted of working with white supremacists to overthrow the government of Dominica, and while in prison he had helped a former South Korean soldier blow up Arviv's, a Toronto club, because the owner wanted the C$950,000 insurance money.

Jung-Hwa would never forget walking through Geneva,

Switzerland, carrying an attaché case with a huge sum of money from North Korean agents. He deposited it into an account. In Vienna he interpreted for the agents and gangsters.

However, the plot fizzled after Yanover collected a payment of U.S.$600,000 and someone tipped off the South Koreans. Yanover kept the money, and Jung-Hwa woke up to realize that this was no sparring match and that he and his young family were at great risk.

The police arrested Yanover in Canada. Meanwhile, his South Korean soldier friend, the one who had blown up a Toronto club, was in South Korea, where the Korean CIA arrested, tortured, and imprisoned him until Canadian officials flew in to ask questions. Jung-Hwa suspected that he himself would undergo a similar interrogation if Canada shipped him to South Korea, where the KCIA wanted to interrogate him.

"Bizarre Death Scheme," screamed a newspaper headline after police announced the plot. Police in eight countries had helped Canada investigate for six months. The story also jumped from the front pages of Korean-language newspapers: "The Assassination of Doo-Hwan Chun was Schemed at Choi Hong-Hi's." The police raided Choi's house, looking for Jung-Hwa and evidence, but the younger Choi was already on a plane to North Korea. As the police spent three hours searching the elder Choi's residence, he claimed that he did not know about the plot.

The KCIA now had good reason to kidnap Choi and his son, and Choi found out that an assassin was assigned to the job. Most Korean-Canadians avoided Choi. KCIA agents called with good-night threats, and protesters gathered in front of Choi's Canadian house, chanting, "Go away pro-North Choi!"

He did just that, moving to North Korea, where he lived for about two years, until 1984.

Wondrous and weird events transpired in those years. He agreed to borrow C$400,000 annually from the North Korean Tae Kwon Do Association.[372] He created his last technique — the flying, tumbling kick — which involved jumping into the air while flipping backwards 360 degrees to strike an opponent with the heels.[373] He also finished his fifteen-volume encyclopedia, even while his adversaries focused on eliminating him.[374] Also in 1984, the North Koreans dispatched a unit to assassinate the South Korean president — yet again — this time in Burma. They narrowly missed him but killed most of South Korea's cabinet.

At the same time, Yanover used the $600,000 to buy diamonds. He testified in court that his goal had been only to steal from the North Koreans. A judge sentenced him to two years in prison for conspiracy to defraud and sentenced his accomplice, Michael Gerol, to one year. Meanwhile, Jung-Hwa Choi remained on the run in North Korea and then in Eastern Europe.

x x x

This was Tae Kwon Do in the early 1980s, when I first began studying the martial art: spies, clubs, gangsters, communists, and, somewhere in there, time to plan flying kicks and an Olympic Games. I did not know the extent of the intrigue at the time. In 1986, for example, the American Taekwondo Association (ATA), which was the largest Tae Kwon Do group in the U.S., was a tool of the South Korean dictatorship. One master instructor told me that the ATA was a tentacle of the Korean CIA, which had been renamed the Agency for National Security Planning.[375] Another instructor told me a story about gargantuan amounts of money flowing from the dictatorship to the ATA.

In 1986, Ron Turchi, a Tae Kwon Do master, was a confidante and right-hand man of the ATA's founder, Huang (Hank) Lee. "I was on call 24/7," Turchi told me.[376] One day, Lee called him with an urgent request — to be head of security for the South Korean dictator's brother, who would visit the U.S. for three or four days. Turchi rounded up a few martial artists, picked up the brother from the airport, and drove him to a hotel in St. Louis, where Lee met them. Lee and the dictator's brother walked into a hotel room and asked Turchi to push a bed across the door. Then Lee pulled out two big bags of cash and handed them to the brother.

"I'd never seen so much money in my life," Turchi said, who found the whole thing disturbing but did not say anything. "I didn't ask questions. In the ATA, we had blind loyalty." His attitude reflected a common one at the time; blind loyalty is useful if you are running a dictatorship and need money and manpower. In those years, South Korea's leader was squirreling away hundreds of millions of dollars for himself.

I now look back on when I started Tae Kwon Do and remember that my uncle did warn me about the problems. I had joined an International Taekwon-Do Federation (ITF) gym near my house in Ottawa. A pioneer instructor named Park Jung-Taek ran it. My uncle, however, had obtained his black belt from a competitor's gym, run by Lee Tae-Eun, one of Kim Un-yong's right-hand men. Being something of a father figure, my uncle told me that I was betraying values that my family held dear because communists (in other words, maniacs and terrorists) ran the North Korean-supported ITF. He did not seem to know or care about the gangsters, criminals, and KCIA agents in his own gym's association. In any case, I was only sixteen years old and listened to him the way one listens to bad news on the radio, wondering when the songs will return.

Still, I scraped together a pound of courage to ask my instructor about the rumours. Grandmaster Park Jung-Taek was not around, so I bravely approached his second-in-command, Phap Lu, a gifted athlete who had been a student of an old Vietnamese master, Nguyen Van Binh. In Vietnam, Lu had heard stories about combat Tae Kwon Do during the Vietnam War, had trained at the Oh Do Kwan in Saigon, and had watched his martial arts friends become secret-service agents, but Lu had landed in a Vietnamese prison, where he was tortured as an anti-communist.[377] He had fled the country when released, arriving in Canada with waves of Vietnamese refugees, not knowing how closely his life mirrored that of Choi Hong-Hi's.

Lu set me straight, saying that the North Korean version of Tae Kwon Do was the traditional one. He told me that the other style, the WTF's, arose decades later and had devolved from martial art to sport. The ITF was affiliated with the North Korean regime, yes, but the WTF was based in a South Korean dictatorship.

All that, of course, had nothing to do with the murder and mayhem.

CHAPTER 14

THE OLYMPIC SUMMER OF LOVE

North Korea threatened a bloodbath if South Korea hosted the 1988 Olympics alone. It demanded that the Games be shared by both countries.[378] After the Soviet Union agreed to join the Olympics, an overly excited South Korean government official blurted to the media that the U.S.S.R.'s participation would act as "a strong shield against bullets." At the time, the Soviet Union was North Korea's ally, and a Soviet official demanded an explanation for the outrageous comment. Kim Un-yong flew to the rescue, saying that the Korean official did not mean "shield" in the military sense. The bullets were metaphorical. Kim welcomed the communists with open arms and began teaching himself how to speak Russian. South Korea, a small country that was suspicious of foreigners — and for thirty-five years had waged a vicious covert war with communists — was opening itself to the enemy.

Choi Hong-Hi was already a couple of years ahead of them. He had been lobbying Olympic leaders to hold a joint martial arts event between his Tae Kwon Do and Kim's.[379] Kim seemed to like the idea. The choice of Seoul as Olympic host had obviously struck a hard blow to North Korea, but Kim believed there was hope of holding a joint Olympic Games. At the very least, talking about a joint event was politically wise for both Kim and Choi because Koreans on all sides always get dewy-eyed about Korean unification.

But Choi, the tornado, had never been a good diplomat, while Kim was a masterful negotiator. Both men had access to money and powerful politicians, however. In 1985, Choi flew to Moscow to meet the chairman of the Olympic Organizing Committee to warn him about "sham" Tae Kwon Do and the "phony" Kim, not knowing or caring that Kim had just been promoted to vice-chairman of an Olympic committee.[380] Choi's lobbying failed, and Kim succeeded in adding Tae Kwon Do to the 1986 Asian Games and the 1987 Pan American Games.[381] In the process, Kim became a powerful member of the International Olympic Committee, and Choi, increasingly marginalized, could not compete with the rivers of money and favours flowing to and from South Korea.[382]

In 1987, the year before the Seoul Olympics, South Korea erupted in protest after police tortured yet another student to death. Millions of Koreans took to the streets. With a long-needed revolution spreading across South Korea, the world wondered if Seoul would be capable of holding a peaceful Games, but South Korea promised "the largest and most successful festival of mankind in peace time."[383] The challenge was the "peace" part.

Politicians Kim Dae-jung and Kim Young-sam decided that democracy should enter stage left, and they met in April 1987 to begin a new democratic party for an upcoming election. The Korean CIA and agents trained in Tae Kwon Do tried to stop them in what is now called the Yongpal Incident, named after the weightlifter who organized it.[384] Politicians in South Korea's regime recruited Lee Seng-wan, a Tae Kwon Do master, to hire fifty hoodlums to disrupt the democratic party's events.

The thugs, backed by the KCIA and ultimately directed by the South Korean president, descended on twenty meetings, destroying furniture and attacking people with clubs. Lee had been a national sparring champion in 1964 and had become head of the Jidokwan, which had been one of the main gyms that had formed Kim Un-yong's World Taekwondo Federation. Not much had changed since the regime's brutal tactics of the 1960s and 1970s. Lee and others were captured and charged. For his role in the 1987 attack on the democratic party, Lee was sentenced to one and a half years in prison, but he later became a powerful man in Tae Kwon Do.

In spite of the violent disruptions, the new political party grew and student protests continued. In June 1987, the South Korean president sent White Skull police (*paekkol*) to break students' heads with clubs, but the protests went on, with four or five million Koreans marching through the streets. The president resigned at the end of the month and installed a replacement, another general, Roh Tae-Woo, who announced there would be direct elections in 1987.[385] As if in response, North Korean terrorists planted a bomb on a Korean Airlines flight from Baghdad to Seoul, killing 115 people.[386] Many expected the North Koreans to target the Olympics, too, and the Americans filled Korean waters with warships.

The Games had to go on though, because the Olympics would unveil Korea to the world, just as the 1964 Olympics had unveiled modern Japan.[387] General Roh Tae-Woo won the Korean election in 1987 after the opposition split the vote, and he went on to steal U.S.$650 million from Koreans over the years.

In 1988, as the promise of violence surrounded Seoul like a fog, Korea's secret service promoted and protected the Olympic Games, whose official emblem meant "Progress through world understanding and peace." Kim Un-yong later wrote, "A total of 81,630 members of military and police forces were mobilized to provide security for 264 facilities."[388] They patrolled the ground, flew through the air, floated on the sea, and hid underwater, with American spy satellites watching the North Korean army's every twitch, everyone prepared for anything short of an invisible nuclear bomb.

* * *

At 1 p.m. on the day of the opening ceremony in 1988, twenty massive balloons — ten metres each across — floated on the roof of Seoul's elegant Jamsil Olympic Stadium, which had been designed to reflect the curves of an ancient, *Chosŏn*-dynasty porcelain vase. The stadium was packed. For the first time since 1976, both the Americans and Soviets were in the Games, along with 157 other countries. Only North Korea and Cuba had boycotted. The balloons depicted huge, grotesque masks as dancers ran frantically to and fro carrying grisly and bizarre masks of their own. The masks were from Korea's ancient history: there was *Choyong*, which repelled bad spirits; *Yangban*, the aristocrat with the open, laughing mouth; and *Halmi*, the old widow.

Suddenly, flames leapt from the stadium floor between the dancers. It was pandemonium. Were the North Koreans finally attacking? No, the dancers were performing a piece called "Chaos," which was followed by 1,008 "Taekwondoists," as they were called, who smashed boards, screamed through techniques, and forced order onto the bad spirits.[389] The Tae Kwon Do ceremony "symbolized the destruction of all barriers," Kim later explained.[390]

After chaos and order on day one, the world watched 184 men and women from thirty-two countries compete in Tae Kwon Do for the first time, at Seoul's upgraded Changchung Gymnasium.[391] This was one of Kim's proudest achievements. He had defanged a martial art into a sport and was showcasing one of Korea's treasures in spite of the country's violent dictatorship. The "sport" part had been one of his goals; he took the "martial" out of the "martial art," toning down the aggression in spite of the gangsters, spies, and violence in Tae Kwon Do's history and the Korean regimes. He also succeeded in highlighting Korea's newfound power: at the end of the Tae Kwon Do competition, Koreans ranked first, with nine out of sixteen gold medals, and South Korea won a total of thirty-three medals at that Olympics, ranking fifth in the world — a spectacular finish for a small country.

But the lopsided Tae Kwon Do results worried many and led to accusations of cheating. Few people were interested in an Olympic demonstration sport dominated by South Korea and full of corruption, and many wondered why it should be an official sport.[392] Viewed from afar, the entire competition looked like a battle mainly between Koreans: Koreans had coached the second-place Americans as well as the Canadian, West German, and Australian teams, to name only a few.[393] In addition, Tae Kwon Do was seen as racist

— or, at best, ethnocentric, favouring Koreans over non-Koreans, no matter what the skill level. In practice, it seemed as if non-Koreans faced an uphill battle in becoming international champions. More tellingly, non-Koreans faced impossible hurdles in becoming leaders in the organizations that ran Tae Kwon Do, which had access to huge Olympic budgets nationally and internationally.

The cheating in particular was maddening. Rumours began that "branch trimming" (*gagee chigee*) had taken place during the 1988 Olympics and 1986 Seoul Asian Games.[394] "Branch trimming" refers to the practice of pressuring judges to rule against the strongest competitors in early sparring matches. This cheating ensured that Koreans did not have to face strong, non-Korean fighters in the final rounds. There would be no revelation of "branch trimming" until 2002, when a vice-president in the World Taekwondo Federation (which ran Olympic Tae Kwon Do) explained it to a journalist, but the rumours had begun circulating during the 1988 Summer Games in Seoul.

Even though the 1988 Olympics showed off Tae Kwon Do's kicks along with South Korea's economy, the International Olympic Committee did not choose Tae Kwon Do as an official sport for the 1992 Games. In response, a desperate Kim Un-yong asked IOC President Juan Antonio Samaranch to consider Tae Kwon Do as an "exhibition sport" for 1992. Kim had created an elaborate plan, one that would have impressed his old mentor, Pistol Park, who had died a couple of years earlier.[395]

"For the growth of Tae Kwon Do it has to be chosen," Kim told Samaranch.

Samaranch's face stiffened, and he replied, "But we've selected the demonstration sports already, and only two are allowed." The IOC could not pick Tae Kwon Do again because a sport could be a demonstration only once.

Kim explained his idea about an "exhibition sport."

"Is it in the regulations?" Samaranch asked.

"No, it isn't," Kim said. "I made it up." He explained how Tae Kwon Do could benefit from the exposure at the 1992 Barcelona Games and how the Olympics could benefit in the process.

"Is it possible?" Samaranch asked. "Did you think about the details?"[396]

Kim had. He had a talent for details (as well as access to a lot of money); it was not for nothing that the IOC had promoted him to its executive in 1988. First, he would reduce the number of weight classes in Tae Kwon Do, thereby decreasing the number of matches and completing the tournament in a day. Second, South Korea would pay for the players' security and expenses.

Samaranch agreed to give it a try and suggested that Kim approach IOC executive members individually to "persuade" each one to support the new idea. After Kim's intense lobbying, the IOC skipped the "exhibition" idea and, bending the rules, included the martial art as a demonstration sport in 1992 — and Kim was soon mired in one of the most publicized corruption stories in Olympic history. Before the press found out about the scandal, however, 128 competitors from thirty-three countries competed in Tae Kwon Do at the Barcelona Summer Games.[397] Tae Kwon Do's leaders made sure that the Korean competitors did not dominate this time. The host country, Spain, did uncharacteristically well, which once again fuelled rumours about unfair judging.

Choi's reaction to the 1988 and 1992 Olympics could be summed up in one word — phony — and he was not just referring to the cheating. Tae Kwon Do had officially become a sport, but he wanted it to remain a martial art. In his view, without punches to the head, jumping kicks, and the hundreds of techniques that distinguished Tae Kwon Do, the Olympic sport was worse than Karate, but his view did not matter to Olympic Tae Kwon Do, which now had tens of millions of practitioners. Choi had fewer than a million. Partly because of the turmoil between Choi and Kim — and between the two martial arts — the Olympics rejected Tae Kwon Do as a sport for the 1996 Games. Choi took that as a positive sign.

North Korea committed to giving Choi C$10 million over ten years, and he became more active.[398] No one knew about the money — neither his family nor his closest disciples, and certainly not his ITF executive, who struggled to cover the expenses of world championships. Choi's wife would tell her children that she did not know if their father was rich or poor.

With the money rolling in, some of Choi's prime instructors asked for a salary hike, and in response, he accused master instructors, such as Park Jung-tae and Han Sam-soo, of spying on him. The accusations seemed bizarre. Park Jung-tae was Choi's top instructor in the world then, and Han Sam-soo had been on an international demonstration team, but Choi accused Han of receiving "some direction for some task of the KCIA" and of being a double spy since 1978.[399]

Choi blurred the boundary between generosity and greed and between fear and paranoia because of his war with South Korea's dictatorship, and he crucified his own pioneering instructors along the way, but he was never into Tae Kwon Do solely for the money. "He was a man of morals," explained Choi's former right-hand man, Michael Cormack. "Money corrupts. I never said General Choi never took the dollar that he shouldn't have, but I can say that when it comes to Tae Kwon Do, every dollar he got, he gave a hundred, in terms of time, effort, et cetera. He gave a thousand. General Choi, anytime, could have made way more money out of Tae Kwon Do if he wanted to."[400]

In 1990, money became important to Park Jung-tae, Choi's former pioneer instructor, after he and Choi had a falling out. Choi had started training Park in 1980, so that Park could introduce Tae Kwon Do to North Korea and Eastern Europe. The end came after they had a talk about money, and Choi went berserk — and Park went from making a good living every month to making nothing.[401]

Park began the Global Taekwon-Do Federation (GTF) but needed help to set up and maintain the large organization. He turned to Americans John Tompkins (one of his close students), Scott McNeely (a sparring champion), and Robert Hardin (who had received his seventh-degree black belt from Park). Hardin had

Park Jung-tae (middle) recruited Scott McNeely (right), Bob Hardin (left) and John Tompkins (not pictured) to help set up the Global Taekwon-Do Federation.
PHOTO COURTESY OF HARDIN.

been training in Tae Kwon Do for thirty years and was a legend of sorts because, with only one fully grown arm, he was a sparring champion and an inspiring instructor in the southern U.S.

By 1993, Park convinced a group of Karate experts in Russia to switch to Tae Kwon Do and his GTF, using a tactic that Choi had long used to speed up the process of creating gyms and national associations. Expanding into Russia was a smart move, given the popularity of the fighting arts there, but the country was being devastated by its worst economic depression in more than sixty years, and criminals were running large parts of the country. The U.S.S.R. had dissolved in 1991, and Russia was on the verge of bankruptcy and civil war by 1993.

Unfortunately, Park and the American trio unknowingly ended up co-operating with the Russian mafia, which ran an international tournament for Park in 1993 — the first tournament for the GTF in Russia. The gangster collaboration was similar to situations in South Korea, West Germany, the U.S., and other countries where martial arts had been prominent among crime syndicates and secret-service agencies.

In September of 1993, President Boris Yeltsin dissolved Russia's legislature and launched a *counter-coup d'état* against his own government. A few weeks later, Park and a team of more than forty Americans joined thirty other national teams for the 1st European GTF Taekwon-Do Championships in a very tense Moscow. "We were jacked up," said Hardin, the senior of the trio. "We had a team doctor, new uniforms, and great athletes."[402] But they had no idea what they were in for.

The trip was important because the U.S. had boycotted the 1980 Olympics in Moscow, and, with the end of the Cold War in 1991, every international sporting event had become politicized. But the Americans did not know that crime was rampant in Russia and that the Russian mafia (mainly ex-KGB agents) was running the Goodwill tournament.

The team arrived at Moscow's airport to find out that there had been a mix-up in arrival times. No one was there to meet them, and only one American athlete made it through customs. The team hunkered down behind bulletproof glass and practised Tae Kwon Do while Hardin negotiated with customs officials. Nervous military personnel watched the athletes as they kicked and punched. Eventually, an official asked Hardin for a U.S.$100 bribe from each American — more than $4,000. A customs official collected the money and inserted the $100 bills into a counterfeit-detecting machine, kissing each bill before slipping it into the machine. Hardin was not amused.

As the team zipped to their hotel near Red Square and the Kremlin (the official residence of Russia's president), Hardin saw homeless people everywhere. The streets looked like the Great Depression in 1930s America. The man in charge of the Goodwill tournament, Sergei Kovaliov, was president of the GTF in Russia, supposedly a fifth-degree black belt in Karate, and the leader of a Russian gang. He treated Park and a dozen members of the team to dinner at one of Moscow's fanciest restaurants, complete with dancing girls and violin players. The bill was approximately U.S.$20,000.

The tournament on days one and two was tough. The sparring was direct and nasty, especially a heavyweight match involving Rick Stanford. "Fighters charged hard, like bulls, destroying everything in their path," Hardin said. "They had no defence. Those of us who were matadors did well." It did not help that everyone drank. From the moment they arrived at the hotel, the Americans faced rivers of vodka, along with demands for bribes and sex.

The two Russian gangsters whom Kovaliov had assigned to protect the Americans kept sexually harassing the women and stealing things from the rooms. Troy Burleson, one of the Americans, broke the finger of one man when he kept pointing it at him. Jay Doolin, Burleson's teammate, grabbed the hair of another and dragged him into a room after the guy attacked someone. Finally, three sedans showed up with six men, former KGB agents, wearing trench coats. Hardin could not believe it — the whole thing looked like a bad movie scene — but he was relieved when they grabbed the two thugs, threw them into the cars, and drove away. The problems stopped.

However, everything got worse on day three. While at the stadium, the Americans heard fighting on the streets nearby. Chaos ensued, and everyone rushed onto waiting buses back to the hotel. People were shooting at each other in Red Square, but the ex-KGB gangsters who were protecting the Americans knew exactly how to avoid problems, where to go, and whom to pay. When officials stopped them at checkpoints, the gangsters paid the bribes, and the police let them through.

The next day, the Russian army attacked the government buildings and shut down the airports. The Americans heard bombs go off. Hardin and a few team members rushed onto the hotel roof to look at Red Square and saw that it was under siege, with smoke rising from bombed buildings. Again, they were okay because former KGB agents and members of the Russian mafia took care of them, but they ended up trapped in Moscow for three weeks. For two of those days, security detained them in the hotel because a sniper was shooting people from somewhere nearby. Soon after, the hotel ran out of food.

During a 1993 tournament, Russian gangsters and former KGB members treated martial artists to a U.S.$20,000 dinner during a *coup d'état* in Moscow. Seated at the table are Linda Park, Park Jung-tae, Bob Hardin, Alison Hardin and Scott McNeely. Standing behind the diners are five members of the Russian team, including Elena Pisarenko on the far right. PHOTO COURTESY OF HARDIN.

You could say that the goodwill mission had gone bad. However, Park Jung-tae's Global Taekwon-Do Federation ended up flourishing in Russia, just as it had in South Korea, Germany, and the U.S. Two years after the tournament, Sergei Kovaliov promoted himself into a Tae Kwon Do master (from a fifth-degree to a seventh-degree black belt), asking Park to okay it. Even with Park's easygoing attitude, such a request was extraordinary. It was like a civilian asking a general if he could become a general. Park approved it.

A couple of years later, Scott McNeely invited Kovaliov to the U.S. for a tournament, but Kovaliov and his team arrived in New York, zipped through customs, and disappeared. No one ever saw them again.

Bob Hardin became frustrated with the politics and problems in the GTF. The Goodwill tournament in particular had been unnerving. "The whole thing was a cluster-fuck," Hardin told me. He participated in one more tournament, in Italy, then left the GTF and started his own association.

CHAPTER 15

"NEED A MEDAL? COME WITH MONEY."

After all the violence, cheating, and Cold War missions in Tae Kwon Do, it seems petty to mention a common problem in the 1990s: stealing. But it was a gargantuan amount of stealing. The financial scandals that erupted showed everyone that not only was Choi Hong-Hi out of control, Kim Un-yong, "the godfather of Korean sport," was too.[403] The martial art was in deep trouble.

I joined Olympic Tae Kwon Do in the early 1990s, when Kim became vice-president of the International Olympic Committee. It was an exciting time for me because the staccato ground kicks of the World Taekwondo Federation were as much fun as its Olympic fever. I had joined a WTF gym run by Yoon Yeo-bong because it was close to my home. In those days, I still looked up to Choi Hong-Hi and his martial art in spite of the bad rumours, but I was also excited about Olympic Tae Kwon Do, joking with my uncle about training for the Canadian Olympic team. Every kid dreamed about joining the Olympics, a dream that fuelled the growth of the WTF.

Tae Kwon Do's leaders were involved in a number of controversies at the time. In a Korean article entitled "Need a Medal? Come with Money," a reporter discovered that one could hire Tae Kwon Do brokers with access to officially sanctioned black belts. One martial artist paid U.S.$10,000 to jump from a fourth- to sixth-degree black belt, which is one level below master.[404] This was in the 1990s, but problems with money and promotions continue to this day. In 2013, for example, the Kukkiwon organized a "Skip Dan Promotion" in Germany that was closed to the public, during which black belts could pay thousands of dollars and obtain multi-dan promotions.[405]

Also, too many sparring matches were unfair. I entered martial arts competitions, both WTF and ITF, and quickly learned that the judging was odd, at best, and that the behaviour of coaches, families, and the audience was a circus sideshow. I knew that Tae Kwon Do was not based on Buddhism or religious values, just as Karate had not been based on religion, in spite of spiritual mumbo jumbo in both, but I did follow Tae Kwon Do's five tenets (Indomitable Spirit, Perseverance, Self-Control, Courtesy, and Integrity). The martial art had sunk far below the standard of these ideals.

In the late 1990s, I finally saw a couple of reasons for the cheating and chaos when journalists dragged the first big scandal into the light of day. Kim Un-yong was implicated in a bribery incident during Salt Lake City's early 1990s bid to host the Olympic Games. Since 1966, the Salt Lake City Olympic organizers had been attempting to win a bid, and in the early 1990s, they realized what they had to do: they heard people involved with the Olympics ask for favours — sex, gifts, money, and sweetheart business deals — so the organizers provided for what was known as The Club. In three damning books, journalist Andrew Jennings and his co-authors wrote about "The Club of the Olympics" and the corruption swirling around them: "The games are controlled by a self-perpetuating oligarchy who travel the world like kings, most taking lavish gifts from cities desperate to cash in on the huge profits the Olympics can generate," they wrote.[406]

Kim and Tae Kwon Do stood at the centre of the Salt Lake City controversy — and would for the next fifteen years — but he saw the scandal as a smear campaign. The media reported that Kim's son, Jung-hoon (John) Kim, had been indicted in the U.S. for accepting $104,000 from Salt Lake City bidders for a bogus company job between 1990 and 1992.[407] The city's bidders, caught by U.S. officials, had been trying to influence Kim Un-yong, who was the most senior IOC official investigated in the scandal. "Federal officials have charged the committee with using an elaborate gift-giving scheme to court I.O.C. members who would vote on the site of the 2002 Winter games," reported the *New York Times*.[408]

Canada's IOC member, Dick Pound, later led an investigation of the charges and saw a shocking side of Kim when, in 1999, Kim confronted him and François Carrard, the executive director of the IOC. They were at an IOC executive board meeting in Lausanne when Kim rushed back to the meeting after a phone call. Kim had thought that the Salt Lake City crisis was behind him, but another piece of evidence had arisen just as Kim was planning a bid to become IOC president. Pound told me that Kim lost it at the meeting:

> He came storming back from where he got the phone call and encountered Carrard on the stairs — and did one of his martial arts poses. They didn't strike or anything like that. Carrard felt himself threatened. Kim came up to where we were, on the second floor, and he did the same thing. He said, "Bastards! Bastards!" He had just lost it. He started doing that stuff. I said, "Kim, calm yourself. Calm yourself!" Samaranch saw what was going on, intervened right away and said, "Kim, go to my office and stay there." Carrard went home or to his office; he was badly rattled by it. I said, "Listen, I didn't join the IOC to be confronted by this kind of shit."[409]

Kim denied that he had struck a threatening pose. Pound said that Kim later sent written letters of apology.

For Kim's part in the Salt Lake City scandal, the IOC gave him a "severe" warning and a "reprimand" for a second deal involving benefits to his daughter.[410] Ten other IOC members — all supporters of Kim — were kicked out of the IOC, a move that declared to the entire world that Kim was a survivor: after every Olympic scrap, he was the last man standing. From Kim's point of view, the smear campaign had failed, but he was angry at the humiliation and angry that he had lost ten supporters who were replaced by twenty people who did not support him.[411] After the severe warning from the IOC, Kim continued his climb up the Olympic ladder and his son left the U.S.

Another well-known Tae Kwon Do son was also on the run around that time. After the failed assassination plot in the early 1980s, Jung-Hwa Choi, the son of General Choi, had moved to North Korea and then Eastern Europe, where he had lived for ten years teaching Tae Kwon Do to instructors.[412] In 1992, South Koreans elected a civilian to lead the country and Jung-Hwa felt it was time to make a move. With help from Russell MacLellan, a Tae Kwon Do black belt and a member of Canada's Parliament, Jung-Hwa cut a deal with Canadian police and gave himself up, knowing Canada would not ship him to South Korea for interrogation and torture. At the same time, his father flew to North Korea, where he attended dictator Kim Il Sung's birthday party, thereby missing Jung-Hwa's trial in Canada.[413]

Jung-Hwa pleaded guilty and said very little during the trial, as per his father's orders. A judge sentenced Jung-Hwa to six years in prison for counselling to murder a president. "Canada must not become or serve to become a place for mercenaries or terrorists," the judge said.[414]

Jung-Hwa could have fought the charge, but he said he pleaded guilty to protect his father, who still denied knowing about the plot. Fighting the charge would have revealed more secrets about General Choi. Jung-Hwa wondered if his father had been some sort of spy, for example. Had his father been a double agent for decades, pretending to work for South Korea but, in reality, co-operating with North Korea? The elder Choi had admitted to talking to North Koreans in 1962, 1968, and a couple of times in the 1970s. In any case, Jung-Hwa Choi spent a year in a Canadian prison, where he worked as an English teacher and administrative clerk — and no one, not even Choi's family, knew that his father had okayed the assassination plot.

Years later, Jung-Hwa said he felt no animosity toward his father, even though the elder Choi never visited him in prison. The principles of Confucianism, especially the duties of a son, were paramount: "There is no such thing as forgiving, it's an absolute — you had to follow him," Jung-Hwa said. "Of course I was very hurt and had a shock that my own father would not visit me — and he would think of nothing of sacrificing his son."[415]

His father's rationale was that Jung-Hwa would inherit Tae Kwon Do in the end. "That's the only reason why he wanted a son," added Jung-Hwa, who knew his responsibilities. "Confucianism tells us that change is bad, we must conserve tradition. General Choi is from an era and his thought process is exactly the same as people who were one thousand years old — very much old world. When we categorize the types of people and the people from different eras, in Korea, we say, 'There are men who studied with the brush, and there are those who learned with the pen.' Of course, now, people learn with computers. General Choi is a man who learned by the brush."

x x x

Meanwhile, Kim Un-yong continued to dream big. After twenty-one years of struggle with Choi and other martial artists, and after decades of threats and negotiations with North Korea, Kim took credit for making Tae Kwon Do Korea's national sport, for globalizing it, and for making it part of the nation's identity. "It was like a dream," Kim wrote. The political benefits of Tae Kwon Do in the Olympics piled up with the gold medals. Winning athletes enhanced South Korea's prestige, increased tourism, and generated income for Korea. During competitions, millions of people heard the matches in Korean, the universal language of Tae Kwon Do.

Kim now shot for a loftier goal: to lead the entire Olympics and replace President Juan Antonio Samaranch. Kim positioned himself as an alternative to the white Europeans who had always dominated the Olympics. A *New York Times* article explained that he "has been a master at rehabilitating his image, coalescing an apparently strong base in the developing nations of Asia, Africa and Latin America, and regaining enough political ballast that some insiders now consider him the favorite to succeed

Samaranch. With Samaranch's Nazi-soldier past whirling around the Olympics, Kim pushed the fact that he would be the first non-white president of the I.O.C. in the more than 100 years of the modern games and the first from Asia."[416]

A vote for Kim meant a vote for non-Western countries, for a diplomat who was a master organizer, and for someone who could negotiate billion-dollar contracts and tricky political mergers. However, it also meant a vote for the Olympics' "perceived history as an autocratic, secretive, corrupt, elitist organization," which, by coincidence, mirrored the history of Tae Kwon Do's organizations. As one former delegate from India told the *New York Times* in 2001: "He has the wisdom of the East and the efficiency of the West."[417] He also had the backing of spies, gangsters, and a dictator or two.

CHAPTER 16

CHEATING IN THE OLYMPICS

Because the IOC had rejected Tae Kwon Do for the 1996 Olympics, Kim Un-yong began a "007 Operation," as he called it, to sneak Tae Kwon Do into the 2000 Games.[418] It was an intriguing name for the mission, as some people believed that Kim was still a high-ranking secret-service agent and many wondered about cheating and corruption under his reign. For the 007 Operation, he would have to counter strong lobbying from martial arts groups in China and Japan, who, as usual, were lobbying for inclusion of their martial arts. Also as usual, Choi Hong-Hi's International Taekwon-Do Federation would try to attend the final, crucial meeting.[419]

There was no time for Kim to individually persuade members of the International Olympic Committee, and the direct support of IOC President Samaranch became imperative once again, this time at a showdown with Choi's people at an IOC General Meeting in Paris.[420] While Choi's fortunes had fallen, especially after the death of North Korea's leader in 1994, Kim's had risen, along with South Korea's.[421] Choi had been lobbying the IOC to reject Tae Kwon Do for the 2000 Games, but he failed once again after Samaranch bent the rules for Kim and Tae Kwon Do.

The subsequent buildup to the Games was rocky, mainly because of cheating allegations around the world. Martial arts officials in Malaysia, for example, warned judges that they would take strict action if there was biased judging, and a riot broke out at the Asian Games after fans in Thailand disagreed with a judge in a semifinal match.[422] For Kim, though, South Korea had expanded Tae Kwon Do from a martial art into an international sport, and he claimed that the mistakes in judging would be fixed.

Meanwhile, Choi had installed security cameras around his Canadian house and rallied his old grandmasters for the final mission of his life — to reunify Tae Kwon Do (the ITF with the WTF) and, while he was at it, to reunify his homeland (North and South Korea).

Ironically, Kim had a similar goal. South Koreans appointed him to their National Assembly in April 2000, and Kim-the-sports-leader became Kim-the-political-leader. There had always been an overlap between Tae Kwon Do and international politics, and now there was an even stronger connection: Kim became a special adviser to the South Korean president, Kim Dae-jung.[423] The venerable Kim Dae-jung had battled dictators all his life, had avoided rogue Tae Kwon Do instructors, and had survived the Korean CIA's attempts to blow him up, run him over, and throw him into the sea. He had finally become president of South Korea and was now negotiating the Korean deal of the century: the Sunshine Policy, which promoted a long list of activities that pointed to the reunification of the two countries. He chose Kim Un-yong, Tae Kwon Do's leader, to be on the North–South negotiation team.

That year, when the two leaders of a divided Korea met for a peace summit for the first time since the countries' creation,[424] Kim Un-yong was standing in the room. He thought that the North Korean leader, Kim Jong Il, was funny and open to new ideas.

"What can we, South and North, do together in sports?" the North Korean ruler asked Kim.

"The Sydney Olympics is soon," Kim Un-yong replied, "and the IOC is proposing that South and North enter together for the opening ceremony."

"Yes, I am well aware of that," the North Korean leader said. "What sports can we do together to top the world?"

"Ping-pong," Kim answered.[425]

The North Korean leader replied that he would get back to him.

Choi Hong-Hi (on left) met Kim Jong Il in North Korea after Kim became the country's leader. PHOTO COURTESY OF JEONG SOON-CHEON.

The two groups did agree that they should co-operate in Tae Kwon Do, however. Driven by a deep desire to end a fifty-year trauma — a desire shared by Koreans in both North and South — the men who ran Tae Kwon Do proved that kicks and punches could play a positive role during political talks. Choi was not in the room, but his organization would agree to Tae Kwon Do demonstrations as part of the Sunshine Policy. Along with family reunions and a railway link between the two countries, there would be cross-border Tae Kwon Do visits.[426]

What few people knew at the time was that the South Korean president had shovelled U.S.$500 million to the North Korean leader as an incentive for the North Koreans to participate in the 2000 peace summit.[427] Alongside these illegal political payments — no one used the word "bribes" — Kim Un-yong helped to "promote inter-Korean sports exchanges," as he put it, by delivering U.S.$1.1 million to a North Korean Olympic official, Chang Ung, who happened to be a leader in Choi's International Taekwon-Do Federation.

While the money flowed to North Korea and its Tae Kwon Do leader, the two Koreas agreed to walk into the stadium together during the opening ceremony at the 2000 Sydney Olympic Games.

They completed the deal at the last minute, but the whole thing would not work without proper uniforms. Both teams had to wear the same outfit, but the deal-making had taken so long to finalize that Korean Olympic officials did not have enough uniforms. They ran from manufacturer to manufacturer during a Thanksgiving holiday to collect 300 uniforms and delivered them at the last minute. "I believe that heaven helped us," Kim concluded.[428] More than half a billion dollars in bribes to North Koreans probably helped, too.

x x x

A couple of months later, in September, 120,000 spectators watched the opening ceremonies of the 2000 Sydney Games and saw Kim Un-yong and Chang Ung, heads of the Olympic Committees and of the Tae Kwon Do organizations in their Koreas, enter the stadium holding hands.[429] Kim was overcome with emotion as he walked near a specially designed Korean flag that merged North and South Korean symbols. He had been planning this moment for more than three months. Two days before the opening Games, after someone had obtained two donated bottles of whiskey — "unification booze" — from the Uzbekistan team, Kim and South Korea's athletes and officials had met their North Korean counterparts for a party in the Athletes Village. No doubt, the liquor would later help to alleviate the pain from cheating during Olympic bouts.

An uncanny part of Olympic Tae Kwon Do is that the host country always seems to do astoundingly well in medal counts: in Seoul in 1988, the South Koreans took most of the golds; in Barcelona in 1992, the Spanish were the best after the Koreans; and at the 2000 Games in Sydney, the Australians won gold in the first Tae Kwon Do match, creating a buzz and "boosting the sport's popularity in an instant," according to Olympic officials.[430] The silver and bronze medal winners at the 2000 Olympics thought that the cheering crowd had swayed the judges.[431] In fact, the alleged cheating was more concrete. A Korean journalist later reported that a Tae Kwon Do official, Lee Chong-woo, had swayed judging in key bouts before the medal matches.

At two Olympics, Tae Kwon Do had been a demonstration sport, so it had not been part of the medal standings and had not generated much world interest, partly because Koreans dominated. To ensure that South Korea would not win the majority of medals at the 2000 Olympics, Tae Kwon Do's leaders had developed a quota system.[432] In 2000, there were four weight categories for men and four for women, and all nations could enter only two men and two women. Australia, however, was allowed to enter double that number — eight athletes — which immediately increased its chances of winning Tae Kwon Do medals. Kim Un-yong had agreed to this arrangement, and Australia won the first gold. He later wrote that Korea had not done as well as expected but that Tae Kwon Do had done well.[433]

However, Lee Chong-woo, who was a World Taekwondo Federation official, revealed a different side of Kim to a Korean journalist in 2002:

> When Korean athletes captured a small number of medals, Un Yong Kim was so distressed that he just looked at me and didn't say anything. . . . At that time, all the Korean athletes in the other sports had been beaten, and the last hope was for Tae Kwon Do. Kim said that "even though we won three gold medals in the four weight divisions, because of the quota system we did not even enter four divisions, so we actually had to give away four gold medals." During these hectic times, the hosting country Australia took whatever they could take, and Un Yong Kim went into a rage.
>
> At that time, as the Vice-President of the World Taekwondo Federation, I was responsible for all technical matters for the Tae Kwon Do competition. When we assigned referees prior to the competition, I was the one who decided most of all who was to be assigned or not assigned [for each match]. I could not openly ask judges to take care of Korea, could I? So when I hit the judges' backs, some were sensitive enough to understand what it meant, while the insensitive ones did not understand at all.[434]

Lee told the surprised journalist, Sung-chul Yook, that the process was called "branch trimming." He explained how it worked and the underlying political motives for it:

> **LEE:** When they were told, "Be fair," they read my intention and sensed it. I was in charge of this kind of manipulation and I carried it out. Without it, we could not have taken any more than one or two gold medals. That sort of thing was accepted and worked out because we were Korean, not from other countries.
>
> **REPORTER:** I watched all three final matches where Korean players fought, and based on what I observed, I believe that all three Korean athletes won.
>
> **LEE:** Only watching the final match would not be enough. In order to understand it as a whole, you have to pay very careful attention beginning with the first match. In this sense, it is not that simple. There are so-called tactics. That is, you kill the strong opponent beforehand. We are not the ones who kill. The judges do. When you tell judges to do their job fairly, they know what to do and they do it. From the beginning of the preliminary games, you have to perform *gagee-chigee* [branch trimming]. If not, at the end you will be in trouble . . .
>
> **REPORTER:** Do you mean that "branch trimming" is inevitable in order for Korea to retain its reputation as the strong Tae Kwon Do country?
>
> **LEE:** Yes, I do. If a formidable person goes out as a judge, it is difficult to do it the way we want. It is also difficult to kill the Korean athlete's opponent at the final match. Therefore, from the beginning, you should have a good grasp as to which country is strong. Assigning judges is a skill. That is, so and so country will be in the competition. So and so

country should not get into the finals. Therefore, so and so should be killed this way.

REPORTER: From the point of view that Tae Kwon Do is a sport which puts its emphasis on courtesy, isn't that "tree trimming" unjust behavior, contrary to good sportsmanship?

LEE: When judges play tricks, the outcome of a match is reversed. If a judge says he did not see [a point], that is the end of it, and he can make repeated deductions of points. For this reason, I did this (moves his hand horizontally across his throat) to one of the judges. He was the one who caused the defeat of a female Korean athlete, by giving her a deduction. I gathered the judges together and instructed them absolutely not to call deduction of points, but to give a *choui* [pre-warning] for the first and second time, and then a *kyungo* warning for the third one. In spite of my instructions, he made deductions. After the match, I shouted at him, "You cannot do that! Do you have a problem?" After this match, the attitudes of the judges changed completely.

REPORTER: Critically speaking, it seems to me that *gageechigee* is a precise way to manipulate results.

LEE: If this was disclosed openly, it would be a disgrace for Korea. But this is a reality. For example, if there were a final match between two strong competitors representing Korea and Germany, we would not make Germany lose in the final. If we perceived that the Korean athlete would have the disadvantage in a match against the German, we would "kill" this German athlete before he reached the final.

REPORTER: I don't think that's fair. Upon hearing these words of the Vice-President, I am worried that Korea might cause some misunderstandings about the way Korea is maintaining a good reputation as a strong power in Tae Kwon Do through the use of result manipulation.

LEE: This is related to the national interest. This is a sensitive issue. When Korean Tae Kwon Do is destroyed, there will be chaos and then athletes' spirit will fall to the ground. Foreign athletes' skills have improved drastically. This [result manipulation] has been possible, because Korea has dominated the leadership . . . There is no fair play.

REPORTER: Do you mean that in almost all the international games . . . this sort of unwritten rule is applied?

LEE: Yes, a country that holds dominant leadership is always a strong country [in that sport's standings] . . .

REPORTER: What is your estimate of how many gold medals our Tae Kwon Do would be awarded if we competed fairly without privilege?

LEE: We would reap half, at the most . . .[435]

After the article was published in April 2002, Lee denied the story, and Olympic Tae Kwon Do officials said that his allegations were groundless. (In July 2008, the World Taekwondo Federation's public relations director, Mr. Seok-Jae Kang, told me that there had been no official investigation as far as he knew.) Sung-chul Yook, the reporter, was threatened and refused to comment in the uproar that followed. Lee had clearly been unhappy with the way things were going in the WTF and had "exploded" in front of journalist Yook, as one grandmaster explained it to me.[436] Lee's denials and the reporter's silence helped quell the controversy.

Many people were careful in their reactions to the article, but some went on record to say they were not surprised, especially because Lee had not run for re-election as WTF vice-president the autumn before.[437] Herb Perez, a 1992 Olympic gold medal winner in Tae Kwon Do and a U.S. Olympic official at the time, read the article and said, "This has been the way Taekwondo is."[438]

U.S. Tae Kwon Do gold medalist Steven Lopez, who fought in the 2000, 2004, and 2008 Games, was more forthright. The *Houston Chronicle* reported that Lopez had heard about matches fixed in favour of Koreans:

> "It's pretty bad, but it's something you have to live with in our sport," he said. "We have to deal with it in our own way, and we're still dealing with it. You have to train two or three times harder and smarter and realize even then that things are stacked against you."
>
> . . . Lopez said he hopes the allegations regarding taekwondo will help clean up his sport.
>
> "Enough people have been double-crossed, and enough people are sick and tired of taking it," he said. "It's time for people to open their eyes and do something about it."[439]

In 2008, I asked David Askinas, the new CEO of USA Taekwondo (which is part of the Olympics), what he thought of the 2002 article. He had not heard about Lee's statements but said, "It would not surprise me. The WTF has had to take a lot of steps to prevent abuses in judging, and, yeah, I've heard stories and read things about bribery — things like that. They've pretty much cleaned that up."[440]

Which was not true. At the 2008 Olympics in Beijing, Canada's Yvette Gonda was favoured to win a medal but lost to a Swedish fighter in her first fight, despite Gonda kicking her repeatedly. Gonda's coach suspected that one of the judges, who was from China, ignored Gonda's points so that a Chinese competitor would not have to face her in the next round.[441] In another match, judges supposedly did not see a clear kick to an opponent's head, and a

British competitor lost her quarter-final match. In the uproar that followed, the WTF reviewed videos and, in a decision noted for its rarity, did the right thing and reversed the decision in favour of the British athlete.[442]

In Canada, WTF Secretary General Wayne Mitchell, was more forthright about "branch trimming" when I talked to him in 2008. "It was an extremely sophisticated way of cheating," he said. He went on to explain that it was accepted behaviour among leaders and common knowledge among some grandmasters. "To them, you had to lobby to get into the inner circle, so that you were the one on the good side of getting trimmed," he said. Some referees knew it existed, but not all knew that there was a name for it and that it was organized. "I think there was a circle of referees, because all it takes is a couple of them, or one of them in a match to not show points for a certain fighter, then, all of sudden, the game is over for you," Mitchell said, adding that Lee Chong-woo, a high-ranking WTF official, had been mad at somebody, leading to his outburst with the journalist. That somebody had been Kim Un-yong.[443]

After the International Olympic Committee once again chose Tae Kwon Do as an official sport, this time for the 2004 Athens Olympics, Kim announced that he would run for IOC president and would cleanse the Olympics of over-commercialism. Expecting votes from thirty-seven IOC members from Asia and Africa and a handful from Europe and North America, he thought he had a chance. His one big worry was that Samaranch, a former ambassador in Spain's fascist government, would betray him.[444] Kim told him, "If you support me or keep neutral, I will win, but if you oppose me, I will lose." He remembered Samaranch's reply: "You are the only friend out of five IOC candidates," and he hugged Kim.[445]

However, controversies about Tae Kwon Do judging refused to die down and the seemingly invincible Kim became the number one target. It did not help that millions of dollars were flowing from more than 170 countries to his martial arts federation with little transparency. Around that time, a group of World Taekwondo

Federation (WTF) executives decided to rebel against the corruption, demanding that the WTF lower its black belt fees. The leader of that rebel group was expelled and began a reform movement.[446]

In July 2001, Kim Un-yong lost his bid to become IOC president, and he blamed Samaranch.[447] The old Salt Lake City scandal had been dusted off and sent to the media, fuelled by claims that Kim had offered approximately U.S.$50,000 in bribes to IOC members.[448] Dick Pound, who had also run for the presidency, had a more frank explanation: "I think Samaranch realized that, by then, with the reputation that Kim had, it would be a disaster for the IOC. He was certainly actively campaigning against Kim, and also against me, in favour of [Jacques] Rogge."[449]

Kim was devastated by the loss to Rogge. Without a hint of irony, he claimed that the IOC remained a stronghold of white people and that the election had been corrupt.[450] Chang Ung, Kim's North Korean IOC compatriot, was also disappointed. Kim had been sending money to him in North Korea.

The game was up, Kim thought, and his world began falling apart. In October 2001, only three months after his IOC loss, he drove to the Seoul Olympic Parktel for an 11 a.m. Korean Tae Kwon Do Association meeting to resolve internal disputes. Dozens of angry Tae Kwon Do masters and students strutted through the hotel lobby, mixing with Kim's supporters.

Kim walked into the hotel and up to the conference hall, leaving in his a wake a cacophony of swearing and yelling between the two groups. Inside the hall, he could not conduct the meeting.

"President Kim, do the right thing and make up your mind!" yelled reformers in the lobby.

"He created Tae Kwon Do from nothing and you dare ask him to retire!" shouted Kim's supporters.

The yelling turned into pushing and grabbing, which I imagine is a potentially dangerous thing among Tae Kwon Do masters.

Kim said nothing, got up, and walked back to the lobby through the swearing and pushing, maintaining his composure. Through the fighting, he made it to his car, but some of the Tae Kwon Do instructors jumped on top of it. Kim sat there.

What did he think as they stood on top of him? Amid the shouting and shoving outside, did he imagine that his supporters should have hired more muscle and that his reign as a Tae Kwon Do king was over? Protestors finally let the car pull away at 11:15, but the shouting and fighting continued, which surprised the foreigners arriving for an innocent international conference in Seoul.

The hotel melee was an undignified display. The problems of Korean Tae Kwon Do — the gangsters, stealing, and unfair tournaments — had spilled onto the streets of Seoul. Three days after the hotel confrontation, Kim was supposed to open the fifteenth World Tae Kwon Do Championship, but the rebel instructors did not care because they thought the last championship, in April, had been a fiasco.

"It is the fault of Tae Kwon Do leaders for not preparing, for ignoring the situation after the April national championship," the instructors told a Korean reporter.

Kim Un-yong also became entangled in the South Korean president's scandal over the U.S.$500 million sent to North Korea for a 2000 peace summit. After President Kim Dae-jung had won the Nobel Peace Prize for that summit, an investigation began. So much money had flowed through various networks — through different companies, government agencies, and sports organizations, including Tae Kwon Do — that it made Koreagate from the 1970s look amateurish.

A few people knew that Kim had been accepting bribes from two businessmen in return for helping them join sports committees and that he had been embezzling millions from the World Taekwondo Federation.[451] No one knew the full details, but coaches and black belts were wondering why Kim's relatives were on staff in Tae Kwon Do organizations, why there was little transparency when it came to money, and why rumours of cheating continued.

But the game was not over for Kim; he was in sudden-death overtime. He resigned from the Korean Tae Kwon Do Association in November 2001, and Koo Cheon-Seo, another politician, took over amid streets fights outside the KTA presidential election. Kim felt as if the last thirty years of his life were flitting around him like a Korean running-horse lamp, the images spinning on a wire, the lamp becoming hotter, the horse running faster and faster on that single wire.[452]

CHAPTER 17

LIKE A CULT

It was a beautiful spring day in March 2001 when I accompanied my Tae Kwon Do instructor, Grandmaster Jong-Soo Park, to Choi Hong-Hi's house in Toronto. Park and I were both nervous. He had always claimed that he had never been part of a plan to kidnap Choi, but the two had never discussed this accusation of Choi's. In turn, Park was trying to forget that Choi and his son had discussed assigning a gangster to kill Park. By now, the General and Park had grey hair and were planning a reunion of masters and grandmasters that month, as Olympic Tae Kwon Do spun out of control.

We stepped out of Park's rusted Mercedes, and I stared at Choi's huge home. There were no trees because Choi hated squirrels. The little rodents had nibbled the cucumbers and hot peppers he had grown in the gardens of his previous homes, and he did not want them scrambling around here.

Park gently lifted the door knocker, straightened his hair, and smiled when Mrs. Choi opened the front door. She bowed and immediately went to get her husband. Inside, we waited in a large hallway leading to four immaculate rooms and a spiral staircase that soared to the second floor. Choi had replaced the cheap furniture that he had bought when he had first moved to Canada with Polish antiques that his son had shipped from Eastern Europe in the 1980s. Beside us on a low shelf were perfect rows of embroidered

Asian slippers. I slipped on a pair just as Choi materialized next to a parchment of calligraphy hanging on a wall.

Choi greeted Park and me with a slight nod. We bowed. His thin limbs stuck out of a plaid shirt and pinstriped pants — he looked like a large puppet. No wonder so many men had tried to crush him. He did not fear for his life as much as in the old days, when he had built a house on a hill to make it difficult for people to attack him.[453] But recently, when Park and Choi had gone out for a meal, Park had been surprised to discover that Choi still considered him a bodyguard every second that they were together; Choi asked Park to accompany him to the washroom, in case someone attacked him there.

Park, Choi, and I settled into the antiques in the living room and talked about Tae Kwon Do. It was difficult to get personal because he was so serious and formal, but I eventually asked him about how he had become a Karate expert.

"Talk a bit louder," he said, waving his hand. "My hearing is not okay." He refused to use his hearing aid.

I loudly asked about the day he had lost his mother's life savings in a poker match with a wrestler — that crazy old story from 1938, back when Choi's Korea was more Confucian and less terrorist.

"Sir, did you ever meet the wrestler?" I asked.

"No, my friend told him that I studied Karate and he would not have a chance with me, so he avoided me." Choi chuckled. "He was just a country boy."

"Did you ever apologize to him?" I asked. I knew that Choi travelled to North Korea a lot, and I assumed that my question would be an easy one. After all, the General constantly preached about courtesy, self-control, integrity, and the other tenets of Tae Kwon Do, and he had broken at least one of those tenets when he had thrown an ink bottle at the wrestler in a desperate attempt to get the money back. But Choi did not reply.

"Sir?" I said.

He turned his head away and stared at the foyer.

Park, who sat beside me, interrupted: "Of course, the General went to the hospital to see if he was dead or alive. That was a *sorry*."

"It was a five-cent bottle made of thick glass," Choi said, looking at me again. He laughed.[454]

In fact, he had met the wrestler, Haak-Soon Huh, in North Korea in the late 1980s, fifty years after the conflict in which Choi had knocked him out with the bottle.[455] To be more accurate, he did not meet him so much as summon him. By that time, Choi was an important person in North Korea and the wrestler was a commoner. During the 1938 poker match, Huh had been Choi's superior. During the 1980s meeting, the roles were reversed: Huh and his wife did not look directly at Choi and, as with everyone else in North Korea, they did not use first names; they addressed Choi as the powerful man he was. Choi assumed they were honoured to meet him. There were no chuckles about poker cheats, stolen money, near-death experiences, and — ha, ha — fleeing like a country boy, nor about how all the fear had led to Karate and Tae Kwon Do. How ironic that one of the world's most popular martial arts was partly due to this wrestler bowing before Choi.

In 2001, between Park sitting in Choi's living room and my inadvertent, impertinent questions, the General was not amused. He sat facing me with his chin tilted, like someone holding court.

But Choi's eyes lit up when he spoke about Tae Kwon Do and his efforts to improve it. He was proud that Tae Kwon Do dominated Karate. He had been fighting Japanese Karate since the Second World War. "They antagonized me then for politics; now they do so because of Tae Kwon Do," he said.

His entire life had been a long war against the humiliation that Japan had inflicted on him and his people and, in 1961, against the humiliation from a South Korean dictator. In many ways, he had been fighting the same ghosts for fifty years. He had great respect for North Korea, partly because its leaders would not let Japan and the U.S. push them around and also because the North Koreans liked his Tae Kwon Do.

"North Korea has original Tae Kwon Do — pure, one hundred per cent," he told me. "That's why they are very good." By pure he meant there was no Japanese or Olympic involvement.

At the time, Choi was on a mission to force masters to learn how to jump over a standing person with no running start, just as the ancient *hwarang* warriors had apparently jumped over walls. Choi wanted his masters to take only one or two steps and leap over an opponent, but even the North Koreans said it was impossible. Some masters of the past, such as Han Cha-gyo, had jumped over a crouched man, but the vast majority could not and would never be able to. Choi's organization had fist fights over the issue, with some saying they should try and others declaring it was a mad expectation. Choi's demand was such an unreasonable request that a group of North Korean masters, those practising so-called pure Tae Kwon Do, told him that it was impossible, and Choi slapped one of them in the face.[456]

Soon after my initial visit, I met Choi in his house again, alone, and he led me to a study, where he pointed to his 1965 and 1972 Tae Kwon Do books. Photos of Jong-Soo Park jumped on the covers. "He was my prize student," Choi said.

A phone rang, but no one answered. He crouched and touched the first volume of his fifteen-volume encyclopedia set. "History is in this one," he said gently. "This volume contains the Theory of Power. This one, hand techniques." He spoke as if he were in a church. "This volume is sparring," he whispered, as the phone rang again. "Patterns, here." He had created a condensed version of the fifteen volumes in the 1980s, he said, because people could not carry around all fifteen, which were more than a foot thick when piled together. "Too heavy," he said matter-of-factly. These were the days before PDFs and smartphones.

He flipped through another volume until he came to the pattern *Tong-Il*, which means "unification." He was proud of this one, the last of twenty-four patterns, because it symbolized reunification of the two Koreas. "See? It's easy to learn," he said, turning the pages slowly. "You follow the photos." We looked at the techniques in *Tong-Il*, the middle punches with the twin fists and the horizontal strikes with the twin knife-hands. If only politics had been as easy as these techniques. I thought of what he had told me in the living room earlier: "To die is pitiful." Choi was eighty-two years old and still fighting.

x x x

Nine months later, in January 2002, I met Jung-Hwa Choi, the General's son and the supposed heir to all things Tae Kwon Do. Their International Taekwon-Do Federation was in trouble, as was the World Taekwondo Federation. While the older man reminded me of stone, his son seemed like water — adaptable, hard to pin down, and transparent. Jung-Hwa lived in the same Canadian city as his father. His home was smaller but just as opulent. I walked into the living room, where he sat in a large golden chair wearing a blue tie and an immaculate white shirt. His wife stood in the kitchen. His right-hand man, Joe Cariati, sat across the room.

After he was released from prison in the 1990s, Jung-Hwa began rebelling against General Choi, partly for personal reasons but mainly because he thought the General was destroying the martial art with Cold War politics. Jung-Hwa had learned from his mistakes, but it seemed his father had not; for decades, they had pushed against one another, against the pressures created by Tae Kwon Do, but both men were now pushing even more.

"I think he had always worried that his son would undo what he had built," Jung-Hwa told me. "Sometimes, I laugh at this, because he had a monopoly in Tae Kwon Do in the 1970s; there were no other competitors, meaning we had tens of millions of members. I can tell you now, we are in the hundreds of thousands," he said, referring to the ITF worldwide. "If this isn't bankruptcy, what is?"[457]

The conflict between father and son was embedded in a Confucian view of family relationships. For example, Choi rarely spoke to his son about personal matters. One morning, however, Jung-Hwa asked his father if he still dreamed about his own father.

"What a silly question," the General replied. "Do you know how old I am? I'm past eighty years old! Do you think I have memories of my father?"

Jung-Hwa had not expected this answer. Surely a parent remains in your heart no matter what your age, especially for someone like Choi, who expected sons to show unwavering obedience to fathers.

"Did you enjoy conversation with your father?" Jung-Hwa pressed. He knew his father had lived under Confucianism, and therefore the boundaries of father-son relationships had been strictly observed, but he wanted to know if his father and grandfather had even talked.

"He was very strict with me, and he was very disciplined, so I had to observe father-son respect, not like you, who are out of line in asking such questions," Choi replied. That was how Jung-Hwa learned that he was to never discuss his father's father.

The elder Choi's latest mission was to merge the International Taekwon-Do Federation with the World Taekwondo Federation as part of the talks to help North and South Korea reunify. Choi expected Jung-Hwa to build a strong relationship with North Korea, but Jung-Hwa did not want to; he wanted to exorcize politics from the martial art.

"He was always trying to ingrain in my head that I must follow North Korea, because they were so helpful towards ITF, and I said, 'I don't see anything that they are helping us with'," Jung-Hwa told me. "In fact, it's weird, sacrificing not only our teaching to them, but becoming outsiders to our own people by following them.'"

In 2001, Jung-Hwa realized the full consequences of defying his father with such comments. They were standing in a hotel hallway in Rimini, Italy. Masters from around the world had recently elected Jung-Hwa as the next president of the ITF, much to his father's surprise. The young man hoped that his father would finally take a rest, would retire perhaps, but as Jung-Hwa stood there, his father, the *chadol*, the small stone, was immobile.

"What's wrong?" Jung-Hwa asked.

"Please get away from me!" Choi said, shooing him away like a servant. "You are not my son!"

For as long as Jung-Hwa could remember, his father had humiliated him with that comment. Sometimes the older man would add that he had sons elsewhere.

Jung-Hwa stepped out of hitting range. Clearly, General Choi was unhappy that Jung-Hwa had become ITF president.

Later, as they drove to the closing ceremony of the Rimini world championship, Choi warned, "I promise you, boy, that I will unite ITF and WTF within one year. When I do, I will give everything to Kim Un-yong. I will never see you become president." At the time, Kim (Choi's lifelong enemy) was trying to become president of the International Olympic Committee.

Jung-Hwa told me that he then saw his father's real face for the first time in his life, and it was not human. The elder Choi despised Kim. Jung-Hwa did not believe that his father was demented. Rather, General Choi was under the influence of something stronger than old age: North Korea. He realized that Choi, a dictator, was going to defy what the elected masters had decided; he would oust his own son.

Jung-Hwa soon quit the ITF and set up his own organization, also called the ITF. He claimed that one-third of the world ITF membership joined him, and he said that his father was lying about an ITF-WTF merger.

Negotiations between the ITF and WTF have often been a joke. The two groups abuse each other and then discuss mergers the way beatings are followed by promises in a dysfunctional marriage. Negotiations between Tae Kwon Do factions began long before Kim Un-yong arrived on the scene; in the 1950s, heated arguments took place between the main martial arts gyms (the *kwans*) in Korea, and in the 1960s between the ITF and the Korean Tae Kwon Do Association. For more than forty years, announcements about merger attempts have sounded like fantasies created by hopeful martial artists around the world who wanted mama and dada to get along.

"Whenever there was unrest in the ITF, or inactivity in the ITF, we would come out with certain statements, such as 'we are going to merge,' or 'our instructors are being invited to South Korea,'" Jung-Hwa Choi later told me. "In fact, I'm one of those who is guilty. I was instructed by my father to write a letter, as Secretary General, to our members around the world that we may be sending a demonstration team to South Korea and that we were looking for people who would like to take part in it. The letter even went further to mention that we may even send ITF members to South Korea to open schools. Of course, there was nothing to back this up."

For its part, the behemoth WTF does not need the pipsqueak ITF, but the leaders of both meet every year or so, elevating hope that the powerful WTF will accept the traditional ITF.

"Those groups are talking at a fairly high level to do a merger," WTF Canada's Wayne Mitchell told me in 2008, "but I don't think it's going to be a merger as much as an absorption."[458] He added that the ITF did not have access to the dollars and resources available to the WTF.

That is an understatement. The relationship is eerily similar to the political history between poor, proud North Korea and rich, suave South Korea. Still, in 2015, the International Olympic Committee and the WTF teased many ITF factions with promises of a merger. I asked Stuart Anslow, the editor of U.K.-based *Totally Tae Kwon Do* magazine, one of the largest in the world, if he put any credence in the recent merger talks: "At first I didn't, then I did, then I didn't," he replied.[459] That summed up many people's attitude.

After a series of negotiations that had the intensity of a nuclear-arms deal, the IOC, WTF, and ITF-North Korea signed an agreement in 2015 to hold a couple of joint demonstrations, but not much came of those talks. Surprisingly, the earth continued spinning.

For his part, back in 2002, Jung-Hwa Choi did not want North Korea to swallow their Tae Kwon Do. Part of the problem was that General Choi had always run the Tae Kwon Do organization like a cult. When his father had visited Reverend Sun-Myung Moon (the leader of the Unification Church, considered a cult by many) to ask for money decades ago, Jung-Hwa was not surprised. "General Choi, I think, would be very happy if he were in the place of Reverend Moon Sun-Myung. You know? Moonie?" Jung-Hwa told me in 2002.[460] "He used to just lambaste Moon. He used to talk badly about him, but now I know it was jealousy. He did go and meet Moon one day. After he returned, he said, 'Why is he bad after all?' Even before that, he told me how, at Moon's snapping fingers, people would just stop moving and come to his command, and how he used to move people around. General Choi was impressed. I said, 'Careful, sir, you're trying to use him, but how can a shrimp swallow a whale?'"

"The ITF organization was an absolute autocracy — there were no questions asked," Jung-Hwa continued. Many Tae Kwon Do instructors agreed with this assessment, usually adding in the same breath that the General was a genius.[461]

"As a matter of fact, General Choi said, 'Buddha comes from India, yet India is mainly Hindu," Jung-Hwa said. "Jesus comes from Israel, but there's not much Christianity there. Ironically, Tae Kwon Do comes from South Korea, but there's no ITF Tae Kwon Do there.' Does that mean he wants to become the fourth saint?"

Jung-Hwa suspected that the darkest part of his father was attracted to North Korea's despotic government, which oppressed millions of people. Once, during a sumptuous meal in North Korea, Jung-Hwa told his father that the economy was backwards, and his father replied, "How can you say that? We eat like this all the time. How can you say this country is poor?"

"This is not an everyday dinner for the common people," Jung-Hwa explained to him. His father refused to listen. In fact, he made it a mission to tell anyone he met that North Korea was doing well. Jung-Hwa realized that his father, who dined with North Korean dignitaries, could not care less for the average North Korean and the gulags that awaited commoners if they complained. Choi's entire life was Tae Kwon Do, and, in his view, Tae Kwon Do needed the North Koreans.

"There are two Generals," Jung-Hwa said as we sat in his living room. "One is the great man General Choi." He was the "founder" of Tae Kwon Do. "The other is a child who grew up in a broken home and who always desired love. When he could not find love from his family, he turned to his disciples." If they failed him, he would feel betrayed, and he would turn on them verbally or physically. As they fell, he rose.

"It is what they call Small Man's Syndrome, in which one has to appear the best, one knows the best, and one has to constantly prove that one is great, even to family," Jung-Hwa added. "Every day, he gave us a sermon, every breakfast and dinner, about how great he was." And the family listened. "One Christmas, he actually told us, 'Why do you believe in God? If you want to believe in God, then believe in my fist.'"

In fighting brutal men all his life, the General had become brutal himself and had wrecked many people — and he had also suffered in the process. It was no surprise that he wanted to be a god. He had a hard time being human.

Not even the North Korean instructors were spared this brutality. "I have seen him really butcher people in front of others," Jung-Hwa said. Once, in 2001 during a Tae Kwon Do seminar, North Korean instructors asked Jung-Hwa to tell his father that they had not prepared a sparring demonstration. Choi had asked them to research new sparring methods, but they came to the seminar with only research papers and they approached Jung-Hwa for help:

> They said, "We know General Choi, so, if you please, can you tell him not to ask us to do any physical demonstration, because we've done only academic research." I said, "I will try." I explained to General Choi, "Is that all right?" and he said, "Yeah, okay." Suddenly, he was in a different mood and, the next day, he called them up to demonstrate, knowing they had not prepared. Of course, their faces turned white . . . They were almost out of their minds, because they were in front of many delegates. General Choi was screaming at them, "Show it in physical form! . . . Shut up! Stop reading! You do the demonstration!" But they weren't hearing General Choi anymore; they were like zombies, reading, and we all cried for them. Then General Choi left. He could not keep his temper, and he started to smash his hand on the wall, screaming. Many people thought he was going to have a heart attack that day — many people wished that he would have a heart attack . . . That was a turning point for many members.

Jung-Hwa knew what he was up against. Splitting from his father and starting his own ITF organization meant a vicious conflict.

For his part, General Choi did not trust his own son in 2001. He thought Jung-Hwa was plotting to kill him.

CHAPTER 18

THE LITTLE GIANT DIES AND TAE KWON DO FALLS APART

A month later, priorities suddenly changed because Choi Hong-Hi was diagnosed with cancer and doctors gave him little time to live. His organization was splintering as fast as the cancer inside him was spreading, and the subsequent developments were a stunning display of what happens when one person rules an organization too long and pits executive against executive, son against surrogate son, in a battle to replace him.

Jong-Soo Park and a handful of other loyal disciples helped the elder Choi day and night. Choi refused to eat much and cried if anyone talked about Jung-Hwa Choi. "My only son betrayed me," he would repeat. It was difficult to feel sorry for him, but I did — and for Jung-Hwa as well.

One day, his son visited him at a Toronto hospital and went into a mild state of shock, as his father's body had deteriorated into just skin and skeleton.[462] Choi looked at him and said, "I don't want to see you, I don't want to see you." Jung-Hwa kept his head down, until his mother, who was in the room, screamed at him. Jung-Hwa could not stand that and left, but he returned to the hospital parking lot on the day when his father was discharged. His mother emerged from the hospital, not escorted by bodyguards or grandmasters, and as Jung-Hwa waited, she walked past him. The younger Choi walked into the hospital and helped the old man to the car. Jung-Hwa was happy that he could briefly hold his father, but it did not end well, as usual, because his mother yelled that he was killing the older man. Jung-Hwa left.

He was the only son and his father's favourite, so this three-year conflict must have nearly killed both of them. Once, in South Korea, when Jung-Hwa was two years old, he was playing on a windowsill and fell off, cutting his head and chin. General Choi had just returned from work when he saw the blood. The family did not have time to find a doctor, so Choi removed his military jacket, wrapped his son in it, and ran many miles to the nearest hospital, forgetting his shoes at home. People wondered at the barefoot madman sprinting past with a bleeding boy.[463]

Now, as cancer spread to Choi's liver and he looked yellow, Jung-Hwa did not accompany him to international seminars, such as the one in Denver, Colorado, where Choi taught from a wheelchair.

In May 2002, as Choi sat in a wheelchair at Toronto's international airport surrounded by disciples and bodyguards and waiting for a plane to North Korea, he did not expect his son to show up. In fact, he still suspected that Jung-Hwa was trying to kill him. He was close to death and would likely never return to Canada. His son arrived at the airport with Joe Cariati and other martial artists, and they walked up to Choi. Standing near him was the obsequious Master Soon-Cheon Jeong (who took photos), Grandmaster Kang-Sung Hwang (who lived in the U.S.), Grandmaster Woojin Jung (publisher of *Tae Kwon Do Times*), Grandmaster Jong-Soo Park, and others, all there to say goodbye to their General — and perhaps for other reasons, too.

Jung-Hwa sat beside Choi and held his shoulders. He felt mainly bones. He desperately wanted his father to stay in Toronto but dared not ask. It had taken all he had just to get to the airport. He tried to think of good memories and the love he had for him. "It's not that scary to touch my father," he told himself, because he had always felt that it would be scary. He touched his father's head. He wished that they could have been closer when he had been a boy and his father a younger man. What thoughts to have ten minutes before departure, Jung-Hwa thought. His friend, a few feet away, was crying. "You know, I never had a Choi family," Jung-Hwa quietly told him.

"Can you apologize to me on the internet?" Choi asked Jung-Hwa, who was taken aback. Jung-Hwa's allies had criticized Choi's men, whom Jung-Hwa had called hypocrites and geishas. There was so much that the two men should have resolved before Choi boarded the plane: how a father could brag about sacrificing his son, why the young man had used the name of his father's martial art, why violence lived in them like desire. Instead, Choi talked about the internet.

"And can you apologize to my boys — to the North Koreans?" Choi asked Jung-Hwa, who assumed that his father wanted to save face and assure the North Koreans that Jung-Hwa was on their side. It was perhaps surreal, and not only because a U.S. president had recently made a speech including North Korea in an "Axis of Evil."

"Sir, let's not talk about this now," his son replied.

Instead, General Choi spoke about North Korea's Arirang festival, a two-month event of gymnastics, dance, and arts involving hundreds of thousands of performers. Arirang celebrated the birthday of the nation's founder, Kim Il Sung, and was open to tourists and journalists. "You will come to see me?" Choi asked him.

The younger Choi did not answer; he would never go to North Korea, not like this.

One of the masters took a photo of Choi and his son at the airport. Their eyes revealed nothing. Choi, the small stone, remained unchanged. But Jung-Hwa later stared at his father's face so he could ingrain it in his mind. Then he pushed the wheelchair to the departure gate, where someone else rolled it away. When saying goodbye, it is a Korean tradition to keep your eyes on visitors for as long as possible, and Jung-Hwa watched as long as he could, watched his father shrink into the distance.

About a month later, on June 15, 2002, as Choi lay near death in P'yŏngyang, North Korea, he dictated his last will, which Jong-Soo Park heard. Choi appointed his successor then: Chang Ung, the North Korean Olympic representative to whom Kim

Un-yong had been sending money. Chang had been a basketball player, not a martial artist, and he towered over the Tae Kwon Do grandmasters.

As Choi lay there he remembered the wrestler, the ink bottle, the flight to Japan, the hardcore Karate training in the late 1930s. "If only I had been as tall as Mr. Chang Ung I could have had less opponents," he said. "My body was so tiny. There were many opponents."

Later, Park heard him say, "I'm the happiest man in the world, the happiest man in the world."[464]

x x x

Choi Hong-Hi received a state funeral in North Korea, which deeply worried his son because few people received state funerals in that nation, and he wondered if his father had been a spy or double spy. Jung-Hwa knew what to do: he would save his father's name and tell the world that Choi had not been a communist. "We are ready to resurrect him once again," Jung-Hwa told me.[465]

The ITF split into three groups: one led by a dictatorship (run by Chang Ung, based in North Korea), a second led by Jung-Hwa (based in Canada), and a third led by senior black belts who refused to join the other two (based in Europe). Afterwards, court battles raged over trademarks and who owned the ITF name as the three groups eroded into smaller factions. All three promoted their own world cups, pumped their own world champions, and claimed that General Choi was on their side, or would have been. In 2016, it still creeps me out that all three post photos of Choi on their websites and at their gyms, as if he were some sort of saint or cult leader, while they fight each other in courts and the media.

A lawyer involved in one of the trademark lawsuits in 2008 told me that everything seemed to be about money: "Everybody wants to know what they're getting. 'What's my cut?' they ask."[466] But money was only a part of it, however. Individual power, national politics, and historical legacies overshadowed the money because the techniques would thrive far longer than the men.

Choi would be an immortal — certainly in terms of internet hits. He was more sad than saint in the end, but he was a founding member of Tae Kwon Do. His legacy is shadowed by a Confucian father, Japanese torture, Korean dictators, Kim Un-yong, and his own demons. But at least he had avoided prison in his later years. His nemesis, Kim Un-Yong, was not so lucky.

CHAPTER 19

WTF LEADERS GO TO PRISON AND TKD FACES OBLIVION

When Kim Un-yong became vice-president of the International Olympic Committee (IOC) in 2003, he became the second-most powerful ego in the Olympics. Given the controversies and corruption that he had survived, he was perhaps as powerful as a wealthy aristocrat of the *Chosŏn* dynasty. "He had the power to do anything," a Korean sports journalist told *Time* magazine. "He was God."[467]

But this was the twenty-first century, and not even a god could prevent media leaks. In 2003, as Tae Kwon Do limped to the 2004 Olympics, rumours spread about Kim using bribes to finance his run for the IOC vice-presidency, and a worse one began that, in exchange for votes to become vice-president, he had undermined a bid by the South Korean city of P'yŏngch'ang to host the 2010 Winter Olympics. Vancouver won it by fifty-six votes to fifty-three, and Kim became a scapegoat for the loss. The irony must have hurt; Kim and his Operation Thunderbird had brought the Olympics to South Korea in 1988, and his 007 Operation had made Tae Kwon Do an official sport at the 2000 Games. He had helped place his tiny country at the top of the international sports scene — not only in Tae Kwon Do but in many sports — and here he was being accused of betraying his country.

That same year, Kim met Choi's successor, the North Korean Chang Ung, at a sports event called the Summer Universiade. They agreed to organize a joint march during the opening ceremony at the 2004 Athens Olympics, replicating the tear-jerker at the opening ceremony of the 2000 Sydney Olympics, but Kim did not make it to Athens.[468]

South Korean officials raided his home and office and found C$1.6 million in foreign currencies in a safe. Reporters mobbed a white-masked Kim as police led him away. In total, prosecutors discovered C$5 million in gold, diamonds, gems, and foreign currency.

Under attack from all sides, Kim resigned from South Korea's National Assembly and from the World Taekwondo Federation (WTF), from which he had embezzled C$676,000 that had been donated by the Samsung Corporation, the same company that had donated funds for the WTF's home, the Kukkiwon, in 1971.[469] He said that the charges were politically motivated, but he did not explain how.[470] "These suspicions are currently under investigation by legal authorities and the truth will soon come out, but, regardless of the facts, I bow my head in deep apology for distressing the nation with my misconduct," Kim said.[471]

The Olympic Committee suspended him.

Internationally, Olympic Tae Kwon Do was facing its worst crisis in history, and, country by country, Kim's network began crumbling as national associations closed and his Tae Kwon Do friends quit.

In South Korea, prosecutors exposed the overlap between organized crime and Tae Kwon Do. After Kim's resignation from the Korean Tae Kwon Do Association, the KTA had elected a new leader, Koo Cheon-Soo, who was a South Korean politician. In December 2003, police arrested Koo on charges of bribing officials and rigging his KTA election to replace Kim. Prosecutors later indicted Koo, accusing him of using 300 "gangsters and taekwondo experts" to stop rivals from attending the election and of paying over U.S.$20,000 to two association officials ahead of the vote.[472] The seventeen delegates who got past the gangsters voted unanimously for Koo as leader of the KTA.

"The Korean Tae Kwon Do Association has been controlled by politicians and criminal gangs," a prosecutor said. "Bosses have influenced the association since the 1990s," he added. "As pressure grew for them to stop doing so, the gangs pooled efforts to make Mr. Koo the association's chairman."[473]

Also arrested was an adviser to the KTA, Lee Seng-wan, the Tae Kwon Do master who had served time in prison for hiring fifty gangsters to disrupt a pro-democracy political party in 1987. Here he stood again, seventeen years later, sentenced to four years in prison for colluding with Koo and two others to prevent KTA members from attending the association's election.[474]

Big bosses of organized crime rings had always been attracted to Tae Kwon Do's money-generating capacity. Ironically, one of the bosses received bribes from a company making electronic protective gear for the WTF, gear that was supposed to decrease cheating and mistakes in Olympic Tae Kwon Do matches. Police also arrested eleven others in the 2003 roundup: three other crime bosses, one politician, and seven criminals involved in a Tae Kwon Do bribery scandal in Taegu city.

In 2002, a Korean journalist had asked Lee Chong-woo, a WTF vice-president, about gang members in the martial art.[475] Lee replied that gangsters gave Tae Kwon Do a bad name and that he, Lee, was a "sinner" for having allowed them in the organization.

> **REPORTER:** You mean, hiring people [gang members] for occasions such as General Assembly Meetings or Board of Director Meetings . . . ?
>
> **LEE:** It is not just for that. There were numerous occasions [sic] disrupted by insignificant issues. In order to ease such a situation, sometimes making these people visible made for better circumstances.
>
> **REPORTER:** You mean, they entered [the organization] because of the age-old factions in Tae Kwon Do?
>
> **LEE:** That's right.

In 2006, Lee Seng-wan (on left) presented an award to Lee Chong-woo, the leader of Olympic Taekwondo who had lamented about the number of gangsters involved in the martial art. PHOTO COURTESY OF JEONG SOON-CHEON.

Choi Hong-Hi and his men no doubt led one of those "age-old factions." Lee ended the interview by lamenting, "For the second stage of Tae Kwon Do, a successor for Un Yong Kim should have come along a day earlier."

A year after this pitiable statement, a North Korean official sent a fax to Kim's office in Seoul, reminding him that he was behind in his "payments" to North Korean Olympic official Chang Ung, the head of Choi's International Taekwon-Do Federation in the dictatorship. Kim, facing jail, told prosecutors about the fax.[476]

In June 2004, two months before the Summer Olympics, a South Korean court found Kim guilty of embezzling more than U.S.$3 million from sports organisations and accepting more than U.S.$700,000 in bribes.[477] Prosecutors accused him of turning his Tae Kwon Do and Olympic organizations into private enterprises and sentenced him to two and a half years in prison — and ordered him to pay a fine of more than U.S.$600,000.[478] His appeal to Korea's Supreme Court shortened the sentence to two years.

His supporters said the investigation and jail term were part of a political vendetta and that Kim was a scapegoat for South Korea's failed bid to win the 2010 Winter Olympics, but no one provided details.[479]

Meanwhile, the U.S. Olympic Committee side-kicked the U.S. Taekwondo Union out of the Olympics, citing a lengthy list of problems with competitions, governance, and finances. Since

1984, the USTU had been head of the WTF in the U.S., a pillar of global Tae Kwon Do from the beginning. The USTU's president, Sang-Chul Lee, a friend of Kim Un-yong's, stepped down during the turmoil, and soon the entire USTU was abolished, along with all fifty state organizations. Around U.S.$1.2 million was missing, and so the lawsuits began.

Non-Korean Tae Kwon Do experts in the U.S. took the opportunity to talk about their disenfranchisement, about the times they were ignored for WTF positions because they were not Korean, and about the ethnocentrism in a martial art that unfairly favoured Koreans.[480] When the battlefield cleared in 2006, the old dysfunctional Tae Kwon Do was gone and a supposedly new organization, USA Taekwondo (USAT), had replaced Lee's organization. USAT paid the U.S.$1.2 million back to the Olympic Committee and established a commission to improve things, especially to bring back the hundreds of pioneers and instructors who had not been corrupt.[481]

"Only a handful of people messed up the organization," said Joon-Pyo Choi, co-chairman of the commission, "but they eliminated all the Korean-American masters and grandmasters who were pioneers in Tae Kwon Do in the USA since the 1950s. That was a big mistake."[482]

The infighting and resignations spread to other countries.

In Canada, Wayne Mitchell, secretary general of the WTF, became heavily involved with the organization during this difficult time: "For Canada, it changed," he said, "and for the WTF it did when Kim Un-yong got caught with his hand in the till, which led to an emergency situation and the IOC saying, 'Clean up your act.' I think a lot of people stood up to the plate and said, 'Enough is enough.'" He added, "Sport Canada was going to stop our funding; we changed our constitution to a democratic one. The new push with the new president is openness and accountability. For the first time ever, you see budgets and books and audits."[483]

This was after fifty years of Tae Kwon Do.

I asked him why there was so much corruption. "I'm wondering if it's the time period they come from," Mitchell replied, "because Kim Un-yong was from the secret service . . . and, you know, South Korea was far from democratic, even though they called it that for a long time."

In the early 1960s, Kim had begun his career in a haze of espionage and corruption rooted in a South Korean dictatorship. Forty years later, he ended his career in the same way but the shadiness rooted in a democracy instead. He and his allies left behind a Tae Kwon Do riddled with organized crime and organized cheating.

"We've moved into a business age," Mitchell said. "It's far smarter to run those organizations like businesses rather than like criminal organizations or an extension of that sort of thing."

That was likely wishful thinking. In 2015, ten years after I first interviewed him, Mitchell was president of Taekwondo Canada and was still issuing statements asking people to trust the WTF: "There are some very serious challenges to overcome in order to build Taekwondo Canada in a positive manner. We wish to build trust and participation," he wrote in an open letter posted in October 2015 on the WTF organization's website.[484]

x x x

After such trials in the WTF, how could its new international president, Choue Chung-won, step into the job with his chin up, even with his martial arts training? Choue had been an executive council member of the Korea Tae Kwon Do Association in the corrupt years since 1999, president of a university from 1996 to 2003, and an architect of a Tae Kwon Do department at that same school.[485]

After winning 106 out of 149 votes from WTF member countries, Choue told the media during his presidential acceptance speech that "now is the time for us to be reborn as a multinational sports organization," as if it were not already multinational.[486] More to the point, he also announced that each member country would receive U.S.$20,000 and each continental Tae Kwon Do union U.S.$50,000 as a "reform fund" from the IOC, as if there was not enough money flowing into vague funds already. Two months later, he met North Korean Tae Kwon Do head Chang

Ung at the 2004 Athens Olympic Games, where South and North Korea joined hands, just as Kim Un-yong had planned.

The immediate challenge for Choue was how to keep Tae Kwon Do in the Olympics because the IOC was considering dropping the sport after the 2004 Summer Games, likely not because of the financial corruption and unfair judging but because of boring sparring matches and the resulting low television ratings. Fighters in Olympic Tae Kwon Do spend most of their bouts bouncing around looking at each other, arms dangling at their sides like noodles.

At the end of 2004, the WTF's new president, Choue, released a 188-page strategic plan that would make Tae Kwon Do more transparent and less boring.[487] He became the first president of the Korea Fair Play Committee (KFPC) in 2005, countering cheating claims: "Fair play is a really important thing," Choue told a reporter. I wonder if Kim Un-yong heard this trope after he was released on parole in 2005 after serving about a year of his two-year sentence.[488]

In any case, the cheating continued. The International Olympic Committee voted for Tae Kwon Do to remain in the Olympics for the 2008, 2012 and 2016 Games, thanks to long negotiations, rich Korean companies, and IOC officials "greasing the wheels with money," as a former negotiator told me. And athletes and coaches still had to navigate potential cheating during bouts. At the 2008 Olympics, for example, they faced so much cheating that a frustrated Cuban competitor kicked a referee in the head after being disqualified for no good reason. The athlete's coach also struck the referee. The WTF took only half an hour to ban both men from Tae Kwon Do for life, in contrast to the weeks and months it usually takes to release rulings about allegations of cheating and corruption.[489]

The 2008 Olympics was a new low for Tae Kwon Do. One of the competitors, Steven Lopez, was also fed up, and he and his coach, Herb Perez, explained exactly how some of the shenanigans took place: before the Olympics, Perez was asked to sign an agreement promising not to file protests at the Olympics, and after a controversial judging call in Lopez's gold-medal match, officials asked Perez not to talk to the press. He refused, explaining the cheating to journalists.[490] But such coach-muzzling tactics must have worked afterwards, as very few coaches complained about the 2012 Summer Olympics.

To decrease judging problems during matches, the WTF had adopted electronic protective body gear for sparring, so that computers, instead of referees, scored matches.[491] The gear records a kick and tallies the score. Unfortunately, the equipment was open to electronic tampering and made the sparring even more boring, as witnessed during the 2012 Olympics in London and the world championships afterwards. Also, martial artists had to buy even more equipment, much of it sanctioned by the WTF, so rumours of financial kickbacks and Olympic cheating continued.[492]

The corruption, cheating, and chaos are not surprising. Tae Kwon Do was born into controversy and thrived among soldiers, gangsters, and secret-service agents for most of its life, even into 2016. Choi Hong-Hi and Kim Un-yong are now gone, but their disciples and legacies continue, as do the struggles to stop corruption and cheating. Perhaps the most surreal development was in 2008, when Lee Seng-wan announced that he had become a director of the Kukkiwon, the world headquarters of Olympic Tae Kwon Do. Lee, who had been imprisoned for working with 300 gangsters and martial artists to disrupt a Tae Kwon Do election in 2002, said that it was time for the Kukkiwon "to reevaluate their personnel and get rid of those who are corrupted."[493] Coming from a convicted criminal, the irony was so blatant that it could mean only one thing: the turf wars in Tae Kwon Do were not yet over.

For decades, Tae Kwon Do's leaders have run the martial art like a cult or a crime syndicate — headed by gods or godfathers — so it is heartening that no one has been recently caught stealing more than C$1 million or planning to assassinate someone.

Still, North Korea uses Tae Kwon Do in its diplomatic and spy missions, and South Korea and its Olympic allies still make vague, multi-million dollar sponsorship deals, but things seem to be getting better — unless, of course, people are just being more careful.

CHAPTER 20

CULTS AND CRIMINALS VS. C. K. CHOI

When I walked into the backrooms of Tae Kwon Do, I discovered a group of soldiers, country boys, and bullies preaching a mix of Confucian clichés and barroom bullshit. But for every one of them, there were always others, like Grandmaster Chang Keun (C. K.) Choi.[494] There are many heroes in Tae Kwon Do, many masters who stood up to stupid spies and gods and gangsters, many who refused to become corrupt or violent — and these masters went on to lead millions of people who empowered themselves through Tae Kwon Do. C. K. Choi is one such hero.

In 1962, as a twenty-one-year-old, he won the world's first Tae Kwon Do championship in sparring and patterns, during a time when bare-knuckled sparring was popular. He won in 1963 as well. He trained day and night and taught the art to soldiers and civilians. He also helped General Choi (no relation) to create Tae Kwon Do patterns in the 1960s and travelled the world with him during national demonstrations from 1972 to 1982, promoting and building Tae Kwon Do. For fifty years he developed training systems for the body and mind, and he wrote books about techniques and morality. He symbolizes everything inspiring about Tae Kwon Do.

The Bodhidharma once said that the farther away you are from the truth, the worse your life becomes and the better you feel; self-deception, like good whiskey, helps to get through delusion,

Throughout his career, C. K. Choi advocated for flexibility and conditioning in both body and mind. PHOTO COURTESY OF CHOI.

corruption, and violence. C. K. Choi does not drink though, so it was a shock to discover that this man with the thick glasses and gentle voice had opened a bar in the roughest part of Vancouver, Canada, in 1987.

Before that, he had stood up to Korean CIA agents when they tried to force him to support South Korea's World Taekwondo Federation in the 1970s. And he had stood up to General Choi when the elder became friends with North Korea's brutal regime in the early 1980s. But long after C. K. Choi moved from South Korea to Canada, he tried to make a living at the Sunrise Hotel, located at Hastings and Main streets in Vancouver — and he had to fight Canadian gangsters and drug dealers for ten months to do so. That year was one of the most challenging of his life.

The hotel was in a desperate state when the forty-six-year-old Choi first saw it. All the windows were blacked out, drug dealers did business inside, and a jailed criminal was threatening to kill the owner. The owner wanted to sell the place as soon as possible, but no one would buy it. One of Choi's Tae Kwon Do students was a police officer and had warned Choi not to purchase it because even the police avoided going inside. At the time, Choi was running a small Tae Kwon Do gym, but he needed to earn a better living. He bought the Sunrise Hotel as a real estate investment, in spite of warnings.

His first conflict was with a fellow who wanted to stay the night. The Sunrise Hotel had many empty rooms, but Choi asked him to leave because he was being rowdy. The man stood up and threw two punches at Choi, who deked out of the way.

"Don't do that," Choi calmly said.

The man tried to punch him again, and Choi moved and hit him. The man fell like a tree.

As a waiter dragged the fellow to the road, a few other gangsters in the bar asked Choi how he had punched the man because they had not seen the technique. They and other gangsters soon discovered that Choi was a Tae Kwon Do master, so, of course, they began picking on him.

Before most challenges, Choi would explain that he was only

trying to clean up the place and make a living. Men tried to bully him anyway, because the old bar had been their hangout and a spot to deal drugs, and they did not like Choi telling them what to do. It did not help that journalists were reporting that the Sunrise Hotel had changed for the better.

One day, a friend of a Hell's Angels biker was drinking in the bar. Choi had renovated the place by now; it was clean and bright, and the fights were easing off as business was picking up. He was sweeping garbage from the floor when he saw a fellow drinking with his dirty boots on a chair.

"Please take your feet off the chair," Choi asked politely.

The man refused, so Choi pulled the chair from under his boots. The man stood up. Choi saw that he had some muscle and put down his dustpan and broom. Most men who attacked Choi were big, just like this fellow. The man took off his jacket.

"Are you ready?" Choi asked.

"Yes," the man said.

Choi had kept his distance, as he usually did in such conflicts, but he sprang forward like a tiger and punched the fellow on the side of the face. The man fell, unconscious.

"Hey, he's better than Bruce Lee!" someone yelled.

When the man came to, he stood up and looked at Choi.

"Please finish your drink and leave," Choi said. The fellow offered to shake his hand. "Not today," Choi said.

There were no broken bones because Choi had hit him on the side of the face, not the front. He was a good enough martial artist that he could pick his targets, and a good enough person that he did not disable anyone. But the fights were more than physical; they were emotional, psychological, and racial. People would yell, "You, Chinaman, go home!" and he'd reply, "I'm not a Chinaman. I'm a good Canadian. I work hard and pay taxes so you can get your welfare cheques." Some men laughed, some tried to hurt him, and some wanted to kill him.

Choi was always reasonable with his challengers, but he kept his eyes open after a fight, as men sometimes returned with knives

In his seventies, C. K. Choi still trains and teaches black belts around the world.
PHOTO COURTESY OF CHOI.

and guns. Once, a man showed up and demanded to know why Choi had beat up his friend.

"He hit my waiter first," Choi said.

"Oh," said the man. "Thanks for explaining. I was going to kill you." And he left.

Finally, after ten months of these challenges, word got around that Choi was a reasonable man. He realized that most of the gangsters were not bad if he spoke to them one-on-one and if he did not step on their pride. Patrons learned that if they did not do stupid things, they could stay at the Sunrise. The place became a success, and Choi sold it two years later, making a profit and turning the Sunrise Hotel into a thriving business free of gangsters.

I tell this story because it shows a simple truth about Tae Kwon Do: Choi used it to minimize violence and to empower himself and those around him, just as so many others had in Korea, Vietnam, the U.S., Germany, and the many other countries where it took off in the late 1950s and 1960s. He is now seventy-seven years old and still travels the world, inspiring and supporting Tae Kwon Do instructors and trying to unify his mangled martial art. When you know about the violence, corruption, and cheating that goes on in the fighting arts — and the number of egos involved — you can imagine how hard his job is. He does not have his own organization and refuses to head one, and he uses his words rather than his fists these days.

Once, in Vancouver in 2006, he was sitting at a table of masters and grandmasters from Olympic Tae Kwon Do.

"When your students ask you who is the founder of Tae Kwon Do, what do you say?" Choi asked.

"It's a long story," one master said.

"No, it's not," Choi said. "If you tell the truth, the answer will be in one sentence."

The master did not respond. Choi has heard similar things in the past, in other countries.

"They all know where Tae Kwon Do came from," he told me in 2015, "but they say it's an old art about two thousand years old — and they talk a lot of nonsense." In his view, the founder of Tae Kwon Do is General Choi Hong-Hi, who received help from pioneer instructors such as C. K. Choi.

Today, Choi is continuing their work. His goals are to maintain the high standards of the art (as they were conceived in the early days) and to unify gyms and associations (or at least to make them open to each other). He works with the Tae Kwon Do Association of Great Britain, which has 20,000 members, and with Darin Gibson's United Traditional Tae Kwon-Do Canada, among others.[495] Most national and international associations do not allow you to train, compete, or test at other gyms. Some of my own instructors have disowned me because I organized events with other instructors. These attitudes frustrate Choi. He has often said it is not in keeping with the true spirit of Tae Kwon Do.

The corruption, cheating, and shenanigans in Tae Kwon Do make life difficult for unrecognized heroes like C. K. Choi, especially when dealing with Olympic egos. In 2010, the president of Olympic Tae Kwon Do invited Choi to a reunion of Tae Kwon

Colin Nonomura (on left) and Darin Gibson (middle) help C. K. Choi test black belts during a test in 2015. PHOTO COURTESY OF GIBSON.

Do's pioneer instructors in South Korea — yet another attempt to show that the World Taekwondo Federation (WTF) was in the process of finally recognizing Tae Kwon Do's pioneers and finally opening Olympic events to all their students. The WTF had been harassing or ignoring the pioneers and their students for so long that Choi did not think much of the invitation, but Hoss Rafaty, "special assistant" to the WTF president, called Choi to say that the WTF would treat the pioneers like heroes in South Korea. Choi believed him. He met Rafaty at a large tournament in 2011 in the U.S., and Rafaty seemed genuinely concerned about the closed-mindedness and greed in Tae Kwon Do.[496]

I interviewed Hoss at that same tournament, in Dallas, Texas, in 2011. He had begun training with one of the International Taekwon-Do Federations (ITF) in the U.S. while running a large ice cream distribution business. He stopped training because he hates violence, he told me, but he was still committed to unifying the WTF with various ITF groups, and he spent more time on Tae Kwon Do than on ice cream. In fact, his life's work seemed to be unification.

Gibson breaks concrete slabs during his Tae Kwon Do test for his eighth-degree black belt in 2015. PHOTO COURTESY OF GIBSON.

"What about the corrupt Kukkiwon?" I asked him, referring to the governing body for the WTF. Parts of the Kukkiwon had been corrupt from day one, and a lot of money flowed from it to the WTF.

"I suggested that the Kukkiwon be cut off," Hoss said, "but people insisted, 'Give us three years to clean it up.'"

"There are Korean gangsters in the Kukkiwon," I replied.

"Yes, but they were kicked out nine months ago," he said.

"Really?" I said. "I heard that they were still there."

"True," he replied. "They have stooges there, but they'll be out."

I admired Rafaty's optimism in 2011 — as well as his generosity. There were wicked tensions between the WTF and the Kukkiwon, but if anyone had a shot at helping, it was Rafaty. He was a successful businessman who had financed the 2011 Dallas tournament (which would lose a lot of money), funded two Tae Kwon Do history films (which were never finished), and poured money into a couple of Tae Kwon Do museums (which were never opened).

Rafaty promised C. K. Choi that the WTF would treat him like a hero at a South Korean celebration for Tae Kwon Do pioneers. The humble Choi did not need that sort of treatment, and he had been through such WTF events before, but he asked for an agenda of some kind. What would the pioneer instructors do while in South Korea for example? Rafaty said that someone would send a document, but all Choi received was a short letter from Rafaty's boss, WTF president Choue Chung-won, that began, "It is with great pleasure that we invite you to the WTF offices in Seoul, Korea, for March 21–23. Please join us in a celebration honouring you, along with a select group of other original, pioneer grandmasters for your contributions as sons of Korea." There was no agenda. Choi refused to go.

Other pioneers did go, including grandmasters Nam Tae-hi and Kong Young-il. However, no one met them at the airport, and there was no media conference. Choi was not surprised. In addition to the WTF downplaying the roles of Tae Kwon Do's pioneers, it rarely welcomes the students (even the world champions) from the pioneers' associations. Rafaty tried to make the Olympics more inclusive, but the head of the WTF said that he did not have the power to intervene in national affairs. And that was that. The same attitude made front pages around the world when, in 2012, the WTF in the U.K. barred Aaron Cook from trying out for the U.K. Olympic team because of a coaching disagreement. The WTF itself had ranked him as the number-one fighter in his category in the world. When he could not compete in the 2012 Olympic Games in London he began a protest campaign.

"It's the same old story," Choi told me of the WTF and the Olympics. "There's no substance behind the talk."

In 2015, the WTF promoted Hoss Rafaty to secretary general, the second-most powerful position in the Olympic martial art. And leaders on all sides — WTF, ITF, and others — still insult each other, criticize each other's students, destroy each other's reputations, sue each other in court, and, when they really get going, threaten each other physically.

"The problem with Tae Kwon Do masters or instructors is that they aren't willing to help others," Choi said in his understated way. He has not given up, and around the world, dozens of pioneers like him have not given up. Given what they have survived, these instructors, more than anyone, represent Tae Kwon Do's tenet of indomitable spirit.

In the meantime, Rafaty announced that the World Taekwondo Federation is likely rebranding itself as World Taekwondo, because the acronym WTF also means What the Fuck.[497]

x x x

Perhaps the most promising developments in the past decade were two North Korean Tae Kwon Do demonstrations in the U.S. (if you ignored the secret-service agents watching the North Korean athletes and each other during the events). The 2007 and 2011 tours were a spectacular demonstration of political diplomacy and the best of Tae Kwon Do (if you ignored the fact that the North Korean athletes might be tortured if they failed in any way). The elite athletes demonstrated tremendous power in breaking boards and showing self-defense techniques. One Korean woman broke her arm while trying to break a concrete block. She raised her finger, as if to ask the audience to give her one more chance — and she smashed the brick. Afterwards, officials rushed her to an emergency room in Cedar Rapids, Iowa, but only after someone called the State Department to avoid an international incident between North Korea and the United States.

Recently, the WTF invited this same North Korean demonstration team to South Korea, part of an exchange of demonstrations. Ri Yong-son, the new president of the North Korean International Taekwon-Do Federation, said that the WTF and ITF would follow an agreement signed with International Olympic Committee President Thomas Bach to respect each other, organize exchanges, and allow athletes to compete in any competition.[498] Such initiatives promote "harmony, friendship and peace," as one press release noted, as though the United States does not have nuclear bombs circling North Korea and North Korea is not trying to develop a bomb of its own.

Once again, Tae Kwon Do is being used to do the impossible: reunite warring countries. But any talk of such mergers and exchanges involves money — a lot of money — which is perhaps the point of such events. Recently, the WTF and the Booyoung Group, a real estate company, signed an agreement for Booyoung to provide a record U.S.$10 million to the WTF over the next six years. Press releases did not mention what the money was for and what the WTF would give in return.[499] Booyoung is owned by one of the richest men in Korea, who was released from prison in 2007 after serving three years for embezzling funds.

Today, much of Tae Kwon Do continues to be run as either a cult or a crime syndicate. In 2012, the North Korean ITF built a museum called the Tae Kwon Do Sanctuary, or as one obsequious magazine put it, "The center of the Taekwon-Do holy land." There, people prostrate themselves in front of Choi Hong-Hi's gravestone. Meanwhile, in Olympic Tae Kwon Do, people tell me that the original nine Tae Kwon Do gyms (the *kwans* in South Korea that merged into the World Taekwondo Federation) are still organized like mafia clans or syndicates.

In 2015, tensions are still running high between the WTF, the Kukkiwon, and the newly built Taekwondowon complex in South

Korea — all three operating separately and in competition for the millions of dollars flowing from the Olympics and from sales of Tae Kwon Do paraphernalia.

Pioneer instructors such as C. K. Choi do not have time for such monumental shenanigans and shady million-dollar deals. Working in obscurity to unite their martial art and to teach original Tae Kwon Do, rebels like Choi empower people though their individual acts. I still picture him walking among children and adults at the three or four tournaments that I have attended with him. He often talks to people at ringside or in the stands long after other masters and grandmasters have returned to their hotel rooms. He sometimes gives the students pointers while laughing, kicking, and punching in his suit and tie, as if he was twenty-one years old again and the martial art did not have a care in the world.

CHAPTER 21

REPRIEVE

When I used to take my ten-year-old daughter to our neighbourhood Olympic Tae Kwon Do gym for her class, we would walk down concrete stairs to a huge basement with padded floors, and we would see Choi Hong-Hi's five tenets in foot-high Korean calligraphy on the walls:

> Loyalty to the king
> Filial love toward one's parents
> Fidelity in friendship
> Bravery in battle
> No unnecessary violence

On a table near the gym office lay a Tae Kwon Do book by Kim Un-yong, and on another wall hung pages of martial arts patterns. Around the world, the work of Kim, Choi, and their pioneers lives on in gyms like this one. Their legacies — good and bad — live in books and hang on walls. My daughter did not know the history, but she practised and had fun anyway.

Often, after class, as she and I would walk home, we would talk about Tae Kwon Do. Today she is eighteen years old and jogs and practises yoga, but in those days we would sometimes train together and chat about martial arts in that way that ten-year-olds talk (everything concrete and just).

"How's the book?" she asked me one evening after class. We were walking along the street, still hot from the punching and kicking at the dojang.

"Fine," I said. "Almost done." She knew I was writing about the men who had started the martial art and the crazy things they had done.

"Were those men bad, Dad?" she asked.

For a second I did not say anything. I usually reserved "bad" or "evil" for murderers and people like them.

"Not all of them were bad," I said. "Some tried their best. They came from a world that's completely different from ours."

"Where?" she asked.

"Korea — old Korea," I said.

"What was it like?" she asked. As we walked along, it got darker outside, but we felt good — that feeling after a workout, when your feet are solid on the ground, your muscles strong, and your confidence peaking — "feeling jumpy," as my daughter would put it.

"Old Korea is hard to understand," I said. "It's on the other side of the world, near China. Tae Kwon Do started with a crazy poker game in 1938, when a young man lost all the money that his mother had given him for school."

"What was his name?" she asked, surprised.

"Hong-Hi was his first name," I said. "His family was very strict, and they didn't have a lot of money. They were so strict you wouldn't believe it. He snuck out of his room one day to go play poker. He lost all the money for his education. His mother had actually warned him not to, but he did."

"Are you serious?" she said.

"Yeah, he was twenty years old, so he should have known better," I said. "After the game, he didn't know what to do. He sat there, looking at a wrestler who had won all the money. Hong-Hi was short — he was about as tall as you — and the wrestler was huge. That's where the bottle of ink came in. Hong-Hi grabbed the bottle, which was near him, and threw it at the wrestler. The bottle hit him in the forehead."

"Wow," she said. "That sounds bad."

"Yeah, it does," I said, "but it has a happy ending."

ENDNOTES

PEOPLE

1 Interview by emails with Dakin Burdick (Jan. 2002).

INTRODUCTION

2 Cumings (2005), p. 61.
3 Choi (1999), p. 525.
4 Kim (2002), p. 5.
5 *Globe and Mail* (Sep. 19, 2001), p. A17.
6 Choi (c. 2000), v. 2, p. 90.
7 Interviews, Jong-Soo Park, from 2001 to 2008.
8 Choi (c. 2000), v. 2, pp. 241, 360. Also, interviews with his children: Meeyun Colomvakos, Sunny Choi, and Jung-Hwa Choi.
9 Interviews, Jung-Hwa Choi (May and Apr. 2003).
10 Choi tried to hide the Karate roots for fifty years. Many Tae Kwon Do grandmasters, including Tae Kwon Do pioneers Nam Tae-hi, Jhoon Rhee, and Duk-Sung Son, have acknowledged the Karate origins.

CHAPTER ONE

11 This scene is from my interviews with Choi's family and details in his memoir (c. 2000), v. 1, pp. 19–55, 34, 71–96, and v. 2, p. 469.
12 Child marriage was a common practice in this part of the world. Choi rarely spoke about his first wife and daughter and did not include them in the first two volumes of his memoirs. I interviewed his first daughter, Song-Jook Choi (May 30, 2003). I also interviewed Choi's friend from the 1940s regarding the family: Lim (Aug. 17, 2002).
13 The Japanese characters for his family name are "Nishiyama," a common name. The name is found in a 1945 court document from the Second World War. His full name was Yuseki Nishiyama, which means "brave stone of the west mountain."
14 Choi (c. 2000), v.1, pp. 26–28.
15 Phap Lu told me this in interview. Jung-Hwa Choi also made the same point.
16 All details of the poker game are from Choi (c. 2000), p. 71.
17 The instructor was Han Il-Dong, and he taught Choi for a year, but there's no record of Han and

no one in T'aekkyŏn has ever heard of him. For more about T'aekkyŏn in general, see Hendrik Rubbeling (2014), Young (1993), p. 53. Ouyang (1997), p. 77.

18 As Cumings (2005) puts it on pp. 21–22, "When they [Koreans] say, 'I think,' they point to their chest. Mind is mind-and-heart or *sim*, a visceral knowledge that joins thought with emotion."

19 Cumings (2005), p. 147.

20 Choi (c. 2000), p. 20.

21 Funakoshi (1988), p. 26.

22 Draeger (1974), p. 12.

23 Choi (1999), p. 14.

24 Also, Choi never published the full name of his Karate instructor and did not explain what he learned. In addition, his right-hand man for decades, Nam Tae-hi, rarely saw him practise martial arts techniques. Interview, Madis (Feb. 1, 2011). See also Madis's article, "Storming the Fortress: A History of Taekwondo. Part Four: The First Korean Schools: The Maverick Schools," published in 2012. Retrieved from the Web in October 2015 (www.fightingarts.com/reading/article.php?id=686). Madis writes: "At that time, it took even exceptional students two years of regular training to achieve the rank of shodan (Japanese: "first degree black belt"; Korean: chodan) according to Hironishi Genshin, one of Funakoshi's premier students in the 1930s and 1940s (Takagi, 1989)."

CHAPTER TWO

25 Song (date unknown), pp. 376–79.

26 Details in this chapter are from Choi Hong-Hi (c. 2000), v. 1, pp. 123–94.

27 Oh (2001), pp. 3–19.

28 Choi (c.2001), v. 1, pp. 130–38. I obtained historical facts from Song (date unknown), p. 2, and interview with Palmer (Jan. 2005).

29 Interview, Lim (Aug. 17, 2002).

30 This dubious story is according to the soldier: Cha (date unknown), p. 30.

31 Choi (c. 2000), v. 1, pp. 148-50.

32 P'yŏngyang Military Court (1945), p. 2.

33 Cumings (2005), pp. 178–79.

34 Levine (2000), pp. 144–45.

35 Interview, Lim (Aug. 17, 2002).

36 Cumings (2005), p. 187.

37 Cumings (2005), p. 198.

38 Interview, Lim (Aug. 17, 2002).

39 Cumings (2005), p. 207.

40 Choi (c. 2000), v. 1, pp. 218–24.

41 Funakoshi (1988), p. 24.

42 Dohrenwend (1997), p. 4.

43 Interviews with Choi's daughters, Meeyun Colomvakos and Sunny Choi (Aug. 22, 2002).

44 Interview, Lim (Aug. 17, 2002).

45 Choi (c. 2000), v. 1, p. 234.

46 Interview, Choi (Mar. 2001).

47 Interview, Colomvakos (Nov. 20, 2002).

CHAPTER THREE

48 Hessler (2001), p. 146.

49 As Cumings (2004) put it: "complete devastation between the Yalu River and the capital" (p. 19).

50 Interview, Lim (Aug. 2002). Choi (c. 2000), v. 1, p. 345.

51 Interviews: Jhoon Rhee (Nov. 2007); Lim Sun-ha and Sandy Lim (Aug. 2002); and Song-Jook Choi (May 30, 2003).

52 The men were called the *yangban*. Cumings (2005), p. 237, and Boettcher (1980), p. 11.

53 Details about Nam in this chapter are from interviews with him (2001 to 2008) and military records. Many martial arts grandmasters, such as Nguyen Van Binh (Aug. 11, 2006) and Jong-Soo Park (Feb. 21, 2008), told me about Nam's experiences during the Korean War.

54 The battalion was in South Korea's 6th Division. Nam was in the 12th Company of the Third Battalion.

55 Nam's battle is well known in South Korea, and the Culture and Welfare Bureau promotes it for children's tours; see "Yongmun Mountain Battle" at the Demilitarized Zone website at kids.dmz.ne.kr/time/time21.asp (retrieved from the Web on Jan. 10, 2016). Other sources on the battle: Song (2004), Seo (2008), and the National Institute of Korean History, which is based in South Korea.

56 In total, two battalions fought for three days on plateaus 353 and 427, according to interviews with Nam Tae-hi, and documents from Song (2004), Seo (2008), and other sources.

57 Interview, Nam (July 2011).

58 Interview, Nam (Dec. 2001).

59 Guo and Kennedy (2004), p. 32.

60 Weiss (2000), pp. 82–84, and Dohrenwend (1997), p. 1.

61 He once announced that he was the founder of Tae Kwon Do, but the claim has been widely disputed. Eric Madis wrote a good essay that reviews his life, rank, and accomplishments: "Storming the Fortress: A History of Taekwondo. Part Two: The First Korean Schools: The Shotokan Schools; Lee Won-kuk and the Chungdokwan," published in 2010. Retrieved from the Web on Jan. 10, 2016. (fightingarts.com/reading/article.php?id=661).

62 Much of this paragraph is from Kang and Lee (1999), pp. 1–3, and Simpkins and Simpkins (2002), p. 6.

63 Talbott (1999), p. 1. The hand techniques do not add to ten, but Lee's point was that there were a small number of techniques.

64 Quotes from Nam in this and the next three paragraphs are from my interview with him in Dec. 2001.

65 Nam and Choi told me about some of the first men who arrived for training. Suk-kyu, Woo Jong-Lim (who would train many great instructors), and Han Cha-gyo (who could jump over the shoulders of a standing opponent) (from Choi [c. 2000], v. 2, p. 96). Also from the Chung Do Kwan were Chang Keun (C. K.) Choi, who helped to create Tae Kwon Do, and Jhoon Goo Rhee, who would later befriend Bruce Lee and rule a Tae Kwon Do empire in the U.S. (from interviews: C. K. Choi [Oct. 31, 2007] and Jhoon Rhee [Nov. 2007]). In addition, many famous athletes from the Chung Do Kwan soon taught or trained with Nam, including Uhm Woon-kyu and Lee Chong-woo (both leaders of Olympic Tae Kwon Do later on) and Hyun Jong-myung (who helped to develop the Olympic style) (from Kang and Lee [1999], p. 2 and throughout).

66 Burdick (1997), p. 39.

67 Cumings (2005), p. 97. the *New York Herald* called this battle "Little War with the Heathen."

68 Choi (1960), p. 20. Interviews with Nam Tae-hi (Dec. 2001).

69 Young (no date): Retrieved from the Web in 2008. (www.blackbeltmag.com/archives/482).

70 Interviews with Nam Tae-hi (2001), Joe Cariati (Jan. 23, 2002), and Parmar Rai (Jan. 23, 2002), and C. K. Choi (Nov. 2007), among others.

71 Song (2004), p. 1.

72 Choi (1960), p. 20, and interview with Nam (Dec. 2001).

73 Ouyang (1997), p.77–79.

74 Cumings (2005), pp. 302–303.

75 Kimm (2000), p. 49.

76 Interview, Rubbeling (Sept. 2012). Young (1993), pp. 61–67, and Ouyang (1997), p. 79.
77 Choi (c. 2000), v. 1, p. 423.
78 C. K. Choi (2007), p. 80, and interviews with Nam (Dec. 2001) and Choi Hong-Hi (Mar. 2001).
79 Choi (c. 2000), v. 1, pp. 428–29, and Simpkins and Simpkins (2002), p. 5.
80 Kang and Lee (1999), p. 11.
81 Choi (1960), p. 21.

CHAPTER FOUR

82 Choi (c. 2000) writes that the meeting took place in a *kisaeng* house, and Nam told me it was the Kugīlgwan *kisaeng* house. Much has been written about the meeting but not the meeting place: Kimm (2000), p. 49; Kang and Lee (1999), p. 12; and C. K. Choi (2007), p. 81. Unless otherwise footnoted, details in this chapter are from Choi (c. 2000), v. 1, 435–37, and interviews with Nam Tae-hi.
83 Many Korean-language sources provide details about the Kugīlgwan and the personalities there:
   1) National Institute of Korean History; retrieved from Web in 2008 (www.history.go.kr/en/main/main.do);
   2) a five-volume culture and history collection from the South Korean government; retrieved from Web in 2008 (seoul600.visitseoul.net);
   3) an article by Yi Pom-jin in the March 20, 2005, issue of *Chugan Chosŏn*; retrieved from Web in 2008 (magazine.chosun.com);
   4) "Thirty-year-old tradition of kisaeng house," in *Minju Sinmun* (May 9, 2006), a Seoul newspaper; and
   5) an article called Pak Maria (who was Yi Ki-bung's wife) from the History Liberation Campaign Centre; retrieved from Web on Jan. 10, 2016 (bluecabin.com.ne.kr/split99/pmaria.htm).
84 See Cumings (2005), p. 356–57, for a caricature of *kisaeng*-loving politicians of this period.
85 Burdick (1997), p. 37–38, lists the meetings.
86 Hyun Jong-myung, who later became part of the World Taekwondo Federation.
87 Choi (c. 2000), p. 435.
88 Choi (c. 2000), p. 436.
89 Interview, Nam (Apr. 17, 2006).
90 Choi (c. 2000), v. 1, p. 436–38. Interview, Jung-Hwa Choi (Jan. 2002). Young (1993) outlines the myths that connect the two arts. Many martial arts leaders subsequently wrote about these myths as though they were reality; Chun (2006), pp. 6–10, for example. However, C. K. Choi (2007) comes closest to the truth.
91 Young (1993), pp. 51–59.
92 "Preface" of Choi (1960) and pp. 18–20 of Choi (1988).
93 Rutt (1961), p. 2, 7, 10–11, 19–20, 53, 63. Also, interview with Rubbeling (October 2014).
94 Rutt (1961), p. 28.
95 Interview, Rubbeling (October 2014).
96 Choi (c. 2000), p. 438.
97 Choi (c. 2000), v. 1, pp. 478–87.
98 "Preface" of Choi (1960).
99 Along with "front stance," "back stance," and "horse stance." Funakoshi (1988), pp. 53–61. Choi (1960).
100 Compare Choi (1960), pp. 73–75, to Funakoshi (1988), p. 53.
101 See for example Choi (1960).
102 Quotes about the *hwarang* in this paragraph are from Choi (1960).

103 C. K. Choi (2007), p. 85, lists the men involved.
104 Interview with C. K. Choi.

CHAPTER FIVE

105 Choi's version of the widely reported coup is in Choi (c. 2000), v. 1, pp. 567–86.
106 Choi (c. 2000), v. 1, pp. 567–86.
107 Cumings (2005), pp. 355–56.
108 Cumings (2003).
109 Park Chong-kyu, Kim Chŏng-p'il, and Kim Hyung-wook were some of the powerful men.
110 Kim (2002), p. 219, 227. Kim (1990), p. 295. Details in this section are from his 2002 and 1990 books.
111 Park Chong-kyu, a martial artist himself, was recruited into the KCIA around 1963. The prime minister was General Song Yo-chan. See Kim (2002), pp. 139–47, 239, 257.
112 Halloran (1973), p. 3.
113 KCIA director Kim Hyung-wook served from 1963 to 1969. See p. 6 of U.S. House of Representatives' hearings about Koreagate called *Investigation of Korean-American Relations, Part 1* (June 22, 1977).
114 Many sources confirmed that Kim Un-yong was in the KCIA, including an investigation by the U.S. House of Representatives regarding Koreagate in the 1960s and 1970s:
   1) *Investigation of Korean-American Relations: Report of the Subcommittee on International Organizations* (p. 76, 356–57);
   2) "Testimony of Pak Bo Hi, Special Assistant to Rev. Sun Myung Moon and President of the Korean Cultural and Freedom Foundation. . ." in *Investigation of Korean-American Relations*, Part 4 (pp. 176-178);
   3) Supplement to Part 4 of that same investigation (pp. 11, 271, 672), which lists Kim as being in the "Korean Secret Service" and a "KCIA official"; and
   4) an article from 1975 that lists Kim as one of the "agents of the Korean CIA," in *Activities of the Korean Central Intelligence Agency in the U.S., Part II* (pp. 63–64). Other sources about Kim in the KCIA: (a) Jennings and Sambrook (2000), p. 187, and Simson and Jennings (1992), pp. 139–140; (b) Interview, Choi Hong-Hi (Apr. 13, 2001); (c) Interview, Jhoon Rhee (Jan. 16, 2008); and (d) Kim (1990), p. 295, and Kim (2002), pp. 151, 164.
115 Burdick (1997), p. 41. Kang and Lee (1999), p. 21.
116 Future Olympic Taekwondo leaders, such as Uhm Woon-kyu, Lee Chong-woo, and Hyun Jong-myung, did not support Choi and Nam's Tae Kwon Do in these early KTA years.
117 Choi (c. 2000), v. 2, p. 18.
118 Interviews, Nam (Dec. 2001).
119 Choi (c. 2000), v. 2, pp. 27 and 36. Details in this section are from Choi Hong-Hi's books and interviews with C. K. Choi, Nam Tae-hi, Jung-Hwa Choi, Meeyun Colomvakos, and Sunny Choi.
120 In the 1950s, Nam Tae-hi had put together Tae Kwon Do's first two patterns, *Hwa-Rang* and *Choong-Moo*, both named after warriors (Choi [c. 2000], v. 1, p. 428). A couple of years later, Han Cha-gyo had created *Ul-Ji*, which is named after a Korean guerrilla general from 1,400 years ago. In 1961, C. K. Choi, who would soon be Korea's first national sparring champion, had helped to create the fourth pattern, *Gae-Baek*, named after a strict general from 1,500 years ago (C. K. Choi [2007], p. 81). In Malaysia, Ambassador Choi imported Kim Bok-Man and Woo Jae-lim to help with sixteen of the twenty-four patterns. The last four of the twenty-four would follow in 1966. For a reliable, concise list of pioneers who taught and developed Tae Kwon Do in the 1950s and 1960s, see the "Early History" chapter in C. K. Choi (2007).

121 Interview, C. K. Choi (Oct 31, 2007).
122 Choi Hong-Hi (c. 2000), v. 2, p. 52.
123 Interviews, Park (2002) and Choi (2001).
124 Interview, C. K. Choi (Oct. 31, 2007).
125 Choi (c. 2000), v. 2, p. 255.
126 Choi (c. 2000), v. 2, p. 146.

CHAPTER SIX

127 Interviews, Nam (Sep. 5, 2006), Nguyen Van Binh (Aug. 9, 2006) and C. K. Choi (2015).
128 For Karate: Draeger (1974), p. 127. For Tae Kwon Do: Choi (c. 2000), v. 1, p. 517.
129 Durand (2004), p. 3. Kang and Lee (1999), p. 8.
130 Cumings (2005), pp. 321–22. Last Korean troops left in 1973: v.1, p.124 of the U.S. House of Representatives' *Investigation of Korean-American Relations, Volumes I and II of Appendixes to the Report of the Subcommittee on International Organizations.*
131 All quotes from Nguyen are from my interview with him (Aug. 9, 2006).
132 "Other Guns," *Time* (Jul. 22, 1966).
133 "Letter to the Editor: Tiger Skins," *Time* (Aug. 12, 1966).
134 Durand (2004), plus other sources online: "Battle at Tra Binh Dong" at www.vietvet.co.kr and "Blue Dragon" in archives of www.talkingproud.us. Both retrieved from Web (Jan. 11, 2016).
135 Details about this battle are from Durand (2004) and "A Savage Week," *Time* (Feb. 24, 1967).
136 Durand (2004).
137 Durand (2004).
138 Interview, Kong Young-il (Aug. 16, 2002).
139 Walson spent three years in Laos during the Vietnam War, during which he survived a helicopter crash. He saved the injured passengers, including a South Vietnamese general, after side-kicking the jammed door of the burning helicopter. From interview, Walson (Jan. 2010 and Nov. 2015).
140 Kimm (Jan. 2000), p. 54.

CHAPTER SEVEN

141 Choi's friend who was South Korean's ambassador to West Germany was Choi Duk-shin, a powerful politician who, since 1959, had been opening doors for Tae Kwon Do in Vietnam, Germany, Egypt, Italy, Turkey, Malaysia, and Singapore. Kimm (Jan. 2000), pp. 50 and 53. Choi (c. 2000), v.2, pp. 86–105, describes the Ace tour.
142 Choi (c. 2000), v.2, p. 96.
143 Interview, Cariati (Jan. 8, 2008).
144 Choi (c. 2000), v. 2, p. 73.
145 Interview, Kong (Aug. 16, 2002).
146 In later years, Choi would ask friends like black belt Robert Walson, an American CIA agent, to accompany the Ace team, partly for security reasons.
147 Interview, Choi (Apr. 2002).
148 Interview, Lu (May 17, 2003).
149 Interview, Cormack (May 2, 2003).
150 Interviews, Jong-Soo Park (2001 to 2008).
151 Interview, C. K. Choi (Nov. 28, 2007).
152 C. K. Choi (2007), pp. 87, 90, 94.
153 Kang and Lee (1999) quoted Lee Chong-woo, head of the Jidokwan (one of the main martial arts gyms in the country), who also told two martial artists: "Choi Hong-Hi was like an authoritarian dictator, so Uhm Woon-kyu and I had to kick him out."
154 Choi (c. 2000), v.2, p. 107.

155 Interview, Rhee (Jan. 16, 2008). Boettcher (1980), pp. 42–53, presents a concise history of two of the cult's projects (the Little Angles and Radio of Free Asia) and of Jhoon's Rhee involvement.

156 Larkin (2003).

157 According to Gregory Henderson in 1968, as quoted by Cumings (2005), p. 361.

158 Interview, Nam (July 2011).

159 Interview, Rhee (Jan. 16, 2008). See also p. 2 of U.S. House of Representatives' hearings called *Activities of the Korean Central Intelligence Agency in the U.S., Part II (*1976).

160 Kim (2002), p. 159.

161 Kim's secret-service colleague was Pak Bo-Hi, who was also Rhee's cousin and the right-hand man of cult leader Reverend Sun-Myung Moon. The American government published a number of previously classified reports about these men and their missions during U.S. House of Representatives' hearings called *Investigation of Korean-American Relations. Report of the Subcommittee on International Organizations* (p. 357), and *Investigation of Korean-American Relations, Supplement to Part* 4 (pp. 350 and 355). See also Boettcher (1980), p. 40). I also interviewed Rhee (Jan. 16, 2008).

162 Rhee was a follower of Moon until 1965, when he was confronted with the movement's limitations, one of which involved restrictions on marriage. "I married in 1966," he told me on Jan. 16, 2008. "You know, if I had remained in there, I could not have married; I would have had to wait for their blessings." He began to fade away from the organization, but as his Tae Kwon Do became successful, he donated hundreds of thousands of dollars to Moon's followers in the 1960s. He finally quit when all hell broke loose among the Moonies, the KCIA, and the American government in the 1970s. See also "Report from the American Embassy in Seoul to the U.S. Department of State" (Aug. 26, 1966) on p. 480 of U.S. House of Representatives' hearings called *Investigation of Korean-American Relations, Supplement to Part* 4 (1978).

163 Government hearings and previously classified documents about Rhee's involvement and related issues appear in U.S. House of Representatives' publications, including:

1) "Statement of Donald L. Ranard, Former Director of Korean Affairs, Department of State" (Mar. 25, 1978), in *Activities of the Korean Central Intelligence Agency in the U.S., Part I* (p. 69);
2) the U.S. House's *Investigation of Korean-American Relations: Report of the Subcommittee on International Organizations* (p. 317, 324, 357) as well as *Volumes I and II of Appendixes to the Report* (p. 397, 1463 1469); and
3) the U.S. House's *Investigation of Korean-American Relations, Part* 4 (pp. 397, 661, 718) and *Supplement to Part* 4 (pp. 81, 104, 255, 301, 593, 607, 664).

164 For Kim Un-yong's role with the radio station, see "Sworn Statement of Kim Chong Hoon" (the station's operations director) in part of the U.S. House of Representatives' hearings about Koreagate called *Investigation of Korean-American Relations: Report of the Subcommittee on International Organizations* (p. 312 and 363). For Kim's role in the cult, refer to a 1965 letter from Earl H. Voss to Arleigh Burke, the president of the cult's foundation, on p. 364 of the U.S. House of Representatives' *Investigation of Korean-American Relations, Supplement to Part* 4. According to Lee Jai-Hyon, a former South Korean embassy official in Washington, the foundation had a cable channel to the KCIA, which also helped to staff the foundation (as noted on pp. 8 and 9 of the U.S. House's *Activities of the Korean Central Intelligence Agency in the U.S., Part II)*. See also a statement from a former ambassador to South Korea on p. 52 of the U.S. House's *Investigation of Korean-American Relations, Part* 4. The powerful American celebrities and politicians who lent their names to these Korean projects — supporters such as former presidents Dwight Eisenhower and Harry Truman — did not know that KCIA agents staffed the projects, that a cult headed them, and that the initiatives were raising money for covert operations.

165 Interview, Rhee (Nov. 12, 2007).

166 From pp. 277–78 of U.S. House of Representatives' hearings called *Investigation of Korean-American Relations, Supplement to Part 4* (1978).

167 Interview, Burleson (Jan. 24, 2008).

168 All quotes from Pat Burleson are from my interview with him on Jan. 24, 2008.

169 From the file of retired Admiral Arleigh Burke, founding president of the foundation, as noted on p. 216 of U.S. House of Representatives' hearings called *Investigation of Korean-American Relations, Supplement to Part 4* (1978). See also a 1976 statement from Robert W. Roland, a former member of the foundation, on p. 15 of *Activities of the Korean Central Intelligence Agency in the U.S., Part II*, which quotes Rev. Moon, the cult's leader, from an April 15, 1965, issue of one of Moon's publications: "Then back to Arlington for a rest and a bite to eat before driving in several cars to the Karate Tournament under the auspices of the Korean Cultural Foundation and the Jhoon Rhee Institute of Karate. About the Karate Tournament: NBC was there and the officials were excited about this new art or sport of Karate, and said they would certainly televise it every year. It will be on a national hook-up May 16."

170 Letter from Roland to the Foundation's president (Jul. 12, 1965), on p. 405 of U.S. House of Representatives' hearings called *Investigation of Korean-American Relations, Supplement to Part 4*.

171 Kim also helped with the Asian Peoples' Anti-Communist League's Freedom Centre (which distributed propaganda about South Korea). The source for Kim's Little Angels spy mission is "Testimony of Pak Bo-Hi, Special Assistant to Rev. Sun Myung Moon and President of the Korean Cultural and Freedom Foundation, accompanied by John M. Bray, Counsel," on pp. 176–78 of U.S. House of Representatives' hearings called *Investigation of Korean-American Relations, Part 4*. See also p. 356 of *Report of the Subcommittee on International Organizations* (1978) from that same investigation.

172 Interview, Rhee (2007).

173 Choi (c. 2000), v. 2, pp. 126–27.

174 Choi (c. 2000), v. 2, pp. 133–36, 165.

175 Interview, Rhee (Nov. 19, 2007). Choi (c. 2000), v. 2, pp. 196–97.

176 Interviews, Meeyun Colomvakos and Sunny Choi (2002).

177 Choi (c. 2000), v. 2, p. 197.

178 Choi (c. 2000), v. 2, p. 219. Interview, Rhee (Nov. 19, 2007).

179 Interview, Rhee (Nov. 19, 2007).

180 Choi (c. 2000), v. 2, p. 71. Burdick (1997), p. 42. Chun (1976), p. 11.

181 Larkin (2003).

182 Choi (c. 2000), v. 2, p. 127. Choi (c. 2000), v. 2, pp. 129, 323, mentions the instructors involved in the East Berlin Incident. Interviews with grandmasters provided details.

CHAPTER EIGHT

183 Transcript of interview with Isang Yun on *Weekend*, a program on NBC-TV (May 1, 1976), reprinted on pp. 70–75 of U.S. House of Representatives' hearings called *Activities of the Korean Central Intelligence Agency in the U.S., Part II*.

184 C. K. Choi (2007), pp. 93–94.

185 "K's Situation," *Der Spiegel* (Aug. 28, 1967), p. 23–26.

186 Besides *Der Spiegel*, many sources extensively covered the incident. In the *New York Times* in 1967 for example: Jul. 5 (p. 8); Jul. 6 (p. 9); Jul. 8 (p. 6); Jul. 9 (p. 1); Jul. 14 (p. 4); Jul. 15 (p. 9); Jul. 23 (p. 5); Jul. 30 (p. 5); Dec. 7 (p. 10).

187 Yang ran the mission with the Korean CIA's third branch (in charge of counter-intelligence and rounding up spies) and the sixth branch (devoted to dirty tricks, sabotage, and assassinations). His role is mentioned on pages 7 and 93 of a U.S. House of Representatives' report called *Activities of the Korean Central Intelligence Agency in the U.S., Part I* (1976).

188 Kuklinski-Rhee (2010), p. 91-99.

189 *Der Spiegel* articles that quote historian Hannes Mosler and others (Aug. 28, 1967), p. 23–26.

190 Choe (2005), p. 1. Cumings (2005), p. 371

191 Interview with John J Keenan Jr. (June 2015). Keenan was a U.S. Army Warrant Officer in Moehringen, Germany, not far from a restaurant that Kim Kwang-il owned and ran. Once, he asked Kim about Kim travelling to and from South Korea and was surprised to learn that he did not have to go through customs in Germany, as a black car met him where the plane landed.

192 Choi (c. 2000), v. 2, pp. 129, 323. Also, Kuklinski-Rhee (2010).

193 Boettcher (1980), p. 354.

194 Isang Yun on *Weekend*, NBC-TV (May 1, 1976), reprinted on pp. 70–75 of a U.S. House of Representatives' report called *Activities of the Korean Central Intelligence Agency in the U.S., Part II*.

195 Choi (c. 2000), v. 2, pp. 114, 117.

196 From *Der Spiegel* (Aug. 28, 1967) and p. 152 of the U.S. House's *Investigation of Korean-American Relations: Report of the Subcommittee on International Organizations* (1978). See also p. 23 of U.S. House's *Investigation of Korean-American Relations, Part 1*.

197 Kim Hyung-wook explained how this worked on p. 38 of U.S. House of Representatives' hearings called *Investigation of Korean-American Relations, Part 1 (1977)*.

198 Choi (c. 2000), v. 2, p. 217.

199 According to Gregory Henderson, as noted in Boettcher (1980), p. 354.

200 Not until a 2006 Truth Commission would the South Korean government admit that the cases were mainly fabrications. The dictatorship released Yun in 1969. See Isang Yun on *Weekend*, NBC-TV (May 1, 1976), reprinted on pp. 70–75 of U.S. House of Representatives' hearings called *Activities of the Korean Central Intelligence Agency in the U.S., Part II*.

201 Choi (c. 2000), v. 2, pp. 143, 145, 149, 243–44, 277.

202 Interview, C. K. Choi (Oct. 31, 2007). Choi (c. 2000), v. 2, p. 135. A number of websites contain information about the meeting. A photo is found at www.lacancha.com/oyama.html (retrieved from Web on Jan. 11, 2016).

203 Kimm (Jan. 2000), p. 54.

CHAPTER NINE

204 Kim (2002), pp. 166–72.

205 Cumings (2005), p. 53. Boettcher (1980), p. 78.

206 Quoted in Simson and Jennings (1992), p. 139.

207 Kim (2002), p. 169. Yook (2002). Kim (1990), pp. 295, 233–34. He later said on a television show: "I accepted the position of KTA President because the Korean government told me to correct the way Tae Kwon Do was at that time." Kang and Lee (1999).

208 Choi (c. 2000), v. 2, pp. 201–4.

209 Kang and Lee (1999).

210 Kim (2002), p. 61.

211 Kang and Lee (1999).

212 Kim (2002), p. 59.

213 Kim (2002), p. 171.

214 From Pak Bo-Hi's sworn testimony as detailed on pp. 491–92 of U.S. House of Representatives' hearings called *Investigation of Korean-American Relations, Part 4* (1978). Photocopies of the cheques are on p. 487: $200 on February 10, 1970; $300 on April 30, 1970; and $300 on June 14, 1971.

215 Park Chong-kyu, also head of the Presidential Security Force. Details of the Plan are found in U.S. House of Representatives' hearings called *Investigation of Korean-American Relations, Volumes I*

and II of Appendixes to the Report of the Subcommittee on International Organizations (p. 519). A British journalist, Andrew Jennings, quoted a former American CIA officer, Philip Liechty, regarding allegations that "the Korean CIA used taekwondo schools as bases for operations and cover for its overseas officers, particularly here in the U.S. There was a period when some of these people were allegedly involved in kidnapping and covertly removing Korean students, protestors against the Park regime, from the U.S. back to Korea." From Simson and Jennings (1992), p. 140.

216 See U.S. House of Representatives' *Investigation of Korean-American Relations: Report of the Subcommittee on International Organizations*, pp. 4, 121. The mastermind behind the Plan in the U.S. and Canada was KCIA agent Yang Doo-wan, who had moved from West Germany to Washington, where he was KCIA Station Chief. Yang had been in charge of the East Berlin Incident, and he oversaw all KCIA activities in the U.S. His alias was still "Lee Sang-ho," and he was a close acquaintance of people in the KCIA-infiltrated cult foundation, such as Pak Bo-Hi (who was Kim Un-yong's colleague and Jhoon Rhee's cousin). See "Statement of Gen. Kim Hyung Wook, Former Director, Korean Central Intelligence Agency (KCIA)," on pp. 29 and 64 of U.S. House of Representatives' hearings called *Investigation of Korean-American Relations, Part 1* (1977).

217 Many have written about the Plan: Boettcher (1980), pp. 157–58, and Cumings (2005), p. 460. One of their primary sources was a Korean embassy official who defected to the U.S.; see the "Statement of Dr. Lee Jai Hyon, Associate Professor of Journalism, Western Illinois University," on p. 10 of U.S. House of Representatives' hearings called *Activities of the Korean Central Intelligence Agency in the U.S., Part II* (1976). See also pp. 1–2 of the U.S. House's *Investigation of Korean-American Relations, Part 3*, p. 505 of *Investigation of Korean-American Relations, Volumes I and II of Appendixes to the Report of the Subcommittee on International Organizations*., and pp. 105–106 of the U.S. House's *Investigation of Korean-American Relations: Report of the Subcommittee on International Organizations*.

218 Kang and Lee (1999).

219 U.S. House of Representatives' *Investigation of Korean-American Relations: Report of the Subcommittee on International Organizations* (1978), p. 239.

220 U.S. House's *Investigation of Korean-American Relations: Report of the Subcommittee on International Organizations* (1978), p. 76.

221 Details in this section are from the U.S. House's *Investigation of Korean-American Relations: Report of the Subcommittee on International Organizations* (pp. 104, 241), as well as *Volumes I and II of Appendixes to the Report* (pp. 716–18).

222 The U.S. House's *Investigation of Korean-American Relations: Report of the Subcommittee on International Organizations* (1978), pp. 234, 242.

223 Kang and Lee (1999).

224 In a December 13, 1971, interview with Dong A Ilbo. See Kang and Lee (1999).

225 According to a former Korean embassy official who provided a copy of the 1976 Plan to American officials, as noted on p. 2 of U.S. House of Representatives' hearings called *Investigation of Korean-American Relations, Part 3* (1977).

226 "South Korean CIA: Power Grows, Fear Spreads," by John Saar, John Goshko, and Bill Richards, *Washington Post*, May 23, 1976. See also Cumings (2005), p. 371.

227 Information in this and the next paragraph is from the U.S. House of Representatives' *Investigation of Korean-American Relations, Volumes I and II of Appendixes to the Report of the Subcommittee on International Organizations*, pp. 540–42.

228 From p. 137 of U.S. House of Representatives' hearings called *Investigation of Korean-American Relations, Part 3* (1977). See also "Statement of Gregory Henderson, Tufts University, Fletcher School of Law and Diplomacy," on p. 8 of *Activities of the Korean Central Intelligence Agency in the U.S., Part I*, from the same hearings.

229 The U.S. House of Representatives' *Investigation of Korean-American Relations: Report of the Subcommittee on International Organizations* (1978), pp. 93–97.

230 "FBI memorandum entitled 'Republic of Korea (ROK) Intelligence Activities in the U.S.,' dated September 9, 1973," on pp. 465–66 of the U.S. House of Representatives' *Investigation of Korean-American Relations, Volumes I and II of Appendixes to the Report of the Subcommittee on International Organizations.*

231 U.S. House of Representatives' *Investigation of Korean-American Relations, Volumes I and II of Appendixes to the Report of the Subcommittee on International Organizations*, p. 131.

232 Boettcher (1980), p. 206 and U.S. House of Representatives' *Investigation of Korean-American Relations: Report of the Subcommittee on International Organizations* (1978), pp. 402–404.

233 Much of this section about Song is from his sworn testimony to a U.S. Congressional subcommittee, as noted on pp. 81–88, 204–13 of U.S. House of Representatives' hearings called Investigation of Korean-American Relations, Part 5 (1978).

234 From pp. 81–88, 204–13 of U.S. House of Representatives' hearings called *Investigation of Korean-American Relations, Part 5* (1978).

235 His name is Limb Man-sung, probably spelled "Lim," but U.S. Congressional documents use "Limb." More about him is available on p. 4 of U.S. House of Representatives' hearings called *Activities of the Korean Central Intelligence Agency in the U.S., Part II* (1976).

236 "Signed Sworn Statement of Chung Tai Bong to Subcommittee Staff," from pp. 214–17 of U.S. House of Representatives' hearings called *Investigation of Korean-American Relations, Part 5* (1978).

237 The chief of the PSF, nicknamed Pistol Park, was a martial artist in Judo and Hapkido and one of the most powerful men in South Korea. He headed many illegal ventures that raised money for covert activities, including threatening American academics who criticized South Korea, stealing $200,000 that was supposed to be a bribe for a U.S. congressman, and, in 1974, handing an envelope with $10,000 in cash to John E. Nidecker, special adviser to U.S. President Richard Nixon, one of many bribe attempts. These details are from pp. 13–31 of U.S. House of Representatives' hearings called *Investigation of Korean-American Relations, Part 5*. For Nidecker's testimony, see pp. 44, 150 of the U.S. House of Representatives' *Investigation of Korean-American Relations: Report of the Subcommittee on International Organizations* (1978). For more details, see "Statement of Gen. Kim Hyung Wook, Former Director, Korean Central Intelligence Agency (KCIA)," on pp. 23–27, 58–59 of U.S. House of Representatives' hearings called *Investigation of Korean-American Relations, Part 1* (1977).

238 U.S. House of Representatives' hearings called *Investigation of Korean-American Relations, Part 1* (1977), p. 25.

239 The U.S. House of Representatives' *Investigation of Korean-American Relations: Report of the Subcommittee on International Organizations* (1978), p. 90.

240 Choi (c. 2000), v. 2, p. 300.

241 "Bruce Lee and I: Martial arts phenomenon Jhoon Rhee talks, Part two," in *Martial Arts Illustrated*. The correspondence between Rhee and Lee was particularly intense between 1967 and 1973.

242 Details in this paragraph are from an interview with Nam (July 2011).

243 Choi (c. 2000), v. 2, pp. 210–11.

244 Choi (c. 2000), v. 2, pp. 210–11.

245 Interview, Nam (July 2011).

CHAPTER TEN

246 Choi (c. 2000), v. 2, p. 394.

247 Choi (1974), p. 453.

248 Young (1993), p. 62, 67.

249 Interview, Nam (Feb. 20, 2008).

250 Interview, Nam (July 2011).

251 The U.S. House of Representatives' *Investigation of Korean-American Relations: Report of the Subcommittee on International Organizations* (1978), p. 92.

252 Choi (c. 2000), v. 2, p. 286.

253 Boettcher (1980), p. 224.

254 Cumings (2005), p. 376.

255 Cumings (2005), pp. 396, 418.

256 Boettcher (1980), pp. 224–27. See also "Statement of Kim Sang Keun, Former Official, Korean Central Intelligence Agency, Accompanied by Mr. Hong Kyoon An, Interpreter," on p. 61 of U.S. House of Representatives' hearings called *Investigation of Korean-American Relations, Part 5* (1978).

257 Pages 105, 109 of the U.S. House of Representatives' *Investigation of Korean-American Relations, Volumes I and II of Appendixes to the Report of the Subcommittee on International Organizations.*

258 Details in this chapter are from:

1) Interview, Rhee Min-hi (Dec. 22, 2007);
2) "FBI Memorandum entitled 'RHEE Min Hi,' dated November 13, 1974" and other FBI memos on pp. 457–66 and 476–77 of the U.S. House of Representatives' *Investigation of Korean-American Relations, Volumes I and II of Appendixes to the Report of the Subcommittee on International Organizations*;
3) "Signed Sworn Statement of Rhee Min Hee (in Korean) to Subcommittee Staff. . ." and articles and testimony from Song Sun-keun on pp. 79–95, 206–07, 218–21 of U.S. House of Representatives' hearings called *Investigation of Korean-American Relations, Part 5* (1978);
4) Documents about KCIA links to the Korean-American Political Association are in previously classified documents in U.S. House of Representatives' hearings called *Investigation of Korean-American Relations, Volumes I and II of Appendixes to the Report of the Subcommittee on International Organizations* (pp. 1506–17) and *Investigation of Korean-American Relations, Part 5* (pp. 210–13);
5) Boettcher (1980), pp. 224–27.

259 Song called them "Karate students" (on p. 80 of U.S. House of Representatives' hearings called *Investigation of Korean-American Relations, Part 5*) and Boettcher (1980) said they were "karate experts" (p. 225), but more accurately, they were students of Korean Karate or Tae Kwon Do, which was popular in the U.S. in 1973.

260 All details in this scene with Kim and Rhee are from p. 80 of U.S. House of Representatives' hearings called *Investigation of Korean-American Relations, Part 5*.

261 Statement of Kim Sang Keun, former KCIA official, on pp. 57–58 of U.S. House of Representatives' hearings called *Investigation of Korean-American Relations, Part 5*.

262 Interview with Simon Rhee (Dec. 12, 2007).

263 Interview with Rhee Min-hi (Dec. 22, 2007).

264 The three sources that linked Rhee to the KCIA were:

1) *Korea Journal* reporter Song Sun-keun, who had been in the hall;
2) a sworn statement to U.S. Congress from Chung Tae-bong, who had been Song's friend and an advertiser in Song's paper;
3) Lee Keun-pal, who had been Kim Dae-jung's personal secretary in the U.S.

265 See "Memorandum, Subject: ROK CIA Activities in the U.S., dated August 17, 1973," on pp. 166–67 of U.S. House of Representatives' hearings called *Investigation of Korean-American Relations, Part 5*.

266 A former head of the KCIA told U.S. investigators that Japan would be a better place than the

U.S. for the kidnapping (on p. 62 of U.S. House of Representatives' hearings called *Investigation of Korean-American Relations, Part 5*).

267 From p. 1 of U.S. House of Representatives' hearings called *Investigation of Korean-American Relations, Part 5*. Many publications report on the following incident, including "S. Korea Admits Kim Abduction Role," from the *Asahi Shimbun* (Oct. 25, 2007), by Yoshihiro Makino. A full report from the NIS (formerly the KCIA) was available in Korean on the NIS website in November 2007.

268 From the U.S. House of Representatives' *Investigation of Korean-American Relations, Volumes I and II of Appendixes to the Report of the Subcommittee on International Organizations*, p. 466.

269 Interview, Rhee Min-hi (Dec. 22, 2007).

270 A number of sources listed the names of some of those involved in the incident:

1) "Threat to Koreans in U.S. By Seoul Stirs Concern," by David Binder, *New York Times* (Aug. 17, 1973), p. 65;
2) The *Washington Post* articles, "South Korean CIA: Power Grows, Fear Spreads," by John Saar, John Goshko, and Bill Richards (May 23, 1976), and "Koreans Here Seek Politician's Release," by Jaehoon Ahn (Aug. 20, 1973);
3) Letter from Kim Sang Keun, a former KCIA official, on p 172–77 of U.S. House of Representatives' hearings called *Investigation of Korean-American Relations, Part 5*;
4) "Statement of Gregory Henderson, Tufts University, Fletcher School of Law and Diplomacy," "Statement of Donald L. Ranard, Former Director of Korean Affairs, Department of State," and information from Kim Hyung Wook, former director of the KCIA, on pp. 7, 11, 13, 39–42 of *Activities of the Korean Central Intelligence Agency in the U.S., Part I*, from those same hearings;
5) See pp. 81, 87 of *Activities of the Korean Central Intelligence Agency in the U.S., Part II*, from the same hearings.

271 "U.S. Knew Immediately of KCIA Role in Kim's Abduction," in *Kyodo News International* (Aug. 9, 1998), which quotes former CIA station chief Donald Gregg.

272 Klein (2007), p. 107.

273 The U.S. House of Representatives' *Investigation of Korean-American Relations: Report of the Subcommittee on International Organizations* (1978), pp. 147–48, 154. See also Boettcher (1980), p. 227.

274 Choi (c. 2000) v. 2, pp. 287–88.

275 Choi (c. 2000) v. 2, pp. 287–88.

276 The members were: C. K. Choi, Jong-Soo Park, Kong Young-il, Pak Sun-jae, and Rhee Ki-ha.

277 Interviews, Walson (2015) and Schroen (2015).

278 Interview, Schroen (2015).

279 Interview, Schroen (2015). Schroen went on to lead many CIA missions in the Middle East and Afghanistan, including a six-man team into Afghanistan two weeks after the attacks on New York on Sept. 11, 2001. See:

a) Page 26 of *Tae Kwon Do Digest*, vol. 1, no. 3, (1974) published by the International Taekwon-Do Federation, Denver, Colorado.
b) Interviews — Gary Schroen | The Dark Side | FRONTLINE | PBS.pdf, from www.pbs.org/wgbh/pages/frontline/darkside/interviews/schroen.html. Retrieved from the Web on Oct. 13, 2015.
c) Choi (c. 2000), v. 2, p. 246.
d) Interview, Jong-Soo Park (Feb. 21, 2008).
e) Interview, Cormack (May 2003).
f) Interview, Walson (Jan. 2010 and Nov. 2015).

280 Interview, Schroen (2015).

281 Interview with C. K. Choi (Oct. 15, 2015).

CHAPTER ELEVEN

282 Kang and Lee (1999), p. 5.
283 Kang and Lee (1999), pp. 30–40.
284 This scene is from Kang and Lee (1999), pp. 30–40 and Kim (2002), 70.
285 Kim (2002), p. 70.
286 Kim (2002), p. 70.
287 Kim (2002), pp. 63, 67.
288 C. K. Choi (2007), p. 101.
289 Choi (c. 2000), v. 2, p. 351.
290 Kim (1975), p. 7.
291 Kim (2002), p. 63.
292 Choi (1988), p. 7.
293 Kim (1975), p. 13.
294 Details and quotes in this paragraph are from my interview with Nam Tae-hi (Dec. 2001).
295 Interviews, Jung-Hwa Choi (Jan. 25, 2002) and Sunny Choi (Aug. 21, 2002).
296 Interview, Rhee (Nov. 19, 2007).
297 Choi (c. 2000), v. 2, p. 241, 360. Interview, Sunny Choi, (Aug. 22, 2002).
298 Interviews, Jung-Hwa Choi (Jan. 25, 2002) and Sunny Choi (Aug. 21, 2002).
299 Burdick (1997), p. 39.
300 Kim (1975), p. 38.
301 Interview, Tae Eun Lee (Aug. 20, 2007).
302 Kuklinski-Rhee (2010), p. 125–130.
303 Interview, Jae-Hun Kim (Jun. 22, 2002).
304 Interview, Rhee (Nov. 2007).
305 Kim (1975), p. 20. Chun (1976), pp. 3, 12.
306 Anslow (2004), p. 50.
307 Kim (2002), p. 53.
308 Interview, C. K. Choi (Nov. 28, 2007).
309 "Conclusion" in the U.S. House of Representatives' *Investigation of Korean-American Relations: Report of the Subcommittee on International Organizations* (1978), pp. 153–57.
310 Information in this section, including the exchange with Kissinger, is from "South Korean Abuses Tolerated," by Don Oberdorfer, in the *Washington Post* (May 17, 1976), from pp. 89–90 of U.S. House of Representatives' hearings called *Activities of the Korean Central Intelligence Agency in the U.S., Part I.*
311 Choi (c. 2000), v. 2, pp. 277–78.
312 "Korean Consulate General: Condemned," by Yung-gil Kook, in *The New Korea* (Nov. 6, 1975), on p. 29 of U.S. House of Representatives' hearings called *Activities of the Korean Central Intelligence Agency in the U.S., Part I.*
313 Boettcher (1980), p. 7.
314 Choi (c. 2000), v. 2, p. 266.
315 In the 1960s and 1970s, Choi had been consistently in touch with North Korean officials in Malaysia, Japan, Sweden, India, and probably elsewhere during a time when such contact was considered treason and punishable by imprisonment or death. Choi (c. 2000), v. 2, p. 271.
316 Choi (c. 2000), v. 2, pp. 271–76.

CHAPTER TWELVE

317 Interview, Cormack (May 2, 2003).
318 See the U.S. House of Representatives' *Investigation of Korean-American Relations: Report of the*

Subcommittee on International Organizations (1978), p. 424. Kim Hyung-wook's testimony is in U.S. House of Representatives' hearings called *Investigation of Korean-American Relations, Part 1* (pp. 10, 31).

319 Cumings' *Japan Policy Research Institute Working Paper No. 20* (2003).

320 Interview, Choi (Mar. 27, 2001).

321 Interview, Cormack (May 2, 2003).

322 Interviews, Meeyun Colomvakos and Sunny Choi (Aug. 22, 2002).

323 Cumings (2005), pp. 140–41.

324 The abductions took place throughout the late 1970s and early 1980s and were widely reported in 2002, when North Korea admitted to the mission. "Kidnappings latest bizarre tale from N. Korea," by Geoffrey York, *Globe and Mail* (Sep. 19, 2002), p. A19.

325 Burdick (1997), p. 37.

326 Cumings (2005), p. 472, ranks the incident with the 1968 USS *Pueblo* crisis in which North Korea seized a U.S. spy ship.

327 "Statement of Gari Ledyard, Professor of Korean Language and History, Columbia University," on p. 18 of U.S. House of Representatives' hearings called *Investigation of Korean-American Relations, Part 4* (1978).

328 Interview, Kong (Aug. 16, 2002). Anslow (2004), p. 48.

329 Interview, Kong (Aug. 16, 2002).

330 Interview, Nam (Apr. 2006).

331 Park and Nam were in the WTF-dominated magazine *Traditional Taekwondo: Official Magazine for the Korean-Style Martial Artist*, published by D.W. Kang in Oklahoma, USA: Winter, 1975.

332 "South Korean CIA: Power Grows, Fear Spreads," by John Saar, John Goshko, and Bill Richards, *Washington Post*, May 23, 1976.

333 Choi (1980), p. 7.

334 Interview, C. K. Choi (Oct. 31, 2007). Kimm (2000), p. 56.

335 Interview, Cariati (Jan. 8, 2008). Choi (c. 2000), v. 2, p. 313.

336 Many details in this chapter are from Choi (c. 2000), v. 2, pp. 342–52, and Choi (1980), which is a long brochure that Choi printed about the trip.

337 Interview, Cormack (May 2, 2003).

338 Interview, Jung-Hwa Choi (Jan. 25, 2002).

339 Choi (c. 2000), v. 2, pp. 336–38.

340 Cumings (2005), p. 379.

341 Cumings (2005), pp. 343, 383.

342 Kang and Lee (1999), p. 46.

343 Cumings (2004), p. 76.

344 Cumings (2004), pp. 1, 2. Cumings (2005), p. 420.

345 Interview, Cormack (May 2, 2003).

346 Choi (1980), a brochure.

347 Interview, Cormack (May 2, 2003).

348 Cumings (2005), p. 227–28.

349 Cumings (2004), p. 159.

350 Choi (1999), pp. 42, 148–49.

351 Interview, Cormack (May 2, 2003).

352 Interviews, Jung-Hwa Choi (May and Apr. 2003).

353 Interviews, Jung-Hwa Choi (May and Apr. 2003).

354 Interview, Jung-Hwa Choi (Jan. 25, 2002).

CHAPTER THIRTEEN

355 Dick Pound, a former leader in the International Olympic Committee, told me his nickname (Mar. 4, 2008).

356 Details about Operation Thunderbird are from Kim (2002), pp. 6, 78, 101–19, 230, and Seoul Olympic Organizing Committee (1989), pp. 29–36.

357 Cumings (2005), pp. 383–84.

358 All quotes from Kim in this chapter are from Kim (2002), pp. 6, 78, 101–19, 230.

359 The KCIA had been renamed the Agency for National Security Planning.

360 See the U.S. House of Representatives' *Investigation of Korean-American Relations: Report of the Subcommittee on International Organizations* (1978), pg. 363.

361 The other four instructors were: Park Soo-nam, Choi Won-chul, Kim Man-keun, and Lee Keum-hong. Kim was secretary general of the World Taekwondo Federation. Lee was a member of the WTF. From: Kim (2002), p. 113.

362 The corruption is documented in "The U.S. House of Representatives, The Olympics Site Selection Process" (2000), p. 453, which notes: "Peter Ueberroth's biography Made in America, describes the bidding process for the Seoul games that Ueberroth saw as tantamount to bribery." Ueberroth was the organizer of the 1984 Los Angeles Olympics and, later, chairman of the U.S. Olympic Committee.

363 "Olympics; Past Scandal Could Haunt I.O.C. Candidate," by Jere Longman, *New York Times* (Jul. 15, 2001).

364 Kim (1990), p. 60.

365 Simson and Jennings (1992), p. 138, argues, "The Seoul games were conceived [partly] from a desire by a military junta to obscure their brutal image . . ." See also Cumings, *Japan Policy Research Institute Working Paper No. 20* (2003).

366 Kim (1990), p. 61.

367 Interview, Cariati (Jan. 2008).

368 Choi (c. 2000), v. 2, pp. 349, 431.

369 Wealthy North Koreans financed Choi's martial art: Chon Jin-shik in Japan gave C$200,000 to Choi for a championship and became a vice-president of the International Taekwon-Do Federation. Chon's nephew, Phang Jin, later became head of the ITF in Japan. This is from interviews with Jong-Soo Park (Jan. 5, 2003 and Aug. 20, 2004) and from a document called "Japan International Tae Kwon-Do Federation, The History, Management, and Training Style," by Mr Kosuke Yamamoto: "It was 1982 when General Choi met a patriot Chon Jin Shik, one of the early Korean immigrants (Korean-Japanese) who succeeded in business, and also known as a former vice president of ITF. At the time, Mr. Chon was grieving about the separation of mother land [into North and South Korea]."

370 Some of this section is from interviews with Jung-Hwa Choi (Jan. 2002 to Apr. 2003) and Michael Cormack (May 2, 2003), and details are from Canadian newspapers, such as:

a) The *Globe and Mail* ("Plot on S. Korean President Foiled," [Feb. 25, 1982], p. 4; and other articles);

b) The *Toronto Sun* ("Cops Plan More Plot Arrests" [Feb. 26, 1982]; "Court Hears Plot to Kill Top Korean," [Feb. 17, 1984]; "Cops Arrest Suspect in Murder Plot: Korean Prez Target," [Jan. 23, 1991], p. 34; and other articles);

c) The *Toronto Star* ("Man Jailed in Disco Bombing Planned Blast While in Prison," [Oct. 19, 1985]; "Disco Bomb Trial Ends With Plea Bargain Bang," [Sep. 13, 1986]; "Mississauga Man, 36, Pleads Guilty In North Korean Assassination Plot," [Jan. 24, 1991]; and other articles).

371 Choi (c. 2000), v. 2, pp. 355, 369–74, 397. Interview, Cormack (May 2003).

372 Choi (c. 2000), v. 2, p. 401.

373 Interview, Choi Hong-Hi (Mar. 2001). Choi (1999), p. 299.

374 Interview, Cormack (May 2, 2003).

375 Interview, Hardin (July 2011).

376 All quotes from Turchi are from interviews with him in July 2011.

377 Interview, Lu (May 17, 2003). "Phap Lu: A Survivor," *Tae Kwon Do Times* (Jul. 1997), pp. 96–105.

CHAPTER FOURTEEN

378 Details in these first two paragraphs are from Kim (1990), pp. 133, 138, 142, and Kim (2002), pp. 119, 157, 274.

379 Choi (c. 2000), v. 2, p. 417.

380 Choi (c. 2000), v. 2, p. 414, 453. Simson and Jennings (1992), pp. 232–33.

381 Kang and Lee (1999), p. 40.

382 Choi was not the only martial arts leader challenging Kim. Many WTF leaders rebelled against what they saw as corruption in the WTF. In 1986, for example, Dr. Dong-Ja Yang, president of the WTF's Pan American Taekwondo Union, asked Kim Un-yong to consider lowering the exorbitant fees for black belt certification. Kim refused, and the WTF ousted Dr. Yang, who went on to start a Taekwondo Reform Movement. See www.tkdreform.com/about.html (retrieved from Web on Jan. 11, 2016).

383 Kim (1990), p. 60.

384 The Yongpal Incident was widely covered by the Korean media. See BBC News for coverage in English, for example "S Korea Taekwondo chief held" (Dec. 5, 2003), retrieved from Web Jan. 11, 2016 (news.bbc.co.uk/2/hi/asia-pacific/3293927.stm).

385 Cumings (2005), pp. 392–93.

386 Simson and Jennings (1992), pp. 147–48.

387 Cumings (2005), p. 332.

388 Kim (1990), p. 237, 261.

389 Seoul Olympic Organizing Committee (1989), p. 394.

390 Kim (1990), p. 237, 261.

391 Seoul Olympic Organizing Committee (1989), p. 145, 271.

392 Jennings and Sambrook (2000), p. 188.

393 Interviews with Joon-Pyo Choi (Nov. 28, 2007) and Young Su Choung (Oct. 2005).

394 Yook (2002), p. 8.

395 Details in this chapter are from Kim (2002), pp. 80, 82, 87–88.

396 Kim (2002), pp. 80, 82, 87–88.

397 Barcelona Olympic Organizing Committee (1992), v. 4, p. 301.

398 Choi (c. 2000), v. 2, pp. 440–41.

399 Choi (c. 2000), v. 2, pp. 496–99.

400 Interview, Cormack (May 2, 2002).

401 Most of the information on the next few pages is from interviews starting in July 2011 with Robert Hardin and members of the 1993 U.S. team that went to Moscow: Scott McNeely, Troy Burleson, Randy Edwards, Rick Stanford, Jay Doolin, Jack Stevens, Chris Gantner, and Benny Broadway. Park Jung-tae died in April 2002.

402 All quotes from Hardin are from my interviews with him in July 2011.

CHAPTER FIFTEEN

403 From Korean-language article in *Sports Hankook* (Dec. 12, 2005), which is affiliated with the *Korea Times Daily*. See Hankooki.com.

404 "Need a medal? Come with money," in the *Hankyoreh* (Jan. 28, 1999).

405 "The businesses of the Korean Kukkiwon Authorities," Peter Bolz, Denmark (Sept. 23, 2015).

Retrieved from Web on Jan. 18, 2016 (www.taekwondo.dk/files/Forbund/Dokumenter_div/2015/Kukkiwon/2015-09-23_Artikel_Peter_Bolz_Kukkiwon_english.pdf).

406 Simson and Jennings (1992), back cover.

407 Jennings and Sambrook (2000), p. 184. In 1999, the *New York Times* reported on the story.

408 From "Sports Briefing: Olympic Games; Testimony: I.O.C. Member's Son Hired to Help Bid," *New York Times* (Nov. 18, 2003). Media around the world covered this story. For example, "IOC on road to credibility: Pound, Samaranch wins vote of confidence as six members booted out," *Toronto Star* (Mar. 18, 1999), p. 1; "Who Will Clean Up After This Man?" *Asiaweek* (Feb. 23, 2001); "Fugitive in games scandal arrested," *Deseret News* (May 21, 2003), p. A01.

409 Interview, Pound (Feb. 12 and March 4, 2008).

410 Jennings and Sambrook (2000), pp. 98, 193. U.S. House of Representatives, *The Olympics Site Selection Process* (2000), p. 518.

411 Kim (2002), p. 26.

412 Interview, Jung-Hwa Choi (Jan. 25, 2002).

413 Choi (c. 2000), v. 2, p. 531.

414 "Cops Arrest Suspect in Murder Plot: Korean Prez Target," *Toronto Sun* (Jan. 23, 1991), p. 34.

415 Quotes in this section are from my interview with Jung-Hwa Choi (Jan. 25, 2002).

416 "Olympics; Past Scandal Could Haunt I.O.C. Candidate," *New York Times* (Jul. 15, 2001).

417 "Olympics; Past Scandal Could Haunt I.O.C. Candidate," *New York Times* (Jul. 15, 2001).

CHAPTER SIXTEEN

418 Kim (2002), p. 52.

419 Kim (2002), p. 272.

420 Kim (2002), pp. 82–84, 272.

421 Also, in the mid-1990s, Korea's ten largest companies — which means ten Korean families — controlled 60 per cent of the South Korean economy (Cumings [2005], pp. 330, 442).

422 "Taekwondo riot demeans new Olympic sport," *China Daily* (North America ed.) (Dec. 10, 1998). "Bangkok judging under the spotlight," *New Straits Times* (Nov. 26, 1998).

423 Kim (2002), p. 289.

424 Cumings (2005), p. 501.

425 Kim (2002), p. 289.

426 "Koreas Agree to Family Reunions," BBC News (Sep. 18, 2001), retrieved from Web Jan. 11, 2016 (news.bbc.co.uk/2/hi/asia-pacific/1549678.stm).

427 Information in this paragraph is from:

a) "South Korean Leader Says Move Was Meant to Aid 'Sunshine' Policy: Payment to North Puts Seoul on Defense," *International Herald Tribune* (Jan. 31, 2003);

b) "Olympic Games: IOC Official In Bribery Row," *Guardian* (Jan. 10, 2004), p. 19;

c) Na (2004).

428 Kim (2002), p. 47.

429 Kim (2002), pp. 7, 37, 39, 48.

430 Sydney Organizing Committee for the Olympic Games (2001), v. 1, p. 133.

431 Sydney Organizing Committee for the Olympic Games (2001), v. 2, p. 270.

432 Sydney Organizing Committee for the Olympic Games (2001), v. 1, p. 134. And from the same committee (2001), v. 2, p. 271: "Had Korea been permitted to enter more categories the results of the tournament may have been different."

433 Kim (2002), p. 295.

434 Yook (2002), pp. 7–11.

435 Yook (2002), pp. 7–11.

436 The interviewee, a grandmaster in Tae Kwon Do, wants to remain anonymous.

437 "Motivation Questioned In Taekwondo Incident," *USA Today* (Aug. 5, 2002).

438 "Taekwondo Official Denies Judging Quotes," *USA Today* (Aug. 7, 2002).

439 Quoted in *The Gazette* in "One Olympic Gold Gains In Value As Scandal Tarnishes Sport," (Aug. 24, 2002).

440 Interview, Askinas (Jan. 30, 2008). In 2011, the WTF remained mired in controversies and Askinas quit or was fired from the USAT in 2011 amid chaos after a financial audit. From: "Under fire, Askinas out as CEO of USA Taekwondo," by Brian Gomez, from *The Gazette*, Colorado, USA (Aug. 17, 2011). Retrieved from the Web on Oct. 20, 2015 (gazette.com/under-fire-askinas-out-as-ceo-of-usa-taekwondo/article/123399).

441 "Judging questioned after Canada's Gonda loses 1st taekwondo match: Canadians lodge protest but it's unsuccessful," by CBC Sports. Canada (Aug. 20, 2008). Web. Retrieved Oct. 16, 2015 (web.archive.org/web/20080822201352/www.cbc.ca/olympics/taekwondo/story/2008/08/19/f-olympics-taekwondo-gonda.html).

442 The match was between Britain's Sarah Stevenson and China's Chen Zhong. From: "Reprieved Stevenson takes bronze," by BBC. The U.K. (Aug. 23, 2008). Retrieved from the Web on Oct. 16, 2015 (news.bbc.co.uk/sport2/hi/olympics/taekwondo/7578208.stm).

443 Interview, Mitchell (Feb. 13, 2008).

444 Kim (2002), p. 19.

445 Kim (2002), pp. 17, 21.

446 World Alliance for Taekwondo Education and Reform Movement, by Dong Ja Yang (www.tkdreform.com/about.html). Retrieved from Web on Jan. 12, 2016.

447 Kim (2002), pp. 17, 21.

448 Kim said that he had been trying to be transparent and to decrease bribery by offering to pay U.S.$50,000 in expenses for IOC members (Kim [2002], p. 30).

449 Interview, Pound (Mar. 4, 2008).

450 Details about the vote and Kim's reactions are in Kim (2002), pp. 8, 30, 32, 95.

451 "IOC Official Jailed for Corruption," BBC News (Jun. 3, 2004), retrieved from Web Jan. 12, 2016 (news.bbc.co.uk/2/hi/asia-pacific/3771931.stm). Also see "Sports Briefing," *New York Times* (June 3, 2004).

452 Kim (2002), p. 5.

CHAPTER SEVENTEEN

453 Interview, Meeyun Colomvakos (Nov. 20, 2002).

454 All quotes in this scene are from my two interviews with Choi Hong-Hi and Park Jong-Soo that month (March 2001).

455 Interview, Jung-Hwa Choi (Jan. 25, 2002).

456 Interview, Cariati (Jan. 8, 2008).

457 All information related to Jung-Hwa Choi in this chapter is from my interviews with him on and around May 28, 2002.

458 Interview, Mitchell (Feb. 13, 2008).

459 Interview, Anslow (Oct. 2015).

460 Interview, Jung-Hwa Choi (May 28, 2002).

461 Interview, Galarraga (Aug. 16, 2002).

CHAPTER EIGHTEEN

462 Details in this section are from my interview with Jung-Hwa Choi (May 28, 2002).

463 Interviews, Meeyun Colomvakos and Sunny Choi (Aug. 22, 2002).

464 Interview, Jong-Soo Park (2002).
465 Interview, Jung-Hwa Choi (May 28, 2002).
466 The lawyer chose to remain anonymous.

CHAPTER NINETEEN

467 "Fighting Dirty," *Time* (Mar. 8, 2004).
468 Na (2004).
469 Kang and Lee (1999), p. 39.
470 "Official Quits and the I.O.C. Avoids Expulsion Vote," *New York Times* (May 21, 2005), p. D6.
471 "Olympic Games: IOC Official In Bribery Row," *Guardian* (Jan. 10, 2004), p. 19.
472 From *Korea Times*: "Taekwondo Head Koo Gets Suspended Jail Term" (Jan. 16, 2004) and "4 Detained in Taekwondo Probe" (Dec. 6, 2003).
473 From *Korea Times*: "Taekwondo Head Koo Gets Suspended Jail Term" (Jan. 16, 2004) and "4 Detained in Taekwondo Probe" (Dec. 6, 2003).
474 "Godfather of Gangsters Controlled Taekwondo Association," *Hankyoreh* (Dec. 5, 2003), a newspaper in South Korea, retrieved from Web in 2008 (english.hani.co.kr or www.hani.co.kr).
475 Yook (2002), pp. 27–29.
476 Na (2004).
477 From "International Olympic Committee Ethics Commission Decision containing Recommendations N° D/01/05," regarding Mr. Un Yong , IOC Vice-President (Feb. 4, 2005) Retrieved from Web Jan. 12, 2016 (www.olympic.org/Documents/Reports/EN/en_report_913.pdf).
478 "IOC Official Jailed for Corruption," BBC News (Jun. 3, 2004), retrieved from Web Jan. 12, 2016 (news.bbc.co.uk/2/hi/asia-pacific/3771931.stm).
479 "IOC's Kim sits in jail forgotten," *Deseret Morning News* (May 28, 2004).
480 Interview, Askinas (Jan. 30, 2008).
481 Interview, Joon-Pyo Choi (Nov. 28, 2007).
482 Interview, Joon-Pyo Choi (Nov. 28, 2007).
483 Quotes from Mitchell are from my interview with him in Oct. 2005.
484 From "President's Statement," by Wayne Mitchell (Oct. 8/15). Retrieved from Taekwondo Canada's website on Oct. 22, 2015 (taekwondo-canada.com/presidents-statement/).
485 Interview, Kwon (2008). "Choue Chung-won Elected as New Taekwondo Head," *Korea Times* (Jun. 12, 2004).
486 "Choue Chung-won Elected as New Taekwondo Head," *Korea Times* (Jun. 12, 2004).
487 From *Korea Times*: "WTF Has Guarded Optimism on Taekwondo's Olympic Status" (Jun. 23, 2005) and "Taekwondo is Sport For Everyone" (Oct. 26, 2006).
488 "Ex-IOC Official Jailed in South Korea for Embezzlement Released on Parole," Canadian Press (Jun. 30, 2005).
489 "Poor Judging Hurts Taekwondo," by Kim Tong-hyung, in the *Korea Times*. South Korea (Aug. 24, 2008). Retrieved from the Web on Oct. 16, 2015 (www.koreatimes.co.kr/www/news/sports/2008/08/253_29893.html).
490 "Mr. Taekwondo Steven López draws energy from London's Olympic buzz: The American, denied a chance at gold when docked a point on a marginal call in Beijing, is fired up for London 2012," by Kevin Mitchell, in *Guardian*. U.K. (Aug. 8, 2012). Retrieved from the Web on Oct. 16, 2015 (www.theguardian.com/sport/2012/aug/08/london-2012-taewkondo-steven-lopez).
491 The electronic scoring system is supposed to minimize "human error," according to WTF leaders like Joon-Pyo Choi (Interview on Nov. 28, 2007).
492 "Sockgate: Public cries foul in Games row," by Vincent Y. Chao and Ko Shu-ling, in the *Taipei Times* (Nov. 19, 2010). Retrieved from the Web on Oct. 20, 2015 (www.taipeitimes.com/News/front/archives/2010/11/19/2003488876).

493 "Kukkiwon is slowly drowning," a question-and-answer article by Jun Chul Shin (Feb. 21, 2008). Retrieved from www.mookas.us/media_view.asp?news_no=1323 in 2008.

CHAPTER TWENTY

494 All information about C. K. Choi in this chapter is from my interviews with him (2007-2015).

495 Including the World Tae Kwon Do Alliance in the U.S., and the Tae Kwon Do Academy of Norway.

496 Interview, Rafaty (July 22 and 24, 2011).

497 World Taekwon Media. "WTF will rebrand itself as World Taekwondo," in World Taekwon Media. United States (Dec. 29, 2015). Retrieved from Web Jan. 18, 2016 (www.wtkmedia.com/wtf-will-rebrand-as-world-taekwondo).

498 Nam, Hyun-woo. "NK taekwondo team invited to Seoul in Oct," in *Korea Times*. South Korea (Sept. 10, 2015). Retrieved from the Web on Oct. 16, 2015 (www.koreatimes.co.kr/www/news/nation/2015/09/663_186589.html).

499 Nam, Hyun-woo. "World Taekwondo Federation gains $10 mil. in sponsorship," in *Korea Times*. South Korea (Apr. 8, 2015). Retrieved from the Web on Oct. 16, 2015 (www.koreatimes.co.kr/www/news/sports/2015/05/136_176782.html).

BIBLIOGRAPHY

Anslow, Stuart. "An Interview with Grandmaster Kong Young Il." *Tae Kwon Do and Korean Martial Arts,* vol. 9, iss. 10 (Nov. 2004): pp. 48–53.

Associated Press. "Attacks Alter Korean Peace Talks." *Globe and Mail* (Toronto, Sep. 17, 2001): p. A17.

Barcelona Olympic Organizing Committee. *Official Report of the Games of the XXV Olympiad Barcelona 1992,* Vol. 4. Barcelona: Barcelona Olympic Organizing Committee, 1992.

BBC. "Reprieved Stevenson takes bronze." BBC. The U.K. (Aug. 23, 2008). Retrieved from the Web on Oct. 16, 2015 (news.bbc.co.uk/sport2/hi/olympics/taekwondo/7578208.stm).

Boettcher, Robert B. *Gifts of Deceit: Sun Myung Moon, Tongsun Park, and the Korean Scandal.* New York: Holt, Rinehart and Winston, 1980. (Boettcher directed the U.S. Congressional investigations of Koreagate in the 1970s.)

Bolz, Peter. "The businesses of the Korean Kukkiwon Authorities." Dansk Taekwondo Forbund. Denmark (Sept. 23, 2015). Retrieved from Web on Jan. 18, 2016 (www.taekwondo.dk/files/Forbund/Dokumenter_div/2015/Kukkiwon/2015-09-23_Artikel_Peter_Bolz_Kukkiwon_english.pdf).

Burdick, Dakin. "A History of Taekwondo." (This essay from 1990 has made the rounds on the internet, but Burdick published a more accurate version in 1997.)

_____. "People and Events of Taekwondo's Formative Years." *Journal of Asian Martial Arts,* vol. 6, no. 1 (1997): pp. 30–49. Pennsylvania: Via Media Publishing.

CBC Sports. "Judging questioned after Canada's Gonda loses 1st taekwondo match: Canadians lodge protest but it's unsuccessful." CBC. Canada: Aug. 20, 2008. Retrieved from the Web on Oct. 16, 2015. (web.archive.org/web/20080822201352/http://www.cbc.ca/olympics/taekwondo/story/2008/08/19/f-olympics-taekwondo-gonda.html).

Cha, Mong-goo. "Escape From Japanese Hakhpyung." *The Church Under Japanese Occupation.* South Korea: date unknown.

Chao, Vincent Y., and Ko Shu-ling. "Sockgate: Public cries foul in Games row," in *Taipei Times* (Nov. 19, 2010). Retrieved from the Web on Oct. 20, 2015 (www.taipeitimes.com/News/front/archives/2010/11/19/2003488876). Choe, Sang-Hun. "Korea Opens Dark Chapter of History: Case of Missing Spy Under Investigation." *International Herald Tribune* (Apr. 5, 2005): p. 1.

Cho, Hee Il. *The Complete One & Three Step Sparring.* U.S.: self-published by Hee Il Cho, 1988.

_____. *The Complete Martial Artist, Volume 1.* U.S.: self-published by Hee Il Cho, 1981.

Choe, Sang-Hun. "Korea Opens Dark Chapter of History: Case of Missing Spy Under Investigation." *International Herald Tribune* (Apr. 5, 2005): p. 1.

Choi, C. K. (Chang Keun). *The Korean Martial Art of Tae Kwon Do & Early History.* Vancouver: self-published by C. K. Choi, 2007.

Choi, Hong-Hi. *Introductory Tutorial to Taekwon-Do* (or *Taekwon-Do Manual*). South Korea: Im Choonsik and Tunshwa Culture, 1960. (In Korean only. This is a reprint of his 1959 book.)

_____. *Moral Guide Book.* c. 2000. (Contains no publication information and was most likely published in North Korea.)

_____. "Road Map to Unification." *Baidal Times.* Canada: self-published by Choi Hong-Hi, 1980. (Choi printed this brochure after his 1980 trip to North Korea. Michael Cormack, who went on the trip, gave me a copy.)

_____. *Taekwon-Do and I, Volume 1, Motherland: The Land in Turmoil.* c. 2000. (Contains no publication information and was most likely published in North Korea.)

_____. *Taekwon-Do and I, Volume 2, The Vision of Exile: Any Place Under Heaven is Do-Jang.* c. 2000. (Contains no publication information and was most likely published in North Korea.)

_____. *Taekwon-Do: The Art of Self-Defence.* South Korea: Daeha, 1966. (This is a Korean version of his 1965 English text of the same title.)

_____. *Taekwon-Do (The Korean Art of Self-Defence): A Text Book for Beginning & Advanced Students.* Hong Kong: Everbest Printing Co and the International Taekwon-Do Federation, 1972.

_____. *Taekwon-Do: The Korean Art of Self-Defence.* Canada: International Taekwon-Do Federation, 1993. (This is his fifteen-volume encyclopedia.)

_____. *Taekwon-Do: The Korean Art of Self-Defence.* (1988). 5th ed. Canada: International Taekwon-Do Federation, 1999.

Chun, Richard. *Advancing in Tae Kwon Do.* (1983). Boston: YMAA Publication Center, 2006.

_____. *Moo Duk Kwan Tae Kwon Do: Korean Art of Self-Defense.* California: Ohara Publications, 1976.

Cumings, Bruce. *Korea's Place in the Sun: A Modern History.* New York: W. W. Norton, 2005. (This is an update of the 1997 book of the same name.)

_____. "JPRI Working Paper No. 20: Korean Scandal, or American Scandal?" *Japan Policy Research Institute* (2003). From www.jpri.org.

_____. "JPRI Occasional Paper No. 31: Some Thoughts on the Korean-American Relationship." *Japan Policy Research Institute* (May 2003). Retrieved from Web in 2008 (www.jpri.org.).

_____. *North Korea.* New York: The New Press, 2004.

Dohrenwend, R. E. "Informal History of Chung Do Kwan Tae Kwon Do." Cited and available widely on the internet, published c. 1997.

Draeger, Donn F. *Modern Bujutsu and Budo: The Martial Arts and Ways of Japan.* Vol 3. New York and Tokyo: Weatherhill, 1974.

Draeger, Donn F., and Robert W. Smith. *Comprehensive Asian Fighting Arts.* Tokyo, New York and London: Kodansha, 1980. (This is a reprint of their 1969 book, *Asian Fighting Arts.*)

Dukes, Terence (Shifu Nagaboshi Tomio). *The Bodhisattva Warriors: The Origin, Inner Philosophy, History and Symbolism of the Buddhist Martial Art within India and China.* U.S.: Samuel Weiser, 1994.

Durand, Lt. Col. James F. "The Battle of Tra Binh Dong and the Korean Origins of the U.S. Marine Corps Martial Arts Program: Lasting impressions of Korean Marines' martial arts skills led to the establishment of the mcmap." *Marine Corps Gazette* (2004). (The *Gazette* is a professional journal of the U.S. Marines. The article is available online.)

The Economist. "New Kicks from Korea." *The Economist,* Vol. 333, Iss. 7889 (Nov. 12, 1994): p. 121.

Edwards, Peter. "He excelled at 'kicking, jumping, smashing.'" *Toronto Star* (Jun. 24, 2002), p. A2.

Funakoshi, Gichin. *Karate-Do Nyumon: The Master Introductory Text.* Trans. John Teramoto. Tokyo: Kodansha International, 1988.

Gomez, Brian. "Under fire, Askinas out as CEO of USA Taekwondo," *The Gazette,* Colorado, USA (Aug. 17, 2011). Retrieved from the Web on Oct. 20, 2015 (gazette.com/under-fire-askinas-out-as-ceo-of-usa-taekwondo/article/123399).

Guo, Elizabeth, and Brian L. Kennedy. "Magic Martial Arts." *Classical Fighting Arts Magazine*. No. 5 (2004), pp. 31–37. California: Dragon Associates.

Halloran, Richard. "Seoul's Vast Intelligence Agency Stirs Wide Fears." *New York Times* (Aug. 20, 1973), p. 3.

Hessler, Peter. *River Town*. U.S.: HarperCollins, 2001.

International Olympic Committee Ethics Commission. "Case No. 04/2007; Decision with recommendation No. d/02/08." Lausanne: IOC, Feb. 15, 2008.

Jennings, Andrew, and Clare Sambrook. *The Great Olympic Swindle: When the World Wanted Its Games Back*. London: Simon & Schuster, 2000.

_____. *The New Lords of the Rings: Olympic Corruption and How to Buy Gold Medals*. London: Simon & Schuster, 1996.

Kang, Won-Sik, and Kyong-Myong Lee. *A Modern History of Taekwondo*. Korean book translated by "Glen U. and students," as noted on various websites, 1999. (This is the World Taekwondo Federation's unofficial history book, widely cited in English, even though it contains no references. Both authors practised Taekwondo and worked with the WTF.)

Kim, Bok-Man. *Practical Taekwon-Do Weapon Techniques: Art of Self-Defense: A Text Book for Advanced Students*. Hong Kong: Sun Light (P. T.) Publishing, 1979.

Kim, Hyung-wook. *Power and Conspiracy*. South Korea: *New Korea Times*, 1982. (Kim disappeared in Germany in 1978 and the *New Korea Times* published his controversial writings about South Korean President Park Chung-hee, Kim's relationship to him, their fallout, and Kim's exile to the U.S.. Kim's book is in Korean.)

Kim, Tong-hyung. "Poor Judging Hurts Taekwondo," in *Korea Times*. South Korea (Aug. 24, 2008). Retrieved from the Web on Oct. 16, 2015 (www.koreatimes.co.kr/www/news/sports/2008/08/253_29893.html).

Kim, Un-yong. *Challenging the World*. Seoul: Yunsei University Publishing, 2002. (This is one of Kim's memoirs, available in Korean.)

_____. *The Greatest Olympics: From Baden-Baden to Seoul*. Seoul: Si-sa-yong-o-sa, 1990.

_____. *Taekwondo: Korea Background Series*. Seoul: Korean Overseas Information Service, 1975.

Kimm, He-Young. *The Hapkido Bible*. Louisiana: Andrew Jackson Press, 1991.

_____. "General Choi Hong Hi: A Tae Kwon-Do History Lesson." *Tae Kwon Do Times*, vol. 20, no. 1 (Jan. 2000), pp. 44–58. Iowa: Tri-Mount Publications.

Klein, Naomi. *The Shock Doctrine: The Rise of Disaster Capitalism*. Canada: Alfred A. Knopf, 2007.

Kuklinski-Rhee, Thomas. "*Introduction and Transition of Taekwondo in Germany* (1960–2000)," PhD dissertation, Department of Physical Education, Graduate School of Korea National Sport University, South Korea, 2010.

Larkin, John. "Cleaning House." *Time* (Jun. 9, 2003).

Lee, Peter H., translator. *Anthology of Korean Poetry: From the Earliest Era to the Present*. New York: John Day and UNESCO, 1964.

Lee, Tae Eun. *Mastering Taekwondo*. 2nd ed. Ottawa: Tae Eun Lee, 1995.

Levine, Alan J. *Captivity, Flight, and Survival in World War II*. U.S.: Praeger, 2000.

MacArthur, Douglas. *Reminiscences*. New York: McGraw-Hill, 1964.

Madis, Eric. "Storming the Fortress: A History of Taekwondo. Part Two: The First Korean Schools: The Shotokan Schools; Lee Won-kuk and the Chungdokwan," published in 2010. Retrieved from the Web on October 22, 2015 (fightingarts.com/reading/article.php?id=661). There are five parts to the series.

_____. "Storming the Fortress: A History of Taekwondo. Part Four: The First Korean Schools: The Maverick Schools," published in 2011. Retrieved from the Web on October 22, 2015 (fightingarts.com/reading/article.php?id=661). There are five parts to the series.

Minford, John, editor and translator. *The Art of War: Sun-Tzu (Sunzi)*. U.S.: Penguin, 2002.

Mitchell, Kevin. "Mr. Taekwondo Steven López draws energy from London's Olympic buzz: The American, denied a chance at gold when docked a point on a marginal call in Beijing, is fired up for London 2012," in the *Guardian*. U.K. (Aug. 8, 2012). Retrieved from the Web on Oct. 16, 2015 (www.theguardian.com/sport/2012/aug/08/london-2012-taewkondo-steven-lopez).

Na Jeong-ju. "Kim Un-yong Claims He Gave $1.1 Mil. To NK IOC Member." *Korea Times*. South Korea (Jan. 6, 2004).

Nam, Hyun-woo. "World Taekwondo Federation gains $10 mil. in sponsorship," *Korea Times*. South Korea (Apr. 2, 2015). Retrieved from the Web on Oct. 16, 2015 (www.koreatimes.co.kr/www/news/sports/2015/05/136_176782.html).

_____. "NK taekwondo team invited to Seoul in Oct," *Korea Times*. South Korea (Sept. 10, 2015). Retrieved from the Web on Oct. 16, 2015. (www.koreatimes.co.kr/www/news/nation/2015/09/663_186589.html).

Oh, Bonnie B. C. "The Japanese Imperial System and the Korean 'Comfort Women' of World War II." *Legacies of the Comfort Women of World War II*, edited by Margaret D. Stetz and Bonnie B. C. Oh. New York: M. E. Sharpe, 2001.

Ouyang, Yung. "The Elevation of Taekkyon From Folk Game to Martial Art." *Journal of Asian Martial Arts*, vol. 6, no. 4 (1997), pp. 76–89. Pennsylvania: Via Media Publishing.

Pratt, John M., ed. *Revitalizing a Nation: A Statement of Beliefs, Opinions and Policies Embodied in the Public Pronouncements of General of the Army Douglas MacArthur*. U.S.: The Heritage Foundation, 1952.

P'yŏngyang Military Court. "P'yŏgyang Hakhpyung Incident Judgment Record." (This Japanese document from 1945 contains details of Choi Hong-Hi's court martial.)

Rubbeling, Hendrik. *Taekkyon — Wie Wasser und Wind*. (A German-language book about T'aekkyŏn's history between 1910 and 1980). Self-published in Hamburg, Germany: 2014.

Rutt, Father Richard. "The Flower Boys of Silla (Hwarang): Notes on the sources." Seoul, South Korea: The Royal Asiatic Society-Korea Branch, Vol. XXXVIII:1-66; Oct. 1961. PDF retrieved on Oct. 26, 2015.

Seo, J. B. Map from www.defence.co.kr. Seoul: Defence Korea, 2008. (Seo runs Defence Korea, a private online initiative.)

Seoul Olympic Organizing Committee. *Official Report, Volume 1, Games of the XXIVth Olympiad Seoul 1988: Organization and Planning*. South Korea: Korea Textbook Company, 1989.

Simpkins, C. Alexander, and Annellen Simpkins. *Chung Do Kwan: The Power of Tae Kwon Do*. U.S.: Tuttle Publishing, 2002.

Simson, Vyv, and Andrew Jennings. *The Lords of the Rings: Power, Money and Drugs in the Modern Olympics*. London: Simon & Schuster, 1992.

Son, Duk Sung, and Robert J. Clark. *Black Belt Korean Karate*. New York: Prentice-Hall, 1983. (This is an excellent review of black belt techniques, especially the mental aspects that should accompany physical training, by Duk-Sung Son, a founding member of the martial art who is based in New York City.)

Song, Hyŏn-suk. "53rd Anniversary of Yongmun Mountain Victory by Blue Star Unit." *Korea Defense Daily* (May 29, 2004). Seoul: Defense Media Agency. (The article is in Korean: www.dema.mil.kr/web/main.do. DEMA is a Korean government body.)

Song, Kun Ho. "P'yongyang Student-Soldiers' Rebellion Attempt." *Modern Korean History*, pp. 376–379. South Korea: Korean Theology Research Institute, date unknown. (Sun-Ha Lim provided this Korean-language document, which lists Choi Hong-Hi in the P'yŏngyang Incident.)

South Korea [Sŏul T'ukpyŏlsi Sa P'yŏnch'an Wiwŏnhoe]. *The History of Seoul Metropolitan [Sŏul yukpaengnyŏnsa]*. Seoul: Sŏul T'ukpyŏlsi, 1977. (This is a set of books about Korean people, culture and history. All five volumes, published by the South Korean government, were available at seoul600.visitseoul.net in 2008.)

Sydney Organizing Committee for the Olympic Games. *Official Report of the XXVII Olympiad, Volume 1: Preparing for the Games.* Australia: Paragon Printers Australasia, 2001.

_____. *Official Report of the XXVII Olympiad, Volume 2: Celebrating the Games.* Australia: Paragon Printers Australasia, 2001.

Talbott, Jeremy M. "Won-kuk Lee: A 'Living National Treasure' of Korea." England: Practical Martial Arts, 1999. Retrieved from Web in 2008 (www.practical-martial-arts.co.uk).

U.S. House of Representatives. *The Olympics Site Selection Process.* Hearings Before the Subcommittee on Oversight and Investigations of the Committee on Commerce, Oct. 14, 1999 (The Need for Reform) and Dec. 15, 1999 (Review of the Reform Effort). Washington, DC: U.S. Government Printing Office, 2000.

_____. *Activities of the Korean Central Intelligence Agency in the U.S., Part I.* Hearings before the Subcommittee on International Organizations of the Committee on International Relations, U.S. House of Representatives. Washington, DC: U.S. Government Printing Office, March 17 and 25, 1976.

_____. *Activities of the Korean Central Intelligence Agency in the U.S., Part II,* June 22 and September 27 and 30, 1976.

_____. *Investigation of Korean-American Relations, Part 1.* Hearings before the Subcommittee on International Organizations, Committee on International Relations, U.S. House of Representatives. Washington, DC: U.S. Government Printing Office, June 22, 1977.

_____. *Investigation of Korean-American Relations, Part 2.* July 28 and August 3, 1977.

_____. *Investigation of Korean-American Relations, Part 3.* November 29 and 30, 1977.

_____. *Investigation of Korean-American Relations, Part 4.* March 15, 16, 21, 22, April 11, 20, and June 20, 1978.

_____. *Investigation of Korean-American Relations, Supplement to Part 4.* March 15, 16, 21, 22, 1978.

_____. *Investigation of Korean-American Relations, Part 5.* June 1, 6 and 7, 1978.

_____. *Investigation of Korean-American Relations: Report of the Subcommittee on International Organizations.* Hearings before the Subcommittee on International Organizations, Committee on International Relations, U.S. House of Representatives. Washington, DC: U.S. Government Printing Office, Oct. 31, 1978.

_____. *Investigation of Korean-American Relations, Volumes I and II of Appendixes to the Report of the Subcommittee on International Organizations.* Oct. 31, 1978.

Weiss, Earl. "Nam Tae Hi: Chung Do Kwan's Quiet Man." *Tae Kwon Do Times*, vol. 20, no. 1 (Jan. 2000), pp. 82–84. Iowa: Tri-Mount Publications.

World Taekwondo Federation. "WTF Reform Progress Updates," WTF. South Korea: WTF (June 2008). Retrieved from Web in 2008 (www.wtf.org).

World Taekwon Media. "WTF will rebrand itself as World Taekwondo," WTM. United States: WTM (Dec. 29, 2015). Retrieved from Web on Jan. 18, 2016 (www.wtkmedia.com/wtf-will-rebrand-as-world-taekwondo)

Yang Te-sam. "Taekwondo Survives, but Faces Major Reforms." *Yonhap English News* (Jul. 8, 2005).

Yook, Sung-chul (and translated by Soo Lee Han). "Chong Woo Lee, Kukkiwon Vice President, Involved in Choosing the Winners and Losers of the Sydney Olympic Games." *Shin Dong-A Monthly Magazine* (Apr. 2002). (The article is available in English at www.tkdreform.com/archives.html. Retrieved from Web Jan. 15, 2016.)

Young, Robert W. "The History & Development of Tae Kyon." *Journal of Asian Martial Arts,* vol. 2, no. 2 (1993), pp. 44–69. Pennsylvania: Via Media Publishing.

_____. "Hee Il Cho: The Martial Arts Were Different Then." *Black Belt Magazine* archive at www.blackbeltmag.com/archives/482 (retrieved from Web in 2008). U.S.: Cruz Bay Publishing and Active Interest Media, no date provided.

INTERVIEWS

Askinas, David, former CEO of USA Taekwondo (USAT): January 30, 2008.

Anslow, Stuart, Editor of *Totally Tae Kwon Do* magazine, in the U.K.: October 2015.

Balkin, Rick, a master in Tae Kwon Do who participated in a Global Taekwon-Do Federation tournament in Moscow, Russia, in 1993: July 2011.

Broadway, Benny, a master in Tae Kwon Do who participated in a Global Taekwon-Do Federation tournament in Moscow, Russia, in 1993: July 2011.

Burdick, Dakin, Associate Director (Teaching Resources Center, Indiana University at Bloomington): Email correspondence in January 2002. Dakin wrote an essay in 1990 called "A History of Taekwondo." He published a more accurate version of it in 1997.

Burleson, Pat, Karate student who trained with Jhoon Rhee in the 1960s: January 24, 2008.

Burleson, Troy, a master in Tae Kwon Do who participated in a Global Taekwon-Do Federation tournament in Moscow, Russia, in 1993: July 2011.

Callanan, Dennis, a Tae Kwon Do student of Nam Tae-hi's in Chicago, U.S., in the early 1970s: July, 2015.

Cariati, Joe, former assistant to Choi Hong-Hi: January 23, 2002 (with Parmar Rai), January 2008 and October 2015.

Chang, Gedo, Hapkido master: See Nam Tae-hi.

Choi, C. K. (Chang Keun), Tae Kwon Do pioneer and assistant to Choi Hong-Hi in the 1960s: October and November 2007 and October 2015.

Choi, Hee Jin, Secretary to Uhm Woon-kyu, who was Kukkiwon President, a Tae Kwon Do pioneer and a founder of the WTF: April 7 to July, 2008.

Choi, Hong-Hi: March and April 2001, including a three-day Tae Kwon Do seminar in April 2001.

Choi, Joon-Pyo, former coach of U.S. Olympic team and former USAT (WTF) commission co-chair: November 28, 2007.

Choi, Jung-Hwa, Choi Hong-Hi's son and a Tae Kwon Do master: January 2002 to April 2003.

Choi, Song-Jook, Choi Hong-Hi's first daughter: May 30, 2003.

Choi, Sunny, Choi Hong-Hi's third daughter: August 21, 2002.

Choung, Young Su, WTF grandmaster and former head coach of Canada's Olympic team: October 2005.

Colomvakos (née Choi), Meeyun (Mia), Choi Hong-Hi's second daughter: Between August 2002 and April 2003.

Cormack, Michael, former ITF executive and former son-in-law of Choi Hong-Hi: May 2, 2003.

Cumings, Bruce, expert in modern Korean history, University of Chicago: email on January 19, 2005.

Di Vecchia, Lenny, one of my Tae Kwon Do instructors: 2000 to 2014.

Doolin, Jay, a black belt in Tae Kwon Do who participated in a Global Taekwon-Do Federation tournament in Moscow, Russia, in 1993: July 2011.

Edwards, Randy, a master in Tae Kwon Do who participated in a Global Taekwon-Do Federation tournament in Moscow, Russia, in 1993: July 2011.

Gabbidon, Alfonso, one of my instructors: 2001 to 2008.

Galarraga, Nestor, Tae Kwon Do master in Argentina: August 16, 2002.

Gantner, Chris, a master in Tae Kwon Do who participated in a Global Taekwon-Do Federation tournament in Moscow, Russia, in 1993: July 2011.

Ha, Kee, former president of Taekwondo Canada and head coach of Canada's 2004 Olympic team: June and July 2008.

Hardin, Bob, a former American Taekwondo Association regional vice-president (1972 to 1983) and head of Global Taekwon-Do Federation tournament in Moscow, Russia, in 1993: July 2011 and October 2015.

Kang, Seok-Jae, the WTF's Public Relations Director at the time, Seoul, South Korea: July 2008.

Keenan Jr., John J., a U.S. Army Warrant Officer in Moehringen, Germany, in the 1960s, was a friend of Kim Kwang-il's: June, 2015.

Kim, Bok-Man, Tae Kwon Do pioneer and assistant to Choi Hong-Hi in the 1960s: August 13, 2002.

Kim, Jae-Hun, WTF master and former ITF instructor: June 22, 2002.

Koh, John, translator and interpreter for *A Killing Art*: 2002–2008.

Kong, Young-il, Tae Kwon Do grandmaster: August 16, 2002.

Kwon, Soyoung, WTF President Choue Chung-Won's Special Assistant at the time: February to July, 2008.

Lee, Tae Eun, WTF grandmaster and former auditor for WTF under Kim Un-yong: August 20, 2007.

Lim, Sun-Ha, and Sandy Lim, friends of Choi Hong-Hi in 1945: Between August 2002 and May 2003.

Lu, Phap, ITF official and Choi Hong-Hi's assistant in 1990s: May 17, 2003 and May 6, 2008.

Madis, Eric, martial arts historian: February 1, 2011 and October 19, 2012.

Maidana, Jose, Tae Kwon Do expert in Argentina: August 16, 2002.

McNeely, Scott, a Tae Kwon Do master who participated in a Global Taekwon-Do Federation tournament in Moscow, Russia, in 1993: July 2011.

Mitchell, Wayne, former Secretary General of the WTF in Canada: October 11, 2005 and February 13, 2008.

Nam, Tae-hi, founding member of Tae Kwon Do: December 2001 (with Gedo Chang interpreting) to July 2011 (with Chris Nam, his son, interpreting).

Nowling, Douglas G., a Tae Kwon Do instructor in the U.S.: July 2011.

Palmer, Brandon, Korean historian: emails in January 2005.

Park, Bu-Kwang, Tae Kwon Do grandmaster: August 16, 2002.

Park, Jong-Soo, my instructor from 1993 to 2006: Interviews 2001 to 2008.

Parris, Richard, ITF master: April 22, 2001 and April 29, 2008.

Pound, Richard (Dick), former member of the International Olympic Committee: February 12 and March 4, 2008.

Rafaty, Hoss, Secretary General of the World Taekwondo Federation in 2015. I interviewed him in Dallas, U.S., on July 22 and 24, 2011, when he was Special Assistant to WTF President for WTF Expansion Project.

Rai, Parmar, ITF black belt and assistant to Jung-Hwa Choi: See Joe Cariati.

Rhee, Jhoon, Tae Kwon Do pioneer: November 2007 to January 2008.

Rhee Min-hi, Tae Kwon Do instructor: December 22, 2007.

Rhee, Phillip, Tae Kwon Do movie star and Rhee Min-hi's son: December 22, 2007.

Rhee, Simon, Tae Kwon Do movie star and Rhee Min-hi's son: December 12 and 21, 2007.

Rubbeling, Hendrik, a T'aekkyŏn expert and historian in Germany: September 2012 and October 2014.

Schroen, Gary C., an American CIA officer in Iran and a second-degree black belt in Tae Kwon Do who helped Choi Hong-Hi and the ITF with a tournament in Iran in 1973: December 15, 2015.

Son, Myung-Soo, Tae Kwon Do instructor: April 21, 2001.

Song, Sung-Keun, Vice-President of the Kukkiwon: July 2008.

Sergerie, Karine, Canada's WTF world champion: May 2008.

Stanford, Rick, a master in Tae Kwon Do who participated in a Global Taekwon-Do Federation tournament in Moscow, Russia, in 1993: July 2011.

Stanley, Craig, Tae Kwon Do master: 2001 to 2008.

Stevens, Jack, a master in Tae Kwon Do who participated in a Global Taekwon-Do Federation tournament in Moscow, Russia, in 1993: July 2011.

Turchi, Ron, former executive with the American Taekwondo Association: July 2011.

Van Binh, Nguyen, Tae Kwon Do grandmaster from Vietnam: August to September 2005

Walson, Robert, an American CIA officer and sixth-degree black belt in Tae Kwon Do in 1974 who helped Choi Hong-Hi and the ITF for many years: Jan 2010 and November 2015.

Yang, Dong-Ja, former executive in the WTF and leader of the Taekwondo Reform Movement: July 2008.

Yook, Sung-Chul, journalist who wrote "Chang Woo Lee, Kukkiwon Vice President, Involved in Choosing the Winners and Losers of the Sydney Olympic Games," for *Shin Dong-A Monthly Magazine* (April 2002): July 7, 2008.

Young Su Choung, WTF Canadian and Ontario coach over the years: October 2005.

INDEX